Permission to Shoot?

Jyoti Belur

Permission to Shoot?

Police Use of Deadly Force in Democracies

 Springer

Jyoti Belur
University College London
Jill Dando Institute of Crime Science
Torrington Place 2-16
WC1E 7HN London
UK
j.belur@ucl.ac.uk

ISBN 978-1-4419-0974-9   e-ISBN 978-1-4419-0975-6
DOI 10.1007/978-1-4419-0975-6
Springer New York Dordrecht Heidelberg London

Library of Congress Control Number: 2010933973

Printed on acid-free paper

Springer is part of Springer Science+Business Media (www.springer.com)

Preface

Police use of deadly force has fascinated criminologists for decades especially in the Western world. While some instances of police killings have been perceived as being acceptable and unavoidable, often they have elicited controversy and anger. The police are more often than not accused of abuse or excess use of deadly force against fellow citizens. If that were the case, few have delved into the question: what makes ordinary, "decent" human beings do horrible things? (c.f. Huggins et al., 2002; Foster et al., 2005a). Further, the question, "how are such 'wrongdoings' on the part of state actors justified in a democratic society?" goes a-begging. The questionable use of deadly force by the police, with a monopoly on state violence, is a universal phenomenon and yet police officers' perspective on this issue has seldom been explored in depth in democratic countries.

This book is about a peculiar feature of Indian policing called *encounters*. An *encounter* is a spontaneous, unplanned "shoot-out" between the police and alleged criminals, in which the criminal is usually killed, with few or no police injuries. However the police "cover story" (Hunt & Manning, 1991) from official sources and cited in the media is *always* the same raising the suspicion that it is a cover-up for facts that might not be legally defensible or permissible. The term *encounter* is not just police jargon but is part of everyday discourse in India and is used by police officers, media, and public to refer to police use of deadly force in circumstances described by one newspaper report as follows:

> '*Mumbai Police pats itself as encounter deaths double*'
> The Mumbai police call it "proactive policing". In everyday parlance, it is referred to as an "encounter" between policemen and gangsters that always results in the death of these gangsters. That these encounters do not have a surprise element, instead are planned, to a large extent, by the police, no longer raises eyebrows. But even by their own standards, Mumbai police have been far too "proactive" in 2001 compared to the past few years...In 2000, the total number of alleged gangsters killed in encounters was 49, and the year before that it was 60. The quantum leap to 94 has certainly sent shockwaves through the under-world. Extremely pleased at this leap, Police Commissioner M.N. Singh said: "Organised crime is well under check. This is the final blow.
>
> *The Indian Express* (December 29, 2001)

Of all types of force used by the police, deadly force is cause of most concern, not only because its consequences are irreversible and irreparable, but because it "affects citizens' attitude toward the police and toward the government in general" (Geller & Scott, 1991), as does all inappropriate use of force. It is important to understand why it is that in a free and democratic society like India, the abuse of deadly force is not only tolerated, but in many ways (both overtly and tacitly) encouraged.

I worked as an officer of the Indian Police Service (IPS) in the state of Uttar Pradesh, which is one of the more backward, illiterate, densely populated, and crime-infested regions of the country. My experience, during training and subsequently in the field, led me to believe that the influence of the occupational subculture[1] is ubiquitous and tangible. There is formal emphasis on the rule of law and due process, but these are viewed by police officers more as obstacles to be overcome in the ultimate quest to tackle crime and law & order problems. The "heroes" or "model cops" to be emulated are those who have proved their "bravery" or "toughness" in the field through dealing with one or more "dreaded criminals" in *encounters*. These messages are rarely articulated explicitly, but are disseminated in more subtle ways, that are nonetheless very powerful. A few young officers even join the police with the aim of joining the ranks of *encounter* "heroes" and tend to use deadly force with less reservation than is mandatory[2].

This pattern is not replicated across India as some states have a much better record on the use of deadly force than others. Areas facing serious challenges from Naxalites (communist rebel groups), organised gangs, very high levels of serious crime (e.g. dacoit[3]-infested areas), and separatist groups or terrorist operations, have a greater tendency to engage in *encounters* than others. Furthermore, the context and circumstances in which *encounters* happen are very different in all these different situations.

Certain states in India that were and some that continue to be affected by counterinsurgency, like Punjab, Kashmir, Assam, and other North Eastern states have different experiences as compared to those affected by militant Maoist rebels. Gossman (2002) describes types of "death squads" that operate in various parts of India, differentiating between out-of-uniform police officers who formed death squads in insurgency ridden Punjab; security forces (army, paramilitary forces, and the police) operating in Kashmir and in Assam, threatening and assassinating militant leaders and other opposition figures; and special police squads operating in Naxal-infested areas. The Naxalite movement began in India in 1969 formed by radical Maoists, who believe that the enemy of class struggle, the power-wielders in the existing social order, have to be eliminated even if that enemy (state agents)

---

[1]Several studies have shown that the police organisation has a particular occupational culture, which is shared by almost all police forces across the world. It is characterised by mission, action, cynicism, suspicion, pragmatism, machismo, solidarity, isolation, etc. (Reiner, 2000a).

[2]Studies by Van Maanen (1973), Hunt (1985) and Harris (1978) found that a similar process of "indoctrination" of new police recruits into the "masculine ethic" and the regaling of war stories featuring violence by instructors was a feature of police training in the USA.

[3]Dacoity is defined under section 391 of the Indian Penal Code as robbery committed conjointly by five or more persons.

may not have directly harmed them. States affected by the Naxal movement include Bihar, West Bengal, Chattisgarh, Andhra Pradesh, Jharkhand, parts of Orissa, Maharashtra, Madhya Pradesh and is spreading to other parts. In these states, especially Andhra Pradesh, special police squads are alleged to have executed suspected militants and prominent activists in custody and "claim that they have been killed in armed "encounters"; for most of these routine killings, no elaborate cover-up was considered necessary" (Gossman, 2002:262).

Another pattern of *encounter* killings was well established in Punjab and Kashmir (during the days of insurgency in the 1980s and 1990s) where the "victim" was detained and tortured for several days before being killed (Mahmood, 2000, Pettigrew, 2000). Gossman (2002:268) suggests, "Government practice of providing cash rewards for police who eliminated wanted militants encouraged the police to engage in extrajudicial killings".

Encounters may be considered by the police to be a natural fallout of routine policing in these "difficult" areas. However, in other parts of the country, especially in some large cities like New Delhi and Mumbai, *encounters* appear to be used more as a deliberate, short-cut method to bypass the delays and uncertainties of processing "criminals" through the criminal justice system rather than being spontaneous shootouts between organised criminals and the police.

Police *encounters* are not only "prized" internally by the police organisation and are sometimes rewarded by the government (either with one-rank-promotions, or bravery medals, and/or other privileges), but also enjoy some societal approval in Mumbai. There have been several examples when the police have been publicly congratulated for "acts of bravery" that have ridden society of a "menace". Most police officers[4] consider their work to be not just a job, but to be a "way of life with a worthwhile mission" (Reiner, 2000a; Skolnick & Fyfe, 1993) – to serve the public and protect society against the forces of evil. Public adulation is a heady stimulant and combined with positive press ratings and organisational approval in the form of allowing such actions to continue unquestioned, can serve to demolish any moral compunctions that the police have towards depriving another person of life.

Police officers are recruited from among ordinary citizens, (albeit at different levels and ranks) and are not inherently evil or natural "killers". The question then arises: how and why do ordinary people kill fellow citizens? The explanations might lie in their difficult working conditions, the demands of the socio-political milieu within which they operate, combined with a spiralling crime problem that have led to a situation where "criminals" are seen to deserve executions. It could even be the case that since most police *encounters* are not subject to detailed scrutiny, the decision to invoke deadly force maybe undertaken lightly, or without considering the full impact of the moral and legal aspects involved.

---

[4]In India a distinction is drawn between the subordinate ranks (men) and senior ranks (officers). However, henceforth the term "police officers" will cover all ranks of police personnel in this book.

There is growing human rights awareness in India and a number of Non Governmental Organisations (NGOs) and pressure groups have over the past few years questioned some of these more dubious police tactics and actions. Over the past decade there has been some public outcry against *encounters* and criminal action has been initiated against some well-intentioned but misguided policemen involved in *encounters*.

Police use of deadly force not only has a very significant impact on the right to life of the victim, but it also affects the life of the police officer involved, in many far-reaching ways – from being involved in criminal or departmental proceedings and inquiries to maintaining their moral well-being. Solving the moral dilemma of using "dirty means to achieve good ends" (Klockars, 1991) is something every police officer has to confront during his/her career in some form or the other. The book examines the truly complex nature of the issues surrounding the police decision to invoke deadly force and explores an area that has profound ramifications for policing, police malpractice, and the social and cultural context in which it takes place.

The aim is not merely to uncover or describe police use of deadly force, but in order to understand the use of force,

> "One must evaluate them [police accounts] from the point of view of the cops who succumb to these moral hazards of their occupation. Doing so requires that the cops themselves be permitted to speak at length and in intimate detail about these issues. As they do, they often advance extremely complex and sometimes highly seductive moral and psychological arguments for their behaviour." (Klockars & Mastrofski, 1991:396)

Therefore, an important part of the research is to explore the different ways in which police officers and people whom I call "claimsmakers" perceived and talked about issues around *encounters*. Various justificatory arguments used by officers clearly indicate that they used a discourse of denial to account for *encounters,* arguments that not only neutralised their actions but also served useful functions for the audience they were intended for. Thus the discourse of denial served two purposes: first, ameliorating guilt or culpability about the action itself; and second, enabled the public to respond to *encounters* not as cold-blooded police killings but as part of a justified war on crime.

Encounters have yet to be publicly perceived as a "social problem" – "a social condition that has been found to be harmful to individual and /or societal well being" (Bassis et al., 1982:2) in India. It is therefore imperative to understand how the phenomenon of *encounters* is socially constructed by "claimsmakers" asking the sorts of questions that Best (1995) explores: what sorts of claims get made; when do claims get made, and by whom; how are these claims received by the intended audiences and under what conditions? By adopting a form of contextual constructionism in the research, this book explores the claims made by officers and "claimsmakers".

The book is set out as follows:

Chapter 1 reviews the literature on police violence, concentrating on studies of police violence in some western democracies, especially the USA, the UK, Canada, and Australia, as well as in other less-developed democratic countries, in Latin America and Africa. The Mumbai police is situated within this wider literature and various models (individual, situational, organisational, and structural) to explain the causes of police violence, that are relevant to the situation in Mumbai are discussed. The "moral dilemma" that arises in situations that call for solutions to a "means-and-ends" problem is explored. The content and nature of policing is intrinsically linked to the use of force, and in many countries has been associated with some form of racial discrimination. The situation in India, and Mumbai, in particular, is more nuanced, in that, the use of deadly force by the police is allegedly directed against "hardened criminals", but the police are often accused of mainly targeting criminals belonging to a minority ethnic community.

Chapter 2 discusses actual examples of police shootings in three big cities, New York, London, and Mumbai in order to draw out similarities and differences in the way the shootings were presented and perceived in these cities. High profile cases of shootings that generated controversy, a lot of media interest, and elicited a strong reaction from the public and the police organisation alike, are discussed in some detail. The subtle nuances of the way the story is presented by the police, interpreted and disseminated by the media and perceived by the public, and the courts in the three cities highlights the universal nature of the problem of police shootings: that is the police are perceived as getting away with abuse of deadly force, not just in former colonies and dictatorial or military regimes but in democracies.

Chapter 3 introduces Mumbai city and its socio-economic and cultural place in Indian life. The city, its size, population, ethnic composition, importance as a commercial trade centre, its manufacturing and service industries, and its special position as the capital of the film industry in India (Bollywood) all demonstrate that Mumbai has a unique social, cultural and economic position in India. The city's contemporary police force has grown out of a colonial legacy of policing based on the model of the Royal Ulster Constabulary. The structure of the police service, as well as the administrative framework that provided the context within which *encounters* emerged and different power structures operated and influenced the politics of day-to-day policing are discussed. The chapter traces the growth of organised crime in Mumbai since the 1970s that led to the use of deadly force by the police, in scenarios constructed as *encounters*. It focuses on the growth and development of some of the leading gangs, and how their activities impacted on citizens of Mumbai. The twin processes of the politicization of organised crime and the criminalization of politics in Mumbai are also discussed.

Chapters 4–6 focus on interviewees' perspectives of *encounters,* their understanding of the term, and attitude towards the legality, morality, desirability, and acceptability of *encounters,* individually and organisationally. Police officers' perception of their role and responsibilities are vital in shaping their attitude towards *encounters* and whether they are willing to adopt or condone these actions. Their perception of how the public respond to the use of deadly force is also important in understanding their justifications for *encounters.* Public opinion is reflected to some extent in the interviews with "claimsmakers", so called, because these particular individuals – lawyers, journalists, judges, politicians, Human Rights activists, and representatives from the industrial associations – actually had made public claims about *encounters* over the period of study (1993–2003). These interviews were used to contextualize the conviction of police officers that society not only approved of and encouraged their actions in *encounters*, but that there actually was a vocal social demand for such proactive action. While there was no consensus on the moral or legal rectitude of police *encounters*, there was a common belief that *encounters* were very effective as a short-term measure to control spiralling organised crime. There was also a belief that even though police actions were suspected, there was very little anyone could do to prevent or punish "wrongdoing". A striking feature of these interviews was the lack of consternation or protest that the police were involved in executing alleged criminals and this appeared to provide the moral impetus to police justifications of *encounters*.

In Chap. 7 perceptions of police officers' perspectives on *encounters* are put together with Stan Cohen's Theory of Denial to demonstrate how officers use denial and justificatory accounts to explain the necessity and importance of *encounters* in Mumbai. Police officers have to live with the fact that they used or condoned the use of deadly force as perpetrators or bystanders and that they act as judge, jury, and executioners against alleged criminals. I suggest that classic denial mechanisms are used to justify their actions to themselves and to their audiences.

The final chapter uses "*their*" (interviewees') reasons to extrapolate "*the*" (structural) reasons for why *encounters* happen (Cohen, 2001:58), why they are tolerated, and identifies agendas for future research. Taking a step back from these stories "the" reasons why police actions were not challenged, and the wider structural and systemic factors that create conditions where killing "hardened" criminals seems to be the last resort for the police are explored. Chapter 8 examines the social and political situation in a commercial, crime-ridden city, preoccupied with protecting its businesses, manufacturing units and service industry as well as safeguarding the life and property of its citizens and speculates on the wider cultural and specifically police sub-cultural factors that made *encounters* both feasible and acceptable. Factors accounting for police abuse of force in Mumbai are compared and contrasted with prevailing conditions in other societies where police executions feature prominently. The experience of different police forces and policy makers in other countries have sought to control police use of deadly force by introducing legal, procedural, cultural, and/or structural changes and their efficacy are discussed. Finally, suggestions for possible solutions to curb Mumbai police's excessive use of deadly force and protect the right to life are offered.

London, UK   Jyoti Belur

Acknowledgements

I would like to thank the Mumbai Police and all the wonderful officers who unhesitatingly agreed to participate in my research project. The interviews were conducted over 2002–2003 and the then Commissioner of Police, Mr. M.N. Singh was magnificent in his support and cooperation. I am indebted to all the officers who were willing to commit time and thought to explore some very sensitive issues around police use of deadly force. Numerous staff in the Commissioner's office were very helpful in collating statistics and other information I needed. I was amazed at the level of openness with which the Mumbai police extended support for the research. I am also grateful to all my "claimsmakers" who were also very generous with their time and opinions on the police and policing issues. I would like to thank the Director, National Police Academy, Hyderabad and the NPA library staff for the generous use of their facilities while conducting background research.

I am grateful to ABC Clio, Oxford Journals and Sage Publications for permission to reprint materials from:

1. (2010) Police 'encounters' in Mumbai. In J. Kuhn and J. Knuttsson (Eds.), *Police Use of Force: A Global Perspective*. Westport, CT: Praeger Greenwood. 52–63.
2. (2010) Why do the Police Use Deadly Force: Explaining Police 'Encounters' in Mumbai, *British Journal of Criminology*, 50(2), 320–341.
3. (2009) Police use of deadly force: police perception of a culture of approval. *Journal of Contemporary Criminal Justice*; 25(2), 237–252.

This research would not have been possible without the guidance and support of Prof. Robert Reiner, Prof. Stan Cohen, and Dr. Janet Foster. As my guides and mentors they skillfully steered me through my attempts to negotiate unchartered territories of research methodology, theory, and academic writing. I am also grateful to Prof. Ken Pease, Prof. Paul Rock, Prof. Graeme Newman, Prof. M. Natarajan, and Dr. Arvind Verma for supporting the endeavour to write this book. I am especially indebted to Prof. P.A.J. Waddington for his incisive and critical comments and suggestions, which have only made the book better. I would also like to thank Prof. Gloria Laycock and my colleagues Aidan Sidebottom and Dr. Lisa Wainer for their help and encouragement during the writing of this book. I am grateful to Welmoed Spahr and Katie Chabalko for their editorial support.

My deepest gratitude I reserve for my parents Sudhindranath Belur and Urmila Belur and my wider family for unconditionally supporting me and believing in me throughout. Finally, I would like to thank Vidhi and Manasvini for their love, patience, and support in making this whole project come to fruition.

Contents

List of Figures

List of Tables

Chapter 1
Police and the Use of Deadly Force

Introduction

The use of force has always been an integral aspect of policing. Distinguishing between the use of justified, legitimate force and illegitimate force raises many complex and delicate moral, legal, and sociological conundrums. Explaining variations in the use of force requires insight into policing and the exercise of discretion that have been at the heart of empirical and theoretical research on policing in the Western world over the last half century.

Police work, almost universally, is characterised by features such as danger, authority, and the mandate to use coercive force that is non-negotiable (Bittner, 1975; Skolnick & Fyfe, 1993). As the governmental law enforcement agency, the police see themselves as the "thin blue line" that separates anarchy from order (Skolnick, 1975). It is often when police act idealistically, with a "sense of mission" (Reiner, 2000a) to control a dangerous and unruly underclass, that the most shocking abuses of police power take place (Skolnick & Fyfe, 1993). The police are armed and potentially dangerous in most countries and while protection *by* the police is generally assumed theoretically, protection *from* their misdeeds and mistakes is more problematic and less well-defined (Manning, 2003). Proper execution of police use of force is essential not only to maintain state order and legitimacy, but also as it affects public perception, attitude, and behaviour towards the police and the government (Friedrich, 1980).

This book analyses the police use of deadly force drawing upon primary research in the city of Mumbai, India. Issues of police violence in Latin America, the Caribbean, and South Africa are similar to those in India given a common background of colonial imperialism, a culture of violence, developing economies, class inequalities, and widespread poverty that they share. Admittedly, there are also some crucial differences between these countries. However, police violence is not necessarily restricted to third world or developing economies. The USA, UK, Canada, and Australia have also witnessed this phenomenon and struggle to deal with it.

The research reported here resonates with early studies on policing in both the USA and the UK. This could be because of certain similarities between the conditions under which the police described in these studies were operating, and the

J. Belur, *Permission to Shoot? Police Use of Deadly Force in Democracies*,
DOI 10.1007/978-1-4419-0975-6_1, © Springer Science+Business Media, LLC 2010

Mumbai police (c.f. Bittner, 1975; Holdaway, 1983; Skolnick, 1966; Westley, 1970, on policing in the 1960s and 1970s). The level of awareness of the police in these early studies on issues such as human rights, due process, and rule of law was, if not identical, at least, comparable. Another reason could be that these studies are pioneering works commenting on the working of the police. Thus, the methods used by these scholars to arrive at their analysis – primarily ethnographic, and incorporating qualitative methods such as participant observation and interviews – are similar to the ones used in this study. This study is one of the first qualitative studies on policing and use of deadly force in India.

Police Use of Force

Manning (1977: 40) suggests that British policing is synonymous with "legal monopoly on violence and is protected to the point of legal sanctioning for the use of fatal force". This is debatable, especially since the British police do not have a legal monopoly of violence – they have greater legal powers than ordinary citizens, but anyone is entitled to use violence in certain circumstances, for example self-defence. Also, the police are not necessarily protected for use of fatal force but their immunity is dependent on the circumstances surrounding the particular incident. Police use of force is quite complex and involves subtle judgements in determining its necessity and legitimacy.

The concept of "the capacity to use force as the core of police role" (Bittner, 1991: 42) is central to understanding police work. Police use of coercive force could be conceived as a continuum, "consisting of a range of control tactics commencing from body language and oral communication, through weaponless physical control, to non-lethal weapons, and finally to lethal measures" (McKenzie, 2000: 182). One way of defining force is, "acts that threaten or inflict physical harm on citizens", which could be measured according to the "severity of harm it imposes on a citizen" from least to most harmful (Terrill, 2001: 2). The terms "police use of force", "police violence", and "police brutality" are often used interchangeably, though they could imply use of force that is either justified or unjustified, legally and/or morally. Public understanding of the term police brutality means anything from the use of abusive language, commands to move on or go home, stop and search, threats to use force, prodding with a stick, approaching with a pistol, or actual use of physical force (Reiss, 1968).

Bayley (1996) suggests an eight-point classification of "police brutality": arrest-related assaults, torture (or third degree), deaths in custody under suspicious circumstances, police shootings, police raids, riot and crowd control, intimidation and revenge, and non-physical brutality. However, police brutality is not necessarily synonymous with use of excessive force – it has more to do with perception of the observer of what is considered unacceptable behaviour. Thus, some of what may be considered police brutality (e.g. use of abusive language) is not necessarily excessive force and in certain circumstances use of what the law defines as excessive force may be perceived by the observer as justified and thus not an instance of police brutality.

The term "excessive" is problematic, and defining it involves value judgements. Various criteria could be applied to an instance of use of force depending upon who is making this judgement, for example, "Judges apply legal standards; police administrators apply professional standards; and citizens apply 'common sense' standards" (Adams, 1999: 62) and human rights activists apply ethical standards. There is also the distinction between excessive use of force ("using force in too many incidents") and use of excessive force ("more force than needed to gain compliance in any given incident") (Terrill, 2001: 22, citing Adams, 1995).

Klockars (1996) suggests that conventional understanding of the term excessive use of force (in the sense of being a criminal offence, or a civil liability, or a public scandal) is inadequate for identifying instances where excessive force has been used. Instead he proposes a new standard to judge extent of force used, "Excessive force should be defined as the use of more force than a highly skilled police officer would find necessary to use in that particular situation" (Klockars, 1996: 8). Klockars (1996: 10–11) offers five arguments in favour of this definition over others: ontological (force that a highly skilled officer would not find necessary to employ in a given situation is not necessary force); personal (no citizen would like force used against them that a highly professional officer would not find necessary to use); professional (highest possible standard of skill acts as the benchmark); administrative (reduce criminal, civil liability, and scandals); and utility (not its ability to punish officers criminally, civilly, administratively, or politically, but its potential to help control abuses of authority by imposing the highest possible standard for measuring its necessity).

Police use of force can be necessary. Policing engenders situations when the use of force or violence may become inevitable. For example, when confronted with situations they are unable to control through other alternative means, such as a riot situation, the police can be left with no choice but to resort to the use of force to disperse rioters and bring public violence under control. However, the amount and mode of violence used by the police in any situation is subject to debate. There will be conflicting viewpoints on the advisability and efficacy of police actions in such circumstances and whether the police did all that was necessary to avoid the use of force to control a situation. It is therefore difficult to predict whether a particular incident of use of force would be perceived as legitimate or as police brutality. As Bayley (1996: 277) notes, "brutality is in the eye of the beholder". This subjectivity makes defining the concept fairly contentious. In general, the only *principled* justification for the use of force is that it is proportionate, i.e. necessary and minimal.

There has been little or no effort made to formally define what is meant by "excessive force", although the police are accused of using it frequently. Bittner's (1975) comment, "our expectation that policemen will use force, coupled by our refusals to state clearly what we mean by it (aside from sanctimonious homilies) smacks of more than a bit of perversity" (cited in Klockars, 1996: 1) reiterates this point. Assuming, at least conceptually, that some police use of force is necessary and justified, Fyfe suggests there are two other kinds of force, which appear to be based on the mens rea of the police – extralegal and unnecessary. "Extralegal violence involves the wilful and wrongful use of force by officers who knowingly exceed the bounds of their office. Unnecessary violence occurs when well-meaning officers prove incapable of dealing with the situations they encounter without needless or too hasty resort to force" (Fyfe, 1986: 207).

Deadly Force

This subject of this book is police shootings, specifically shootings in a situation of direct confrontation between the police and "criminals" and not in a riot control or public disorder situation, where the circumstantial and situational factors precipitating the use of deadly force, are quite different. The fascination of police brutality or violence for criminological research in the USA goes back 30 or 40 years, when anyone doing research on the police was assumed to be studying either police brutality or police corruption (Klockars & Mastrofski, 1991: 394). Deadly force as the most extreme form of police violence has attracted its fair share of attention. Deadly force can be employed either through the use of firearms, other lethal and non-lethal weapons, or the improper use of holds or restraining techniques, but here the focus is limited to the use of firearms.

Police use of deadly force in a public order context (Jefferson, 1987, 1990; Waddington, 1987, 1991) is somewhat different from that used in direct confrontation with alleged criminals. For example, Waddington suggests that the policing strategy in most public disorder cases is "to maintain or restore order" and the particular strategy adopted depends on the "nature of the disorder, whom it involves, and where and when it occurs" (Waddington, 1991: 145). In most riot situations the police primarily aim to disperse, or arrest, or (more rarely) incapacitate offenders (Waddington) not just in the UK, but even in India. A policy of "negotiated management" (Vitale, 2005) is preferred, whereby maximum effort is made to issue warnings to the crowd and to give them ample opportunity to disperse on their own without a show of force. While major cities in the USA have had a variety of response to policing demonstrations and riots, the New York Police Department (NYPD) has increasingly moved towards a more "command and control" model in which the police "micromanage" the demonstration in order to minimize the disruptive effects, while adopting a more forceful paramilitary style of policing to contain large demonstrations (Vitale). In the UK, police are deployed in public order situations, not as an assembly of individuals but in squad formation under a hierarchy of command similar to that in the military, theoretically making them a more formidable force (Waddington, 1991).

Policing civil disorders often engenders fear, anger, and frustration; heightening anxiety for police officers who are too close to the action to be objective, and heightened emotions on the part of the public makes the situation more volatile. Therefore, stricter supervision, command, and control of such operations are required (Waddington, 1991). Only when the mob is very violent or in an uncontrollable frenzy do the police resort legitimately to the use of deadly force, ideally, in a controlled, precisely targeted, and methodical manner. This is the theory: in practice, force may be misused.

In contrast to this, a sudden confrontation between police and "criminals" can be more fluid, with greater discretion on the part of individual officers to use deadly force, though admittedly, some riot situations may flare up and some confrontations with criminals may be planned operations. However, principles that ought to govern the use of deadly force by the police are universal and not contingent upon the situation under which it has to be employed. Lessons can be learned from those police forces that have designed policies and structured training promoting good practice in order to avoid excessive or unnecessary use of force.

Geller and Scott's (1991) review of previous studies on police use of deadly force finds that these focused on one or more of the following: *counting* (identify the incidence of police involved shootings); *describing* (characteristics of shooting incidents and their participants); *explaining* (why certain shooting patterns emerge); *controlling* (identification and assessment of strategies to reduce police shootings). Studies that *describe* and/or *explain* the use of deadly force by the police are of particular relevance to this study as the aim is to identify whether any similarities characterise such use. Green and Ward (2004) suggest that theories explaining police violence in the context of western countries such as the USA, UK, Australia, and Canada seek common fundamental and apparently universal features of policing as the cause for police deviance, despite key differences in policing histories and styles. They should thus, be applicable in "widely different cultures, economies and political systems" (Green & Ward: 69).

Geller and Scott (1991) examine use of deadly force as a result of police shootings of civilians, and shootings of police officers by civilians and other police officers in the USA. They too acknowledge definitional problems associated with deadly force, such as: whether it refers exclusively to use of firearms or includes all force capable of causing death; whether incidents occurred while an officer was on-duty or off-duty; and whether they were officially or personally motivated. If seen as deviant behaviour, then use of force can be perceived either as police crimes or state crimes (Green & Ward, 2004).

Police Deviance or State Crime?

The labelling perspective says "whether an act is labelled deviant depends on the response of others to the particular act" and is "not the quality of the act itself but the consequence of it" (Becker, 1964: 9). However, Kappeler, Sluder, and Alpert's (1998) normative definition goes further in suggesting that it is not just behaviour, but the social context in which the behaviour occurs, the formal and informal rules of conduct, and the perception of the behaviour as violating existing social norms that explains why an act is considered deviant. Therefore behaviour is deviant when it is perceived as such either by the victims, or because it outrages the public and its morality, or when the police cannot account for it in a court of law or inquiry. Behaviour that may be perfectly acceptable in terms of police culture may be seen as deviant by an outsider. Until deviance is acknowledged and there is a desire for change, particular police behaviours cannot be addressed.

Punch (1996: 56) defines *organisational deviance* as involving "serious and deliberate practices conducted with a measure of deception, stealth and cunning... in order to achieve formal or informal organisational goals. These can be acts of commission or omission and they are frequently supported, overtly or covertly, by senior management". Thus when the police organisation supports and promotes abuse of deadly force, it is a form of organisational deviance where job-related criminal activities during the course of their work are possible because the very nature of police work, characterised by individual discretion and low level visibility, supports it (Sutherland, 1949).

Ross (2000a) defines state crime to include cover-ups, corruption, disinformation, lack of accountability, and violations of domestic and/or international laws, carried out by the state or by any state agency on its behalf (Friedrichs, 2000). The fact that the police in their capacity as representatives of the state violate the laws that govern their working makes abuse of deadly force a state crime (Chambliss, 1989; Green & Ward, 2004; Menzies, 2000). This research suggests *encounters* incorporated all the elements described as state crime, though this was neither widely recognized nor condemned in official or public discourse. Even when police killings in cold blood were deemed to be illegal and undesirable by those interviewed, this recognition did not prompt a public response decrying it. There were a few incidents when police actions were questioned by the media and in the courts of law, but *encounters* were not seen as a social problem. A major object of the research was exploring whether a form of socio-political complicity existed in what appeared to be a state crime. Recognizing that *encounters* are state crimes would benefit the police organisation in reassessing their own actions and policies, especially in a climate of growing awareness of human rights issues. One of the officers interviewed recognized the proliferation of the use of deadly force as, "a ticking time bomb waiting to explode" and that it would cause a lot of damage, in terms of legal action, as well as loss of public confidence in the police, if allowed to continue unchecked (T 33: Senior Management Officer).

In Mumbai, police use of deadly force in *encounters* was not widely perceived as a form of deviance, either by the police officers, the media, or public discourse. Nor was it recognized as a state crime in the sense of being acts that are *mala in se* or *mala prohibita*. Although, *encounters* were not seen as a social problem, they are problematic in many ways. Any analysis of police deviance involves distinguishing between actual misconduct and mere appearance of wrongdoing (Kappeler et al., 1998). This would involve making a judgement about the apparent merits of the police action in every instance. However, the research concentrated on understanding the police and public's perception of deviance and not on providing evidence of actual police misconduct in *encounter* situations. Making any judgement or accusations of actual police misconduct in particular cases would have to be based on a greater degree of proof about each one than was accessible. Since there was little independent evidence to substantiate claims of actual deviance, the analysis avoids travelling down that particular slippery slope.

Besides, public perception of what was acceptable deviance in police conduct was of greater fascination in the Mumbai context. People appeared to know, or it was common knowledge, that the police used excessive deadly force against criminals. This was evident in public discourse, in the interviews conducted during the research, and in the way that media portrayed such events, even bearing in mind the warning to beware of "sensationalism and distortion often present in media accounts of police activities" (Kappeler et al., 1998: 3). Evidently either people were unaware or did not want to know the actual extent and nature of the deviance involved in such *encounters* – and this study investigates why.

The main causes for a sustained pattern of excessive violence in the Americas appear to be corruption and political interference in the police (Chevigny, 1995). According to Chevigny a particular kind of corruption in which predatory crime, being "bent as a job" (predatory corruption – Punch (1985)), fused with a distorted sense of "mission", being "bent for the job" (combative or strategic corruption – Punch), was responsible for most police violence not only in New York, but other cities he studied in the Americas. Instances where police abuse of force did not cause political ripples, but rather was the outcome of political directives, underline the importance of political backing for such abuse of force to be sustained and continue unpunished.

The police are often in effect allowed to get away with blatant abuse of force. Prosecutions of officers may be rare even in cases of excessive use of deadly force in many countries, and convictions rarer still (Blumberg, 1989; Geller & Scott, 1992; Uldricks & van Mastrigt, 1991). Factors responsible for low rates of culpability for police officers in many instances of excessive use of force are: frustration with the criminal justice system which appears to provide a magical cloak of immunity for police officers; the relatively small number of complaints made against the police; difficulties in substantiating complaints; complete control of investigation by the police themselves; the "code" of silence that ensures officers go to great lengths to protect fellow officers; the greater credibility commonly attached to a police officer's account of events as opposed to that of an accused criminal; jurors frequently feeling more sympathetic to an officer than the complainant, and sometimes even intimidation of witnesses, lawyers, magistrates. Thus there is often a lack of public accountability for police actions, (Box, 1983; Cheh, 1996; Chevigny, 1995; Klockars, 1996; Muir, 1977). In Mumbai too very few officers have received a serious criminal sentence in *encounter* cases (until recently), another instance where the police have been allowed to get away with excessive use of force.

Police Shootings

Reviewing the literature on police shootings in the USA, Geller and Scott (1991: 453) suggest that, "the most common type of incident in which police and civilians shoot one another in urban America involves an on-duty, uniformed, white, male officer and an unarmed black, male civilian between the ages of 17 and 30 in a public location within a high-crime precinct at night in connection with a suspected armed robbery or a 'man with a gun' call" (citing Geller & Karales, 1981a). Clearly therefore gender, race, and age of the police officer and of the "suspect", as well as the situational factors and circumstances that lead up to the incident appear to be important. Also important are structures of race and class inequality and the culture of racial antagonism that flows from this.

Police use of violence as a type of informal punishment for defying police authority, or as a form of "street justice" or vigilante justice has been reported by researchers (Chevigny, 1995; Skolnick & Fyfe, 1993; van Maanen, 1978; Westley, 1970). Geller and Scott (1991) found that the most common reason given by police officers for shooting (ranging from 65 to 73%) was self-defence or defence of another person's life because that is the only way of making it legally acceptable (they cite Fyfe, 1978; Geller & Karales, 1981a; Horvath, 1987). However, while there have been substantial number of shootings when the victim was unarmed, this does not mean that the officers necessarily knew or believed that he was unarmed.

Fyfe (1981a) describes a continuum from elective (the officer decides whether he wants to shoot or not) to non-elective shootings (where the officer has no choice but to shoot). Research also suggests that police have used deadly force in situations such as flight without resistance, warning shots, shots to summon assistance and felonious shootings (Geller & Scott, 1991 citing Geller & Karales, 1981a, 1981b; Meyer, 1980). Geller's (1989) study found that officers' reasons for shooting ranged from gun use threat, to use of threat of other deadly weapons, fight without other resistance, other reasons for intentionally shooting, accidents, mistaken identity, and a stray bullet. However, Chevigny's (1995: 213) conclusion that the worst abuses occur when "the police, impatient with the workings of the courts, simply dispose of suspects in bogus 'shootouts'" comes closest to describing the actual prime motivation behind police *encounters* in Mumbai though officers cited many of the other reasons stated above for shooting.

Studies of police shootings also found that virtually all civilians shot at by the police were male (Geller & Scott, 1991), but Geller and Scott do not mention whether all the officers doing the shooting were predominantly male. Though they found that shootings seemed to occur "predominantly in public locations" this did not ensure that they were always witnessed by the public (Geller & Scott: 462). Fyfe's study of New York shootings found that uninvolved witnesses were rarely present at public locations when deadly force was used, perhaps in part because most of the shootings occurred at night (Fyfe, 1981a). Location was of interest in Mumbai as often officers justified the legitimacy of an *encounter* on the basis that it occurred in a public place, either in daylight or even if, as Fyfe's research found, it was in the middle of the night.

Researchers have found that race was a crucial element in shooting incidents and hat black people were more likely than their white counterparts to be involved in police-related shootings (Fyfe, 1981b; Geller & Karales, 1981a; Robin, 1963). Some research studies found this to be rooted in systematic racism (Takagi, 1974). Others suggest the possibility that blacks and Hispanic minorities were disproportionately involved in violent crimes and therefore were represented in higher numbers in police shootings (Alpert, 1989; Fyfe, 1978, 1981b; Matulia, 1985).

They also were disproportionately more unemployed and likely to spend their time on the streets exposing them to confrontation with the police and involvement in shootings (Milton, Halleck, Lardner, & Albrecht, 1977). All these factors reflect wider structures of racial inequality. Other researchers observed that race was not a controlling factor in a patrol officer's decision to shoot, nor were there significant differences in the race of the victim given similar situational factors (Binder, Scharf, & Gavin, 1982; Brown, 1984). Various findings regarding the connection between police shootings and race are highly contradictory and do not conclusively show any correlation between the two.

Mumbai Police and Deadly Force

Police use of deadly force through *encounters* in Mumbai is a special case. Not only do they seem to be cases of arbitrary street justice where the police act as judge, jury, and executioner, deciding to do something about the "crime problem" by eliminating alleged criminals, but they appear to do so with the blessing of the general public, the media, and the political leadership. However, Mumbai is not unique. Chevigny (1995) and Mars (2002) found similar situations in cities in Brazil, Argentina, Jamaica, and Guyana. Chevigny's (1995) research was conducted during a time when parent countries had (at least nominally) democratic elections; possessed a free press, but faced problems of immigration – forced or voluntary; rapid urbanization and industrialization; the after-effects of colonialism and serious problems of crime; which provoked outcries for repressive police action.

Chevigny found that the fear of crime had become a governing political issue in these countries and there was a talk of a "war on crime" with a corresponding conception of the police as combatants. There was universal lamentation about the courts not being tough enough and the need for tougher measures to control crime – rhetoric that also has resonance in many western industrialised countries. Chevigny calculated what he called "disproportionate violence ratios" on three counts:

> If the number of killings by police is a large percentage of all homicides, that suggests that the police may be using a disproportionate amount of deadly force in relation to the actual hazards of their work and of life in the city; if the number of civilians killed is enormously larger than the number of police killed, that suggests that the police may not be using their weapons exclusively in response to threats from gunmen, as is so often claimed in official accounts of police shootings. Lastly, if the police kill many more than they wound, that suggests the use of deliberate violence against some of the victims.
>
> Chevigny (1995: 15)

However, the city police in the countries studied by Chevigny (Brazil, Argentina, and Jamaica) had emerged from serving under or still functioned under strong dictatorial or authoritarian regimes. Unlike these countries, India, though a former colony, has been a viable and functioning democracy for over 60 years. Police killings have not been at the explicit political behest of dictatorial or authoritarian regimes.

Indeed the dynamics of *encounters* have more in common with the way Skolnick and Fyfe (1993) describe the functioning of the Special Investigation Section (SIS) of the Los Angeles Police Department (LAPD) between 1965 and 1992: a period in which its tally reached 28 dead and 27 wounded in 45 separate shooting incidents. The targets or "clientele" of this squad were outgroups – robbers and burglars who had no defenders in the public. Descriptions of the detailed surveillance operations, stories not tallying with forensic evidence, weapons planted on the suspects after the incident, excessive use of lethal force, bungled investigation reports, missing radio communication etc., seem to indicate that the main intentions of the officers of this unit were to eliminate the suspects from the very beginning and to cover up their mistakes or errors in the operations (Skolnick & Fyfe). This is similar to the Indian and the Mumbai context. Just as officers in the LAPD, no officer in Mumbai had been criminally convicted for *encounters*, though this situation is rapidly changing.

Despite similarities between Mumbai and the LAPD a variety of differences are also apparent: police in the US-based studies usually targeted victims belonging to a distinct ethnic minority or a lower social class. Chevigny (1995) concludes that racism was well and alive in LAPD in the aftermath of the Rodney King incident in 1991 and a majority of the city's populace had the police it wanted. Thus police violence has been held to be disproportionately racially oriented in Los Angeles than would appear at first glance in Mumbai. The population in India is largely undistinguishable in terms of racial characteristics, but is deeply divided on the basis of religion, caste, and region. However, since information on the ethnicity or religious identity of the victims of police *encounters* in Mumbai is not openly available, it is difficult to arrive at any conclusions about their religious affiliations or social status. There appears to be a popular perception in Mumbai that the police target youths belonging to the minority religious community (Muslim) and those who are socially disadvantaged. Unavailability of detailed data has resulted in broader trends about the police organisation's use of lethal coercive power, especially against socially, ethnically, and politically disadvantaged groups, remaining relatively unexplored.

The situation in Mumbai was a complex matrix of factors, involving "encounter specialists" who had celebrity status, a permissive police organisation, and a larger permissive culture that accepted and even encouraged violence. Making sense of this world required a combination of various theoretical approaches to understand this particular form of police use of deadly force.

Explaining Police Violence

Explaining police violence is like fitting together pieces of a jigsaw with various theories accounting for one or the other aspect of the phenomenon. Theoretical explanations for police violence are pitched at different levels and can be classified as macro, meso, and micro theories and are interconnected. Macro-level theories, essentially sociological and structural explanations, take into account social, political, economic, and cultural factors that create circumstances that allow and legitimise police use of force. These factors, in turn have an impact on the ethos of the organisation and the subculture of the police institution, which though universal in some sense, is also influenced by local factors and conditions.

Meso-level theories explain police violence in terms of the organisational culture that encourages or tolerates such use. In turn, the organisation, its culture, rules, procedures, and allegiance to rule of law and accountability affect an individual officer's attitudes and "dispositions" to act in certain ways, varying according to individual officer personalities. The officer then has to make a decision about whether or not to use force, given the immediate nature and factors present in each police citizen interaction. Thus, micro-level theories explain police violence in terms of individual officers' psychological make-up, and/or the situational exigencies in which they have to exercise their judgement.

Three main types of explanations for police violence are – sociological and structural, organisational and subcultural, and individual and situational (Green & Ward, 2004; Terrill, 2001; Uldricks & van Mastrigt, 1991; Worden, 1996) which form the building blocks for a fully social theory of police violence to account for *encounters*. One attempt to synthesise these theoretical approaches and provide a rounded explanation for police violence is Chan's (1996, 1997) exposition of the theory of *field* and *habitus*. Chan suggests that the interaction between the *habitus* and the *field* encompasses factors affecting police decision to use violence at all three levels.

The different levels of explanations for police violence are interrelated as depicted in Fig. 1.1.

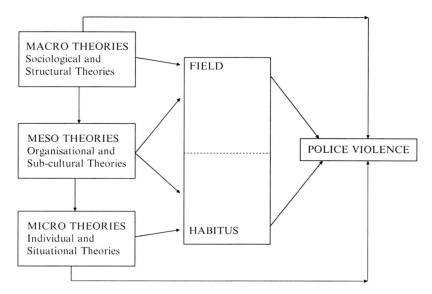

Fig. 1.1 Theories explaining police violence

Sociological and Structural Theories

Sociological theories aim to develop understanding of the problem of police violence beyond the micro-processes of individual action and organisational culture that ask the question: "Why do the police do it?" These theorists aim to answer the question "why are they allowed to do it?" by referring to a broader socio-historical framework.

Box (1983) suggests that acts of violence or brutality cannot be carried out in isolation by officers, but by their very nature can be carried out (and concealed) with the active or passive support of peers and superiors. Presenting of police violence as "defending society against bad elements" provides officers with immunity from prosecution or conviction in many cases. Box (1983: 85)goes on to say that a break-up of the victims' social characteristics revealed that "the 'target' population is not random, but it is drawn from the economically marginalized, politically radical, and ethnically oppressed". Thus, police violence according to Box tends to increase in proportion to the elite's fear of disorder, and the more fearful the elite, the more likely they are to tolerate illegal violence against potentially dangerous groups. Thus in societies with extremely unequal social structures, such as some Latin American countries, the fate of the socially marginal (children, homeless people) is regarded with indifference by the state and the middle class public alike (Chevigny, 1995; Green & Ward, 2004). Even in strong democracies like the UK, Scraton (1987) and Jefferson (1990) found that dehumanisation and demonisation of dissident and marginal groups seeks to construct an "authoritarian consensus" among the "respectable majority", which allows them and the government to authorise or condone coercive measures.

Another social trend in some western democracies has been the growth of paramilitary policing to control social disorders. The demand for and the subsequent creation of specialist elite units, whose training and culture "heightens the very features of the police culture that are most conducive to violence: the perception of danger, fear of outsiders, isolation, secrecy, intense group loyalty and pleasure in 'warrior fantasies'" (Green & Ward, 2004: 80, citing Jefferson, 1990; Kraska & Kappeler, 1997; McCulloch, 2001). The increased threat of terrorism globally has meant that this trend has intensified. Historically it has been demonstrated that measures originally justified on the basis of countering terrorism are quickly absorbed and translated into everyday policing (Green & Ward, 2004).

On the other hand, weak democracies like Brazil, Argentina, and Jamaica do not have an effective monopoly of violence. In such states corruption combined with the public fear of high levels of crime resulting from desperate poverty and impatience with the criminal justice system "makes an explosive brew of state power and vigilantism". As a result, police often act like vigilantes themselves, using violence, including deadly force against the poor and petty criminals "in an effort to intimidate and deter crime and thus to create a semblance of order" (Chevigny, 1995: 143). Skolnick and Fyfe (1993) also trace the source of police brutality in the USA to the American vigilante tradition. Bowden (1978) strikes at the heart of the matter when he suggests that "what might appear on the surface to be *spontaneous* acts of police vigilantism are often in effect managed, supervised, or condoned by governments for their ulterior political motives" (Bowden: 94). Bowden feels that the promise of a rapid return to equilibrium as the attractive outcome of instant justice enables policemen to bypass the legal restraints upon them and rationalize the act of dispensing justice to "those whose guilt the police are sure of" as upholding the law (Bowden: 94).

Chevigny (1995) found in his study of police use of deadly force in the Americas that the police were aware of the illegitimacy of their actions and the international norms that bar it except as a last resort. The authorities invariably claimed all shootings were justified on the basis of self-defence or at least the suspect possessing a deadly weapon.

Mars' (2002: 174) research on police violence in Guyana found that "the enduring influence of colonial rule remained a cogent factor in terms of understanding what appears to be a police occupational subculture of violence". As a quasi-military arm of the state, the police force was encouraged and rewarded for the use of violence to quash internal disturbances. Even after independence in Guyana, the culture of violence was strengthened and legitimised by the state to further its political tyranny, preventing the development of the police as a public service.

Brogden (1987) found that a colonial style of policing can be employed in cases of internal colonialism, implying that policing of particular ethnic or national minority groups within a society are subjected to policies similar to colonial exploitation and subjugation. Thus, minorities often experience harassment, intimidation, oppression, and brute force, a situation that could be said to have arisen in the Deep South in the USA, in Catholic ghettos in Northern Ireland, and in Britain's inner cities (Brewer, 1994). In India, Dhillon (2005: 45) suggests that post-colonial policing is different from the colonial version only "in design not in character".

Organisational and Subcultural Theories

These theories are grounded in the explanation that the police, like other organisations, have their own subculture, which on the one hand can create a "violent" officer, and on the other protect the officer's actions from external censure. Several police scholars have identified key cultural characteristics – mission, action, cynicism, suspicion, machismo, isolation, solidarity, loyalty, pragmatism, and conservatism (summarised in Waddington, 1999a; Reiner, 2000a). These characteristics are core elements of the central police culture, caused by the structural features of police work such as authority, danger, pressure for results, which gives rise to a certain "working personality" (Skolnick, 1966).

The nature of the organisation and the emphasis on factors such as loyalty and secrecy protects officers who are violence prone. "Closing ranks" or erecting a "blue wall of silence" are techniques by which the organisation shields its officers from being under scrutiny or being prosecuted or punished by outside investigating agencies. It can also be argued that certain police organisations appear to have either an overt or tacit policy, or have specialist units that support the use of force by police officers in certain situations. Chevigny's (1995) study on use of deadly force by the police in parts of the USA, Brazil, and Argentina is an illustrative example.

Chan (1997) suggests officers use a body of "organisational knowledge", identifying four types, to help carry out their day-to-day activities. "Dictionary knowledge", (schemas to rapidly classify people and situations), "directory knowledge" (how such people and events are normally dealt with), "recipe knowledge" (combining informal moral code of the police and pragmatic recommendations and strategies to stay out of trouble), and "axiomatic knowledge" (operative goals and values of the organisation, which may differ for the senior and rank-and-file officers) are part of the occupational subculture. These "simplified summaries of information about the social world" termed "typifications"[1] by Holdaway (1996) can often harden into stereotypes. The fact that the police act on the basis of such knowledge is not unique to any particular organisation but is part of a universal cop culture (Reiner, 2000a; Skolnick & Fyfe, 1993; Waddington, 1999b). There may be such common themes in police culture in liberal democracies, but they vary in intensity and there are intra- and inter-organisational and situational differences (Bowling & Foster, 2002; Chan, 1996; Reiner, 2000a; Waddington, 1999a).

However, officers can choose how they resist or adapt to the culture up to a point. Police officers have a degree of autonomy but act in structured situations and with particular predispositions (Chan, 1996). Norms of the "canteen culture" are not necessarily translated into operational practice (Waddington, 1999b) but permit the use of force by providing techniques of neutralization to explain their conduct (Kappeler et al., 1998), and the emphasis on solidarity and silence ensures that officers feel obliged to cover-up and protect colleagues whose conduct they may otherwise disapprove of (see Holdaway, 1983; Punch, 1979; Worden, 1996). The "operational code" (Reisman, 1979) that evolves in the police organisation enables officers to resolve dilemmas of this sort by constructing and reconstructing their daily reality with "guile, craft, and craftiness" (Punch, 1985).

A systematic understanding of the organisation's operating code – a powerful normative order embodied in an "unwritten set of rules and procedures that prescribe what can or must be done and which are enforced by informal peer sanctions and control" and how it subverts organisational goals and sanctions (Reiss, 1977: Foreword) would be essential in understanding how it operates amidst the prevailing political culture to encourage deviant practices such as *encounters*. Police subculture, while not universal and monolithic (Reiner, 2000a), is nevertheless ubiquitous in that "core elements of police talk remain recognizably the same" across jurisdictions (Waddington, 1999a: 111). Countries that are socially, politically, and culturally diverse, share significant features of the subculture for "what unites officers across so many jurisdictions is the experience of wielding coercive authority over fellow

---

[1] A concept originally put forward by Sudnow (1965) to describe typical features of "normal crimes", which provide some form of "proverbial characterization" for the police.

citizens and that… entails taking actions that would otherwise be considered exceptional, exceptionable or illegal" (Waddington, 1999a: 112).

Individual and Situational Theories

There are two types of individual theories. The "rotten apple theory" states that the attitudes and personal characteristics of some officers make them prone to use more violence than others, and it rests on the assumption that a majority of police officers are not violence prone but work within the limitations of law. The other strand of individual theories, the "fascist pigs theory", suggests that only people with certain dispositions, such as authoritarian personalities, are attracted to police work due to its nature so that a majority of officers are violence prone (Uldricks & van Mastrigt, 1991).

The individual theory espouses that "violence prone" or "problem" officers who manifest a *propensity* to use force, and who could be expected to continue to manifest this propensity given invariant conditions are responsible for a "lion's share of the use of excessive force". This explanation found empirical resonance in the findings of the Christopher Commission (1991), Los Angeles (Toch, 1996), Newark (Scharf & Binder, 1983), Jamaica (Chevigny, 1995), and Israel (Herzog, 2000). In Mumbai too, a few "encounter specialists" accounted for a disproportionately large number of *encounter* deaths.

It is questionable whether only a few officers can be blamed for using excessive force. However, individualistic explanations find favour with the police and politicians as they enable them to narrow the focus on a few officers and obfuscate other more serious organisational and larger social issues. It allows them the possibility of being seen as doing something about the problem (should it be socially desirable to do so) by either eliminating or retraining a handful of "problem" officers – solutions that are economical, instantaneous, and populist.

Huggins, Haritos-Fatouros, and Zimbardo's (2002) study of violence workers in Brazil identified three types of masculinities amongst officers – masculinities they term "personalistic", "bureaucratic", and "blended". While they do not suggest that "masculinity itself caused violence or it structured certain kinds of atrocities", they felt that it had a place in police atrocity studies (Huggins et al.: 85). Officers possessing "personalistic" masculinity saw themselves as passionate true believers, whose mission in life was bettering society and protecting it from criminals. They possessed an internal commitment to civilian communities but their feminine, caring side was balanced by their self-image as macho policemen who abhorred physical and mental weakness.

Officers possessing "bureaucratic" masculinity operated as if their masculinity was subordinate to and an extension of the needs and prerogatives of the organisation. As "institutional functionaries" they sought to compartmentalize work and self into separate categories and valued violence merely for its instrumentality in achieving the most appropriate and efficient social control ends. Such officers felt "good" police were "professionals" who know how to employ torture within proper bounds.

Those officers who possessed a "blended" masculinity showed signs of personalistic cops but neither identified positively with the communities they policed, nor with the organisation. They shifted loyalties and were available for purchase. Such officers carried out off-duty executions, which they sought to present as professional legalisms. A confusion of roles led these officers to believe that off-duty executions were legal acts of bravery and not illegal vigilantism at all. Huggins et al. (2002) felt that the personalistic policeman epitomised by "Dirty Harry" (see below) presents himself as acting independently of the police organisation and taking the law in his own hands to do "good". By taking personal responsibility he excludes the police institution, and by extension the state, from atrocities. The "institutional functionary" erases personal responsibility by embedding violence within a complicated bureaucracy. His discourse about violence makes his role in the violence and his organisation's relationship to it, invisible by making it inevitable in achieving desired goals. Blended personalities drew upon first one and then the other kind of legitimation for their violence, switching easily between formal and informal control systems. As an explanation this approach to masculinity appears logical, but this study is unclear about how much of this masculinity is brought into the job by the officer and how much of it develops as a result of the nature of the job and the organisational as well as social context within which the officer operates.

Situational theories examine the characteristics of the situation in which police have used force, concentrating on the age, race, gender, class, of the "suspect" and the officers involved. In some cases the demeanour, status and behaviour of the suspect, seriousness of the offence, the experience level, attitudes and disposition of the officer, visibility of the encounters, numbers of officers present at the scene, and characteristics of the neighbourhood where the interaction takes place play an important role in analysing the outcome of instances where police have used of force (Sherman, 1980). Force is used "in accordance with the dictates of an intuitive grasp of situational exigencies" (Bittner, 1991: 48). These theories deal with the issue of who is more likely to be at the receiving end of police violence (minorities and people of lower class and status) and under which conditions violence is more likely to be used (the nature of the encounter and the presence or otherwise of witnesses). Terrill and Mastrofski's (2002) research found that situational aspects of the police–citizen encounter along with other factors such as *who* the citizen is, and the officer's background characteristics influence police behaviour. Officers with higher education and/or more experience were less likely to employ violence. However, poor, non-white, young males were treated more harshly, whatever their demeanour during the encounter.

Many studies involving empirical research on deadly force concentrate either on the "split second decision" (Geller & Karales, 1981a) or "exit" decisions (Bayley, 1986) made by police officers, analysing the entire nature of the police–citizen interaction in five phases (Scharf & Binder's, 1983).[2] Fyfe (1986) describes the "split-second" syndrome that affects police decision making in crisis, which

---

[2] Also see Fridell and Binder (1992).

provides an after-the-fact justification for unnecessary police violence, and by its very nature and assumptions inhibits development of better techniques and expertise to take such decisions. The split-second syndrome is based on certain assumptions: no two police problems are alike, hence there are no general principles that can be applied to specific situations; given the stressful and time-constrained nature of the problem, certain inappropriate decisions are to be expected, for which officers cannot be criticised, especially by outsiders who have no appreciation of the burdens upon officers; if the citizen intentionally or otherwise provokes a police officer, he and not the officer, should be held responsible for any resulting violence.

Another way of looking at situational theories is by focusing on the victim, which rest on the presumption that certain individuals are more prone to be at the receiving end of police violence than others. Green and Ward (2004: 70) draw upon the work of Muir (1977) to explain that three of the four paradoxes of coercive power that frame Muir's analysis of policing revolve round the premise that "the harder it is for the police to threaten a person with some kind of non-physical harm, the greater the likelihood that they will resort to physical force". Thus when confronted with the "dispossessed" (nothing to lose), the "detached" (who don't care about what they have to lose) and the "irrational" (those who don't understand the threats they face) the police do not have to invoke violence, but they often do. Thus the paradox of dispossession means that the police believe that for people described as "police property" (Lee, 1981) "persons of marginal status or credibility" (Skolnick & Fyfe, 1993), "marginais" in Brazil who are both socially marginal and outlaws (Chevigny, 1996), violence is the only language they are said to understand. The fact that they are disempowered and lack the credibility or the "political" clout to mobilise the media or petition the courts and challenge police actions, makes them more vulnerable to police violence (Chambliss, 1994; Kappeler et al., 1998). Officers' detachment and cynicism towards van Maanen's (1985) "assholes" or Choongh's (1997) "local dross" means that such individuals are perceived as beneath contempt where complaints made by them are not a cause for concern, thus making them the subject of greater violence than necessary. The paradox of irrationality means that not only are the police more likely to use force against those who resist their authority due to drugs, alcohol, or mental illness, but also use of excess force or fatal shootings can be attributed to a temporary loss of control, adrenalin, heightened emotions, or a "combat high" (Chan, 2000; Hunt, 1985; Warren & James, 2000).

Green and Ward (2004) suggest that another reason why police officers tend to use more force than is necessary for restraint or self-defence is Muir's fourth "paradox of face", where "the nastier one's reputation, the less nasty one has to be" (Muir, 1977: 41). Defiance of police authority, especially in the presence of onlookers, provokes punishment, sometimes despite the threat of complaints (Chevigny, 1995; Friedrich, 1980). This contest over "face" is presented in the literature as not just a masculine phenomenon but as Hunt (1985) and Westmarland (2002) found, even women officers had to deal with it.

On the whole, situational theories are of limited value for this research, apart from being part of the justification put forward by some officers to explain use of force decisions. The situational nature of the citizen–police *encounter* is not explored, especially as *encounters* took place, usually shrouded in secrecy, in circumstances where it was either not possible or not feasible to observe them, and also because they appeared to be pre-planned and pre-determined operations rather than the spontaneous result of situational determinants.

Use of Force: A Moral Dilemma

Another way of approaching the problem of understanding use of force decisions is by viewing it as a "classic police dilemma" – the "Dirty Harry Problem" (Klockars, 1991). The Dirty Harry problem originates from the film *Dirty Harry* (1971) where Inspector Harry "Dirty Harry" Callahan is placed in a series of situations where he has to make decisions about whether "bad" means can justifiably be used to achieve "good" ends. The troublesome aspect of this problem is not "whether under some utilitarian calculus a right choice can be made, but that the choice must always be made between at least two wrongs and in choosing either the policeman inevitably taints or tarnishes himself" (Klockars, 1991: 415). Thus by choosing either to act or not act, the police officer is guilty of wrongdoing.

Policing involves situations where the use of force is legitimate and necessary, not only in the eyes of the police officer employing it, but approved of by the on looking public: legitimate means employed to achieve approved goals. However, there are other situations that call for the use of dirty means, including the use of force as a last resort in order to achieve a good end. A genuine moral dilemma results – genuine because it "is a situation from which one cannot emerge innocent, no matter what one does – employ a dirty means, employ an insufficiently dirty means, or walk away" (Klockars, 1991: 413). Such a moral dilemma is a familiar and recurring one to police officers the world over, and the danger, according to Klockars lies not in being wrong (that will be the inevitable result), but in deluding oneself that one has found a way to escape an inescapable dilemma. The consequences for police officers could be: loss of sense of moral proportion, failing to care, turning cynical, or allowing their passions to lead them to employ force indiscriminately, crudely, or too readily.

Skolnick's (1966) policeman as craftsman, who sees himself as a master of his trade, tries to solve the dilemma by denying the dirtiness of its means, justifying its use for achieving good means. This worrisome aspect of Skolnick's craftsman (Klockars, 1991: 422) was what appeared to have been adopted by the police officers in Mumbai. The only way to put an end to the moral problem is by punishing officers who adopt dirty means regardless of the ends they aim to achieve. However, even while putting forward this solution, Klockars admits that insisting that policemen should be punished for having employed dirty means, which appears to be the only way to discourage inappropriate behaviour, creates a Dirty Harry problem for ourselves and for those we urge to effect such punishments (Klockars).

According to Miller and Blackler (2005), police use of deadly force in the USA may be morally justified under three conditions: self-defence, in defence of others, and to uphold the law (in cases of the fleeing felon or the armed suspect). However, they feel that while police use of deadly force to ensure that the law against serious crime is upheld may be morally justified in American society, it is problematic because the issue of which crimes are sufficiently serious to warrant police use of deadly force if the law is to be upheld has to be decided. Besides, it places a great deal of responsibility, not to speak of the opportunity for abuse, on individual members of the police to dispense punishment of death – a sort of justice without a trial. For these reasons Miller and Blackler feel that "upholding the law" has neither moral nor legal justification for use of deadly force. Although the US Supreme Court decided in 1985 that shooting a fleeing felon who posed no immediate danger was unconstitutional (Chevigny, 1995), it appears as if the moral justification for the same has led to the police perhaps continuing the practice, only now disguising or presenting it as self-defence.

Synthesis

Most explanations discussed provide a partial picture of why police violence exists and is tolerated in any society. It is difficult to separate the personality traits of individual officers from the situational and organisational influences that contribute towards creating "dispositions" to act in certain characteristic ways in similar situations (Toch, 1996). Therefore a theory that combines all three approaches to explain police violence would be welcome for being more well-rounded and complete.

Chan's exposition of Bourdieu's theory of *field* and *habitus* (Chan, 1996, 1997), drawing on Skolnick's (1975) work and building on the "fully social" theory of deviance (Taylor, Walton, & Young, 1973), provides a reformulated explanation for police violence. Chan (1996: 115) borrows Bourdieu's concept of *habitus*, "a set of 'dispositions' which integrate past experience and enable individuals to cope with a diversity of unforeseen situations" (citing Wacquant, 1992: 18). It is the "feel for the game" (Bourdieu, 1990: 11) that enables social actors to act *as if* they were calculating rationally, even when lack of time, information, etc. make rational calculation impossible, as they typically do in police decisions to use force (Manning, 1997). The context within which officers act as if they were calculating rationally constitute what Chan, following Bourdieu, calls the *field* of policing: the structure of social relations within which officers struggle to exercise power and authority, stay out of trouble with their superiors, and remain on good terms with their peers. The *field* includes "historical relations between certain social groups and the police, anchored in the legal powers and discretion the police are authorised to exercise and the distribution of power and material resources within the community" (Chan, 1996: 115).

Chan (2000) describes police occupational culture as a "penal culture" (Garland, 1991) that constructs and supports a notion of justice that legitimates violence as a form of punishment. Garland (2001: 163) discusses the culture of control of "high crime" societies (mainly the UK and the USA) and the "crime complex" – a "distinctive cluster of attitudes, beliefs and assumptions" which produces a series of psychological and social effects that influence politics and policy. In such "high crime" societies people exhibit high levels of fear and anxiety about crime and their frustration with the criminal justice's inability to deal with criminals appropriately prompts the demand for stronger action and greater punitiveness. Garland accepts that the instrumental and expressive nature of these punitive strategies differ according to national, historical, and cultural differences (also Sutherland, 1949). However, Melossi (2004) argues that the cultural embeddedness of the discourse on penalty is confirmed by his analysis in the Italian (Catholicism) and North American (Protestant ethic) cultures, but in a way that appears different from any cultural determinism, making this a more complicated argument than would appear at first glance.

Chan (2000: 105) suggests, "the three social dimensions – position (*field*), disposition (*habitus*) and interaction – combine to provide an explanatory framework for understanding police violence". Thus, police violence arises out of a combination of factors: at the conjunction between the point of interaction (situational factors), the police officer's dispositions (a combination of personal traits and attitudes cultivated within the police subculture) and the context (structural, political, and historical factors) within which they operate.

Summary

Explaining police use of deadly force is complicated and ambiguous, especially defining police violence, police brutality, use of excess force, use of deadly force, and abuse of force as police deviance or state crime. The situational, cultural, legal, moral, and operational aspects of use of deadly force by the police make the phenomenon more complex. Additionally, a culture of complicity and approval within the police organisation, the criminal justice system, and society at large, makes it increasingly difficult to acknowledge this form of police deviance as a larger problem of state crime.

This chapter describes the theoretical background to the study of police use of deadly force. Relevant literature on police violence from other countries, especially the USA, UK, Australia, and Canada is discussed. A review of research on police use of deadly force reveals three major approaches to explain police violence: sociological and structural theories, organisational and subcultural theories, and individual and situational theories. Additionally, the nature of police violence as a moral dilemma of the ends and means variety is explored. However, these theories provide explanations at different levels using different units of analysis – society, organisation, and individual. While insightful, the macro, meso, and micro explanations on their own only provide partial accounts for police violence. A more rounded explanation capable of addressing the problem of police violence at all these different levels is desirable. Thus the concluding section of the chapter discusses how Chan's (1996, 1997) use of *field* and *habitus* as a synthesis of all these approaches, is one way of integrating the explanation for police violence at all levels.

Chapter 2
A Tale of Three Cities

Introduction

Police shootings are not restricted to colonial or repressive regimes. In democratic states, however, police shootings often engender controversy, especially if the latter are perceived as being questionable. To illustrate this process, particular incidents of police shootings in three major cities (New York, London, and Mumbai) are discussed in terms of construction of police accounts and the social reaction to these shootings. Common themes running across these police shooting stories are highlighted while acknowledging differences in context.

New York and London, as major international financial and business centres, have long been considered global cities; increasingly, however, other cities are emerging as "new geographies of centrality" with Mumbai being one of these emerging global centres of power (Sassen, 2000). Policing in these large metropolitan cities plays an important role in the making and sustaining of their preeminent status as global players. All three city police forces, the New York Police Department (NYPD), the London Metropolitan Police Service (the Met) and the Mumbai Police have their distinct individual characters that arise from an interaction among their history, reputation and work ethic, and the unique contextual setting of the cities they serve. All three have also been involved in controversial police shootings and embroiled in complicated legal proceedings as a result. The circumstantial and situational backdrop to the police use of deadly force in these different cities and indeed in different incidents in the same city are varied but there are some common threads that bind the case studies presented. This chapter does not attempt to conduct a comprehensive analysis of police use of deadly force in the three cities, instead it focuses on how particular cases were presented, the social reaction to them, and the wider relevance of the apparent similarities in the cases.

Secondary sources (media reports, academic articles, and official documents) are used to analyse the social construction of these shootings. Focusing on reported police version of events and the media and public responses to them, these particular cases are chosen based on the impact they had on cities of comparable importance and size (see Chap. 3). Thus, allowing for a discussion of not only some of the circumstances in which the police shoot to kill, but also the various ways in which systemic protection

J. Belur, *Permission to Shoot? Police Use of Deadly Force in Democracies,*
DOI 10.1007/978-1-4419-0975-6_2, © Springer Science+Business Media, LLC 2010

is offered to the police when this happens. In addition, highlighting similarities in the construction of mitigating circumstances to account for questionable use of deadly force draws out the wider relevance of focusing on the accounts of police officers in Mumbai when justifying the use of deadly force in the chapters to follow.

Police Shootings in Three Cities

Before unpacking the issues surrounding particular shooting incidents, certain common features were identified in the cases discussed in the three cities:

1. The police were involved in controversial shootings where an innocent (or allegedly) person was the "victim".
2. The facts and sequence of events were accessible to the public through the construction and reconstruction of officer accounts and interpretation of the evidence by the media and the legal system. This process is mediated by powerful political forces that shape the debate and also whether and how the "story" will be accepted or contested, thus determining what "realities" and whose "realities" are being represented (Lawrence, 2000b).
3. Police officers involved tend to justify the use of deadly force via accounts that they think will be acceptable to their audiences and "make them look good". This is sometimes deliberate, but often the result of distorted perceptions and mistaken memory recall given the stressful nature of the incident.
4. The cases have been specifically chosen because they created controversy and continue to be subject to intense scrutiny. The real and alleged glaring mistakes made by the police in use of force incidents were highlighted by the media and activists.
5. The strength of the adverse public reaction to the shootings and demands for inquiries and reforms are indicative of democratic forces at play and highlight the media's role in the social construction of these incidents.
6. Though officers involved had to stand trial or face inquiries, they were seldom convicted or underwent disciplinary proceedings. The judge or jury preferred to give the benefit of doubt to police officers, despite clear mistakes in judgement and operational procedures identified in the incidents discussed.
7. Most controversial shooting incidents were followed by reforms in some or all of these – operational procedures, policy, legislation, and firearms training.
8. Finally, the question still remains whether similar procedural shortcomings that characterised these incidents would be highlighted in other cases where the "victim" was a criminal or terrorist and therefore considered "undeserving" or "fit for elimination".

New York: Shootings of Amadou Diallo and Sean Bell

Many police departments in the USA, including NYPD either do not maintain accurate and reliable data on use of force incidents, or if they do, access to it is severely restricted (Kane, 2007). This makes it difficult to comment on a particular department's record on the use of force and compare and contrast firearms discharge records across police departments. An analysis of 42 cases of police shootings recorded by the NYPD over a period of 4 years (2003–2007) showed that the average age of the deceased was 31 years, 41 were male, 35 of the 42 shot by the police were of Black or Hispanic origins, whereas seven were White, and the most common reason for the shooting was because the deceased either possessed or used a weapon (Gill & Pasquale-Styles, 2009). Evidently, the overrepresentation of minority communities, especially Black, in these figures has been a source of tension between the community and the NYPD. I now discuss two cases that aroused a great deal of controversy and exposed the NYPD to severe public criticism.

According to media reports, Amadou Diallo, a 23-year-old black unarmed street peddler, was shot 41 times in February 1999 by four NYPD officers belonging to a "tactical squad" in the Bronx area of New York. It was one of a series of police shootings in which four other black, unarmed men were shot dead by the police in the previous 13 months. The officers, who were on patrol, testified that one officer observed Diallo ducking back into his own doorway, an action considered as "acting suspiciously" by the officers. Officers reportedly believed he matched the description of a "young black man" wanted for rape committed a year ago. The police officers' version suggests that as they stopped the car and approached the young man, identifying themselves as police officers, Diallo "acted suspiciously" and withdrew, at the same time reaching into his waistband. One of the officers shouted "Gun", and believing he was retrieving a gun, all four officers began firing, totalling 41 shots and hitting Diallo 19 times (Harring, 2000). Diallo was neither armed nor the suspected rapist as events subsequently revealed.

Echoing the Diallo case, Sean Bell, another 23-year-old black unarmed man, was shot in the early morning hours of November 2006, outside a Queens Strip club by a group of five NYPD officers. According to media reports of the police story, a group of nine officers of the NYPD's Club Enforcement Initiative rode out in unmarked cars to stakeout Club Kalua in the Queens area in order to set up a prostitution or drugs bust. Three undercover officers went inside the club and were supported by the others waiting in cars outside. At this time Sean Bell's bachelor party was in full swing inside the club; he was to be married later that day. During the course of the evening undercover officer Isnora, observing the actions of a "fat" man in a white baseball cap had reason to believe that the man was carrying a gun. The undercover officers in the club were unable to make any arrests and at around 4 a.m., the officers decided to leave.

Officer Isnora reportedly observed Sean Bell and two companions, Guzman (the fat man in the white baseball cap) and Benefield get into an argument with a group of other men outside the club. Isnora was also said to have overheard Guzman say, "Yo, get my gun". As the officers followed the men outside the club, Benefield was observed speaking on the phone (the officers said they thought he was calling for backup) just as all three men got into a parked car. Isnora followed the men as he called for police backup. Police cars drew up on either side of the road where Bell's car was parked, confining the car carrying the three men. Reports suggest the men then got into the car which began to move, injuring one police officer, before crashing into a minivan in an attempt to get away. Ostensibly believing the men to be armed, Isnora shot first, firing 11 rounds. Four other cops also fired, discharging 50 rounds at the car hitting Bell fatally four times, Guzman 13 times, and Benefield thrice, causing serious injuries to the latter two. There was no return fire from the three men in the car and as it later turned out, none of them were armed (Kolker, 2008; *The New York Times*, 2006). Potentially mitigating circumstances for the shooting were discussed in the subsequent trial. Three of the five officers involved in the shooting of Bell were black but the fact that white police officers were participating in the shooting, the incident was generally perceived as a racist shooting and analogies were drawn to the previous Diallo shooting.

London: Shootings of Harry Stanley and Juan Charles de Menezes

The London Metropolitan Police, a largely unarmed force, has had relatively fewer incidents of police shootings as compared to either the NYPD or the Mumbai police. In the period between 1999 and 2009, 12 people were killed by the Met. Two significant shootings were of Harry Stanley in 1999 and Juan Charles de Menezes in 2005. Both these cases generated controversy and were subject to intense scrutiny.

Harry Stanley was shot dead on September 22, 1999 as he walked home from the pub. He was carrying a table-leg wrapped in plastic, which was earlier mistakenly identified as a sawn-off shotgun by a member of the public who called 999 (Emergency Services) with the information. Two officers (Inspector Sharman and Constable Fagan) of the Armed Response Unit responded to the call. On seeing Stanley carrying what appeared to be a shotgun, they challenged him and each fired one shot. One shot struck Stanley in the left hand and the other hit his head, killing him (IPCC, 2006b). Following the progress of how witness and officer accounts, forensic evidence, and expert testimony were used to construct and reconstruct the shooting makes interesting reading and reinforces the point that presentation of accounts and their interpretation ultimately determine what is considered justifiable and from whose viewpoint.

In the second incident, Juan Charles de Menezes, a 27-year-old Brazilian electrician was shot dead on July 22, 2005 by a group of Special Operations Metropolitan Police Service (MPS) officers in the train at Stockwell Tube station. In the wake of the July 7, 2005 bombings in London, intelligence reports suggested that Hussein Osman was a suspected failed suicide bomb attacker in an incident at Shepherd's Bush station on July 21. Surveillance officers were observing a communal block of flats where Osman was said to be living. They were supported by officers from the Anti-Terrorist Branch to arrest and de-brief suspects if possible and specialist firearms officers to provide firearms cover (IPCC, 2006a). On the morning of July 22, as a young man (Juan Charles de Menezes) left the block of flats, plainclothes officers unsure whether this young man was Osman, followed de Menezes as he got onto a bus (Kennison & Loumansky, 2007). Officers following de Menezes observed him getting off a bus, speaking on his mobile phone and running back to catch the bus, actions that appeared to be classic counter-surveillance behaviour.

In the immediate aftermath of the shooting, witnesses told TV reporters that the young man shot by the police, was wearing a suspiciously bulky overcoat, had jumped the ticket barriers and had run when challenged by the police to stop. Media reports suggested that officers chased de Menezes into the underground station where they had temporarily lost sight of him. Eyewitness accounts claimed three plainclothes officers followed him into the train and shouted, "Get down, get down". The officers then allegedly tripped de Menezes, pushed him to the carriage floor and shot him in the head seven times (Thompson & Phillips, 2005). As it turned out, de Menezies was not a suicide bomber and there were several inaccuracies in the media reports revealed in the Independent Police Complaints Commission's Report (IPCC, 2007).

Mumbai: Shooting of Javed Fawda

Mumbai police's record on police shootings or police *encounters* will be discussed in detail in the following chapters. However, of the hundreds of shootings done by the police over the years, one of the most controversial cases was the shooting of Javed Fawda in 1997. According to the official version, Abu Sayama, alias Javed Talib Shaikh, also known as Javed Fawda,[1] was shot dead in an *encounter* on the night of August 26, 1997 by a team of officers from the Crime Branch, Mumbai Police. According to the evidence of the officers involved in the *encounter* (The Aguiar Commission Report, 1998), they were acting on a tip-off that Fawda and his associates were expected in the Ballard Pier area of Mumbai late at night in order to commit a crime. Fawda was known to the police for his affiliations with a local organised crime group. Police officers planned to lay a trap to arrest them at the scene. Two teams of four and six officers of the Central Intelligence Unit (CIU) set off in cars at around 11 p.m. The teams took position at either end of Sprott Road (where reports indicated Fawda would operate). Some officers alighted from the car to take up hidden positions to observe passing vehicles. At about a quarter past midnight, officers observed a white car stopped on the road and the person sitting in the passenger seat alight. Recognising this person as Javed Fawda, one officer brought out his service revolver and walked towards him saying, "Javed bhaagna nahi" [Javed don't run]. Allegedly, Fawda whipped out a weapon from his waist and fired one shot at him. The officer fired back rapidly in self-defence. Another officer fired a shot at Fawda, who returned fire shattering the windshield of the police car, before collapsing on the ground. In the meanwhile, his associates in the car made a quick getaway. One officer managed to fire a shot at the passing vehicle. In all the police

---

[1] "Fawda" (Hindi), literal meaning rake, was a nickname that referred to Javed's protruding teeth.

claimed to have fired six shots; on the other hand a pistol, with three live ammunition rounds, was recovered from Fawda. Police officers claimed to have taken the injured Fawda to the nearest hospital, where he was declared dead on arrival.

Comparing the Three Contexts

Though the shootings by the police in New York, London, and Mumbai occurred under different circumstances, there are superficial as well as structural similarities that span across the wide differences in the geographic, socio-economic, political, and cultural factors across these three cities and police forces.

Ethnic Minority Victim

Four victims in the cases discussed belonged to a minority community. Diallo and Bell in New York were black, de Menezies in London was Brazilian but mistakenly identified as being of Asian origin, and Fawda was a Muslim man in a city with a majority Hindu population. Initially, there was a brief suspicion that Stanley was Irish (at a time when the Irish Republican Army (IRA) was a threat in London), but was actually of Scottish origin. However, whether Fawda or Stanley was visually as clearly distinguishable from the majority population as in the other cases is unclear. All three city police were accused by the media of targeting men belonging to minority communities that were stereotypically associated with crime and/or terrorism.

Brunson (2007) suggests that policing in the United States has an almost Pavlovian[2] response to race, implying that police officers are conditioned to suspect black men as criminal or dangerous, regardless of their involvement in criminal activities. Skolnick, as early as 1966, referred to American police officers' suspicion of black men as "symbolic assailants" – a suspicion which leads to overpolicing in different forms, from frequent stops and searches through to use of excess force. Racialisation of policing has a long and extensively documented history in the United States (see Jones-Brown, 2007). The consistency with which young black men continue to be disproportionately killed by the police gives rise to questions whether these are indeed isolated "mistakes" or whether the police display a pattern of stereotypical responses to black males.

This is not to suggest that the police display a deliberate prejudice against ethnic minorities. Research showed that background factors such as racial segregation, homicide rates, size of police force, high levels of deprivation, large ethnic minority populations (Liska, 1992) as well as levels of community violence and community

---

[2] Referring to Ivan Pavlov's famous conditioning experiments in which he "trained" dogs to associate the ringing of a bell with receiving food, eventually "training" the dog to salivate on hearing the bell ring, even in the absence of food.

composition (Smith, 2004) have an impact on police use of force. Liska and Yu (1992) hypothesise that larger the non-white population the greater the threat to the interests of the white population. This in turn is directly related to the extent of repressive measures adopted by the police. Thus, the NYPD's record on use of force against young black men might be anchored in wider reasons but it does not refute the allegation that police operational decisions are based on racial profiling. Correll, Park, Judd, Wittenberg, Sadle, and Keesee's (2007) research showed that police officers' racial bias in the USA is rooted in the community's shared racial prejudices and stereotypes. Despite this, officers are less susceptible to racial bias while invoking the decision to shoot as compared to the general population.

In 2005, De Menezes was mistakenly identified by Met officers as a suicide bomber whom they had under surveillance. Evidence presented to the Independent Police Complaints Commission (IPCC) revealed that de Menezes was never properly identified because a surveillance officer was relieving himself at the very moment he was leaving his home. There was considerable confusion about the identity of the man under surveillance and incorrect racial profiling meant officers mistook a person of Brazilian origin to be of Asian origin and thus "racially suspect"; even though he was also identified as being a white male by one of the officers in the surveillance team (Pugliese, 2006). In New York, the police policy of "racial profiling" (Skolnick, 2007) and inaccurate racial profiling by officers in London could arguably be considered responsible for the "mistakes" that occurred in the police shooting incidents described (Banks, Eberhardt, & Ross, 2006; Vaughan-Williams, 2007). On the other hand, critics of this view might justifiably argue that both the Diallo and de Menezes cases were of specific mistaken identities and had nothing to do with racial profiling.

In the case of Javed Fawda, racial profiling was not a clear option as there are no overt racial characteristics marking Muslims out as different from the majority Hindus, though they might be distinguishable on the basis of facial hair and clothes. However, the predominantly Hindu-dominated Mumbai police have often been accused of targeting Muslim minorities. "Police officers, particularly at a junior level appeared to have an in-built bias against Muslims" was the damning finding of the Inquiry Commission's Report into the religious riots in Mumbai (Srikrishna, 1998: 3.13) a few years prior to Fawda's shooting. In Fawda's case, there were allegations that the Mumbai police had targeted a Muslim youth who had putative connections to organised crime.

It has been argued that the police tend to shoot civilians who have been disproportionately involved in serious criminal activities and explained in terms of officers' exposure to dangerous places and persons (Fyfe, 1980; Sherman & Cohen, 1986; Sherman & Langworthy, 1979). Research has found a link between civilian homicides and police shootings alternately known as the "community violence" perspective (Sorenson, Marquart, & Brock, 1993) or "danger-perception" theory (Macdonald, Alpert, & Tennenbaum, 1999). Accordingly, those perceived as having a greater involvement in violent crime are more likely to be targets of police shootings, thus explaining the greater likelihood of police shooting victims belonging to ethnic minority communities.

Mistaken Identity and Beliefs

Diallo was an unarmed street peddler standing outside his own doorway in the Bronx when he was shot. NYPD officers believed that Diallo matched the description of a suspect wanted in a year-old rape case. When approached by the officers, he was seen to have "acted suspiciously" and they believed that he reached out to his back pocket to withdraw a gun. The officers had made wrong judgements on both counts in Diallo's case.

Similarly, Bell and his two associates were emerging from a strip club where they were celebrating the imminent nuptials of Bell later that day. Officers staking out the night club believed one or more of them possessed illegal firearms. As Bell got into an argument with another person outside the club, police believed that it would end up in trouble involving guns. The three men got into a car and allegedly as they moved off officers shot at them in an attempt to stop them from making a getaway. But none of them were found possessing weapons at the time.

In London, a member of the public informed the police that Stanley was carrying a sawn-off shotgun and officers who responded also believed that the table-leg wrapped in blue plastic looked like a shotgun. Though Stanley was actually Scottish, the reporting member of the public thought he was probably Irish and by implication an armed terrorist. Stanley's reaction on being challenged led them to believe that their personal and the public's safety were in danger as Stanley raised his arm carrying the wrapped object. Officers were accused of acting in a prejudicial manner because they believed him to be an armed Irishman, in the wake of the IRA violence in London at the time. However, the officer's testimony, that he was unaware Stanley was Irish, was accepted by the Surrey Police (Surrey Police, 2005).

In the second British incident, police operatives followed de Menezes because they mistakenly identified him as Hussein Osman, a suspected suicide bomber. His suspicious behaviour on the way to the station was considered classic counter surveillance. It was believed that he had entered the underground train in order to unleash a suicide bomb attack. It was alleged that officers believed de Menezes was wearing a bulky overcoat in the middle of summer and was carrying a backpack, ostensibly similar to those used in earlier bomb attacks, and reacted in a suspicious manner when challenged by the police (Gregg, 2006). The IPCC enquiry revealed that de Menezies reboarded the bus because Brixton station was closed and had called his associate to inform him that he might be late for an appointment (IPCC, 2006a). CCTV images revealed that de Menezes walked calmly into the station and was neither wearing a bulky overcoat nor acting suspiciously. It was also later revealed that the reports of de Menezes jumping the barrier were attributed to a ticket collector who had mistaken an armed officer vaulting over the barriers for the "victim" (de Menezes) and briefed the media accordingly. There are no CCTV images once de Menezes entered the platform area, but the IPCC investigation concluded that this was a result of technical faults and that there were no cover-ups on the part of the police. Confusion about actual orders issued and some lack of co-ordination between the various teams of officers meant that instructions to "intercept and stop the suspect from getting on a train" were interpreted as stopping the suspect "at any cost", allowing armed officers to shoot de Menezes under operation Kratos, which was the Met's adopted policy of "shoot-to-kill" when dealing with suicide bombers.

It was alleged that in 1997, the Mumbai police killed Abu Sayama, alias Javed Abu Talib Shaikh, a humble peanut vendor, mistaking him for some other notorious gangster Javed Fawda. However, the notion of mistaken identity was dismissed by the Aguiar Commission but there were several questions raised about the extent of danger to the officers by Javed allegedly reaching towards his waistband on being challenged by the police.

While the NYPD and the Met police had mistaken the identity of Diallo and de Menezes, the Mumbai police were accused of mistaking Javed Fawda for a dreaded criminal linked to the Abu Salem gang while his family claimed he was a poor street vendor struggling to maintain his family amidst extreme poverty (Rattanani, 1997). There was a great deal of confusion around the establishment of the identity of the "victim". Family members alleged that the deceased person was neither a criminal nor called Javed Fawda, instead was called Abu Sayama. On the other hand, the police claimed that the deceased was Javed Shaikh, also known as Javed Fawda on account of his protruding teeth. Police records of fingerprints of one Javed Talib Shaikh, previously arrested and charged with murder, matched the fingerprints of the deceased person. The Judge presiding over the Inquiry Commission ruled that there was no case of mistaken identity and that the person killed, Abu Sayama, was also perhaps known as Javed Fawda (The Aguiar Commission Report, 1998).

However, the inquiry into this allegation and its subsequent dismissal makes interesting reading as it showed the complex conditions in which the Mumbai police had to, and continue to, operate in establishing the identity of a person under difficult circumstances. Circumstances such as the absence of centralised personal criminal or DNA records, a huge city characterised by a large floating population where fake identities can be purchased easily, where births and deaths are not neces-sarily registered in the municipal offices, where ration cards[3] of dubious authenticity (the main document establishing identity and residence, especially amongst the poorer and illiterate classes and slums) proliferate unchecked, where no social security records are maintained for the population, where enrolment in compulsory education is not enforced, and where police registration of criminal cases is often haphazard and misleading at times.

In all these cases, the police were accused of misjudging the danger posed by the "suspect" and of using excessive deadly force against them. The relatively large number of bullets fired by the officers in most of these cases was repeatedly cited by the media almost as if it demonstrated the "trigger happy" nature of policing in these cities. However, research into the use of lethal force by police officers has

---

[3] These were issued to families to enable them to purchase government subsidised essential commodi-ties such as sugar, kerosene, oil, rice, etc. in the years after independence when such commodities were in short supply. In this case, the ration card presented to the court to establish Abu Sayama's identity created more confusion as it claimed a different name for Javed's father from that in the police records and the Missing Person report filed by his sister on August 28, 1997.

demonstrated that perception, judgement, and reaction times of police officers in stressful situations can be hugely complex (see, e.g. Bumgarner, Lewinsky, Hudson, & Sapp, 2006; Lewinsky, 2002; Lewinsky & Hudson, 2003b). Testing officer reaction times under laboratory conditions demonstrated that the more stressful the situation the more slowly a person is likely to respond to changes in the situation. Thus, once officers begin shooting under perceived stressful conditions, while doing many other activities simultaneously and sequentially, their reaction time to stop shooting will be longer (Lewinsky & Hudson, 2003a). This might explain the large number of bullets fired in some of these cases.

Special Police Squads

In all incidents discussed, questionable deadly force was employed by officers belonging to special squads and not regular beat or patrol officers. In New York, the Street Crime Unit tactical squad (Diallo) and undercover plainclothes officers, part of the Club Enforcement Initiative (Bell); in London, the special arms unit (Stanley) and undercover surveillance officers from special branch and armed officers from specialist firearms department (CO19), who formed part of Operation Theseus (de Menezes); and in Mumbai, special Crime Branch officers (Fawda) were involved. In all these cases, the officers involved were part of some special tactical operational teams, by necessity, in many cases.

Punch (1985) has described in detail a number of earlier police scandals around what he calls "strategic corruption" and misconduct that have emanated from special police units and have enveloped the police forces in both New York and London. Specialised units, whose operations are often cloaked in secrecy, possess a sense of invulnerability from outside supervision and control. They are especially prone to becoming "unduly creative" in their quest for achieving high results. Such creativity might lead them to break rules, circumvent the law in many cases, often becoming outright corrupt. The numerous examples of such units point to the necessity for stricter supervision of such units and demanding greater accountability and transparency in their operations (Punch, 2000). Though accountability mechanisms have existed in democratic states to ensure that these units work within the law, especially in cases where deadly force has been employed, the actual operational details of these units are often fiercely protected by the police organisation. Although, the lack of transparency as compared to ordinary policing might well be a prerequisite for the effective functioning of these units.

Post Facto Construction of Plausible Story

In the cases discussed there were allegations, especially in the media, that a plausible story justifying the use of force was carefully constructed by the police. Official accounts are mainly produced for various audiences using publically acceptable and legally justifiable reasons for shooting (Waegel, 1984). This was more evident in the officer testimonies and accounts presented before the courts and inquiry commissions looking into these incidents. Several discrepancies in the official version and evidence gathered from other sources, gave rise to the suspicion that sometimes despite careful construction of an acceptable story, not all loopholes were plugged. The conflict between witness and officer accounts and the physical evidence in police shootings can be scientifically explained in some cases (*Panorama*, 2006), but inevitably raises suspicion that perhaps there was some manipulation of facts.

Bumgarner et al. (2006: 13) found that academic studies broadly tend to consider police violence as "always a matter of misconduct and usually a matter of criminality". Similar doubts were raised in the particular cases discussed. Research has indicated that hindsight bias (i.e. perception of an incident is influenced by the outcome knowledge) plays an important role in the way an incident is perceived by the actors involved and others observing or commenting on it (Villejoubert, O'Keeffe, & Alison, 2006). In incidents where the "victim" was not found in possession of a weapon, observers perceived less danger to the police officers on the scene and police use of deadly force tends to be considered less justifiable under those circumstances. Research has also lent support to the contention that stressful situations such as shooting incidents can distort officer perceptions in different ways leading to accounts conflicting with each other and with the facts (Beehr, Ivanitskaya, Glaser, Erofeev, & Canali, 2004; Lewinsky, 2002; Lewinsky & Hudson, 2003a, 2003b).

In the Diallo case, Harring (2000: 11) openly suggests that police officers had to "fabricate a story to cover the 'roust'. The 'young black rapist' cover story served well since it easily permitted stopping and questioning any such person in the Bronx". Further, Herring adds that since undercover officers blend in with the community and "look more like thugs", Diallo's reaction on being challenged by them could scarcely be called "acting strangely" as they perhaps routinely failed to identify themselves as police officers. This would cast severe doubt on the justification of shooting as a "reasonable exercise of self defence" as the "provoker of a violent encounter cannot then claim self-defence" (Harring, 2000). Waegel (1984) found that police occupational shared knowledge that accounts centring on suggestive moves that have worked in the past often led to similar accounts being applied again to explain subsequent incidents. Perhaps this may have led officers to say that the suspect (Diallo) appeared to reach towards his waistband. However, while no weapon was recovered from Diallo he was found with his wallet in his hand, which lends credibility to the police story that Diallo reached in his pocket to withdraw something that they thought was a gun.

In the Sean Bell case, plain clothed officers again said that they had reason to believe that Bell or his two friends were in possession of a gun/s and were about to engage in violence against another individual or make a getaway when challenged by the police. But no guns were recovered from the three individuals from the car nor was there any corroborating evidence to support the police apprehension that a violent confrontation was imminent.

In the Stanley case, officers were allowed to confer with a solicitor, as per the national procedure operating at the time, before writing up their accounts of the shooting. Though there were inconsistencies in the officer accounts which cannot be adequately accounted for, there was also considerable consistency in the two accounts, giving rise to the allegation that they were fabricated in order to justify the shooting. The IPCC ruled that there was no evidence of deliberate attempts to falsify the evidence, and "perceptual distortions" might account for the discrepancies, the remarkable consistency in the accounts might be the result of either sharing of mistaken recollections or accounts being substantially correct. The accusation of post facto construction of a plausible story in the Stanley case was initially upheld by the Surrey police investigations on the basis that the officers' very accurate and detailed descriptions of Stanley's movements were inconsistent with the forensic facts. However, graphic visualisation techniques and expert testimony were used to explain that Stanley might have reacted to the first shot in his hand and turned away in the split second (a classic response to a bullet shot received while facing the attackers) before the second bullet hit him in the back of the head (Surrey Police, 2005). These findings were independently confirmed by a behavioural scientist, Lewinsky, who claimed that this interpretation of the forensic evidence was most consistent with the reports of the shooting.

In the de Menezes case, officers justified shooting him in the head several times because they believed that he was a suicide bomber and posed a grave threat to public safety. However, as it was subsequently established, this was incorrect. More incriminatingly it was revealed that the Brazilian electrician had already been restrained by a surveillance officer before being shot seven times in the head and once in the shoulder (Cowan, Campbell, & Dodd, 2005). This combination of factors adds weight to the assertion that the story was a post hoc construction to justify the shooting. However, the IPCC (2006a) enquiry established that the shooting was not pre-meditated nor was it authorised by the operational commander but resulted from the confusion created by a plainclothes officer trying to restrain de Menezes in the carriage. On the other hand, Kratos actually permits summary execution of potential suicide bombers in public interest, thus making this case slightly different from the other cases discussed.

Police officers in Mumbai said that they fired in self-defence only when they were attacked by Fawda, who was suspected of intention to commit a serious crime. A pistol with live rounds was allegedly recovered from Fawda by one of the officers, but this evidence was improperly recorded, diminishing its evidentiary value. In addition, there was no documentary or physical evidence to back up the story that a police vehicle had been damaged in the incident. Additional evidence of other officers involved in the incident and eyewitness accounts were not recorded in the original police investigation. There was also no attempt to locate and recover the escaped white car in which Fawda's accomplices allegedly got away, and the vehicle registration number reported was found to be incomplete. No traces of blood were found either on the spot where Fawda allegedly collapsed or in the vehicle that is said to have transported him to hospital. In addition, there appeared to be no explanations for why Fawda got down from the car, as no one was seen waiting for him, nor were there any suggestions that he had got down to check the car because it had broken down. Finally, no evidence was presented to corroborate police intelligence that Fawda was coming to Sprott Road to either kill someone, or deliver guns/explosives, or meet a potential extortion victim. There was little to corroborate the police story which appeared to have been constructed post hoc.

In all the cases, the police chose to present their story as an example of non-elective shooting in self-defence (or defence of others in the de Menezes case). While in the New York and London cases, officers were mistaken in their beliefs, about the victim's identity, their possession of deadly weapon, or that they were about to attack the police or pose a grave threat to people's life or property. In Mumbai, doubts about Fawda's mistaken identity were erased by the Aguiar Commission but the authenticity of the *encounter* was not. Crucially, officers in New York and London admitted to making a mistake in identifying the victim but maintained that the use of force was justified under the circumstances. On the other hand, Mumbai police continued to assert that Fawda was a "hardened" criminal who possessed a firearm and fired it when challenged by the police. This made the use of deadly force against him justifiable in their eyes, even if the Aguiar Commission was not satisfied that it was either reasonable or necessary to do so.

Raising Dust

In the Diallo and de Menezes cases, there were "leaked" media reports that these men were illegal immigrants. There were attempts to discredit Diallo by saying that he behaved suspiciously when challenged by the police either because there were allegations of drug use or that there were some irregularities in his immigration status (Sturcke, 2007) indirectly hinting that somehow his illegal status provided mitigating circumstances or justified his shooting in some twisted way. Diallo was accused of having lied to the immigration authorities and one of theories accounting for the shooting was that being an illegal alien, he thought that the four police officers were actually Immigration officers, coming to catch and expel him from the country. He therefore acted suspiciously, becoming inadvertently responsible for his own shooting (Rivera, 1999).

Similarly, there were tabloid reports alleging that de Menezes had a forged visa stamp on his passport (*The Sun*, 2005) intending to prove that he was a man with something to hide and was afraid of the police. It was a tentative argument that sought to back the police version of events that de Menezes ran when challenged by police officers. However, this particular story was not highlighted prominently in the mainstream media. It was not seriously suggested that because the two men were illegal immigrants, they deserved their fate; but there was some attempt made by the police to cast doubts about the antecedents of the victims, in order to defend their "over" reaction to perceived "suspicious" behaviour.

In the cases of Sean Bell and Javed Fawda too, there were police attempts to divert attention away from their mistakes by adding "mysterious twists" to the story: in the case of Bell, there were rumours of a "mysterious fourth man" who got away and who presumably was in possession of a gun. The fourth man was never found and attempts to find him were a wasted exercise (Gardiner, 2007). Officers in Mumbai too maintained that the white car that brought Fawda to Sprott Road escaped from the scene and though one officer noted down a registration plate number and even shot at the car as it passed by, no car of that description or number was ever found (The Aguiar Commission Report, 1998). In both cases, valuable police time and resources had been spent on looking for what could be called "red herrings" in an attempt to deflect attention away from the actual shooting incident.

Policing Policy

While some of the shootings were perhaps the result of some official or unofficial departmental policy, all of them could be considered to be a part of a larger call for extraordinary police responses to deal with a "war-like" situation. In New York, it was a war on drugs or crime, in London, it was part of the war on terrorism (O'Driscoll, 2008) and in Mumbai, a war on a combination of organised crime and terrorism. One of the main justifications put forward by the police was that the shooting was commensurate to the level of threat or danger posed to society by certain members, be it criminals or terrorists. In these cases, mistakes might occur, but the resulting deaths would count as collateral damage in the "war" being waged by the police (see, e.g. Button, 2005).

In New York, the official firearms policy notwithstanding, a tendency to shoot "suspicious" black men first and ask questions later seemed to operate – something that was perhaps internally tacitly accepted in the department. Organisational support may have been indirect in the reluctance of the Commissioner to take disciplinary action against the officers, but the detectives union president, in fact criticised the City Mayor for having "rushed into judgement" when he expressed the opinion of many New Yorkers that "excessive force" seemed to have been used in the Sean Bell shooting (Haberman, 2008). Research has long recognised that the police tend to use disproportionately greater force against Black (as against White) suspects, including lethal force (Geller, 1982; Smith, 2004). However, NYPD's aggressive policy, especially of stopping and searching black men, is not guided by racial profiling but based on similarity of appearance to a suspect identified by witnesses or victims, according to officers (Skolnick, 2008) – an explanation offered by the officers in the Diallo case. The overly aggressive style of policing by the NYPD has a history of causing friction with the local minority communities and cases such as Diallo and Bell only aggravate such tensions.

In the Stanley case, officers were said to have been compliant with the national procedures before and in the immediate aftermath of the shooting incident. However, as a result of the investigations, these were found to be faulty and were subsequently reformed (IPCC, 2006b). When the officers involved in the incident were suspended, nearly a quarter of all armed officers in the Met threatened to lay down their arms in protest creating a crisis for the Met. One of the reasons for this protest was reportedly because they wanted some clarity in the guidelines telling them what they should do under similar circumstances (Allen, 2004). The Crown Prosecution Service (CPS) and IPCC ultimately decided that there was insufficient evidence to either prosecute or initiate disciplinary proceedings against the officers.

In the aftermath of the 9/11 terrorist attacks in the USA, the London Met had adopted a clearly defined policy called "Operation Kratos", which advocated a "shoot-to-kill" policy to tackle suspected suicide bombers (O'Driscoll, 2008). The de Menezies shooting was a direct result of the application of this policy. The shooting was supported by the then Commissioner of the Met, Ian Blair, who called it a "tragic mistake". The Met was accused of obstructing the IPCC inquiry by restricting access to the investigators for almost 3 days after the incident (Vaughan-Williams, 2007). There was systemic reluctance to prosecute or even condemn the act of the officers involved in this incident by the CPS in 2006.

In Mumbai, police officers interviewed during this research explained that there was a tacit organisational approval for adopting a policy of eliminating "hardened" organised criminals in "*encounters*", which will be explored in the chapters to follow.

Regardless of an explicit or implicit policy supporting police shootings, all three police organisations shared a similar attitude that condoned these shootings and attempted to protect the officers involved in the shooting. The tendency for police organisations to protect their officers and erect a "blue wall of silence" has been well documented in the USA, UK (Punch, 1985; Skolnick, 2008) and, as this research showed, in India.

Trial by Smoke

In all three cities, investigations were conducted in the discussed cases of police shootings and officers faced trial in New York and Mumbai. Though democracy demands accountability, there is a suspicion that courts and juries are ultimately inclined to find police officers not guilty of criminal conduct in these cases.

In New York, police officers involved in the shooting of Diallo and Bell were prosecuted and underwent trial by jury and judge, respectively. Harring's (2000) hugely critical assessment of the Diallo case identified several problems with the trial. To begin with, a consequence of the massive public reaction to the Diallo shooting was that the venue of the trial was shifted to Albany primarily as a conservative reaction to the heavily minority juries in the Bronx. The judge granted the motion to shift the venue to Albany and the prosecution's decision not to contest the motion was considered inexplicable and incompetent. Harring further suggests that the prosecution failed at successfully cross-examining the officers; challenging the officers' claim of self-defence; and raising the "race" issue which was foremost in the public discourse. Instead of the officers being found guilty of excessive use of deadly force, the NYPD officer training and firearms control policy were considered responsible for the terrible "accident". The trial of the officers in the Diallo case "served as a context to legally justify New York's 'aggressive policing' policy, concluding that the killing of Diallo was an 'accident', an unavoidable consequence of good police work" (Harring, 2000: 9). Finding police officers not guilty of criminal conduct in such cases has been the norm in most jurisdictions, as all these cases illustrate. However, there have recently been a spate of cases in India where officers have been charged with and the courts have found police officers guilty of murder in *encounter* cases.[4]

The trial of three police officers in the Sean Bell case in 2008 also began with a request for a change of venue. When this motion was denied by the court, the officers preferred instead to waive a trial by jury and exercised their right to have a bench trial, in which a judge alone determines guilt or innocence. Presumably officers did not expect to have the support of minority jurors in the Queens area (Kolker, 2008). The judge of the State Supreme Court found the officers not guilty of criminal behaviour but was critical of their "carelessness and incompetence" (Haberman, 2008). Police critics alleged that there was a racial element involved, even if the officers involved were black, because their approach towards three white men walking out of the club would have been very different. Stereotypes associated with young black men makes them more susceptible to being at the receiving end of police use of force (Kolker, 2008, citing Reverend Sharpton). The judge, in his ruling, gave greater credence to the officers' testimony that they believed they heard one of the victims mention possession of a weapon while he did not find the testimonies of the other two "victims" (Benefield and Guzman), who denied any such talk "believable" (Baker, 2009). A year after the verdict, federal prosecutors had still to reach a decision whether federal charges were to be brought against the officers and who, in the meanwhile, had requested that internal departmental proceedings against the officers be stalled until a decision was reached. Civil lawsuits against the officers initiated by Bell's fiancee and the other two victims have also been forcibly delayed in the process (Baker, 2009).

In the Stanley case, there were several investigations into the incident: an independent investigation of the case by the Surrey police, two inquests, three reviews into the investigation carried out by the Crown Prosecuting Service, a number of court challenges made to the decisions taken in the case, further investigation by the Surrey police and finally an IPCC report on whether the officers involved should face disciplinary proceedings. Officers were accused among other things, of misjudging the situation resulting in inappropriate actions, exaggerating the perceived threat posed by Stanley, and collaborating after the incident to produce fabricated accounts to justify the shooting. Charges against the officers were found to be unsubstantiated and the officers neither faced trial nor disciplinary proceedings due to insufficient evidence.[5]

---

[4] The Delhi *encounter* case which occurred in 1997 where ten officers were imprisoned for life in 2007 for mistakenly killing two businessmen. Several senior officers were arrested for murder in *encounters* in Gujarat, India, in 2007 and the case is pending trial.
[5] See, for example *The Guardian* (2005), "Policemen Escape Charges Over Table Leg Killing", October 20, 2005.

Following the de Menezes shooting in 2005, the IPCC conducted an independent investigation into the incident. This 6-month investigation highlighted "failures in procedures and communications" in the operation and the IPCC recommended that the CPS would like to consider whether the conduct and actions of some officers might be liable for criminal prosecution. However, after reviewing the evidence, the CPS announced its decision to only prosecute the Office of the Commissioner of the Metropolis for breach of the 1974 Health and Safety at Work Act (IPCC, 2006a). There were to be no criminal charges brought against any of the officers involved in the shooting. A trial by jury in 2007 found the MPS guilty of a "catastrophic series of errors" during the operation that led to firearms officers shooting de Menezes. The MPS was fined and ordered to pay costs after the jury found it had breached health and safety rules and failed in its duty to protect members of the public in the killing of the innocent Brazilian. However, unusually the judge ordered the insertion of a caveat in the jury's decision that the senior police officer in charge of the operation should not be held personally responsible for the tragic accident (Sturcke, 2007).

In 1997, alarmed with a growing number of *encounters* two civil rights bodies, the People's Union of Civil Liberties (PUCL) and the Committee for the Protection of Democratic Rights (CPDR), along with the Samajwadi Party,[6] petitioned the Mumbai High Court to conduct an inquiry into these *encounters*. The High Court found prima facie evidence of a disturbing pattern in police actions in *encounters* and ordered an inquiry into two of them (the killings of Javed Fawda, and Sada Pawle and Vijay Tandel in 1997). Judge A.S. Aguiar carried out the inquiry in 1998. His report was made public in September 1998. The Judge found the *encounters* to be fake. One of them, he said, may never have taken place in the way described by the police, and in the other, the victims appeared to have been unarmed.

There were two parts to the case of Javed Fawda: first, of mistaken identity, and second, deliberate police murder. As mentioned above, while the court found that there was no evidence to support the charge of mistaken identity, the inquiry found adversely against the police that "the deceased Javed Fawda, alias Abu Sayama, alias Javed Abu Talib Shaikh was not killed in the encounter as claimed by the police. It is doubtful whether any such encounter took place" (The Aguiar Commission Report, 1998, paragraph 148: 30). The commission found several weaknesses in both the documentary and forensic evidence, raising serious doubts about the authenticity of the police account. Cross-examination of the police officers revealed that when they went to allegedly arrest Fawda, they were unaware that he was a known gangster or dangerous criminal, which meant that there was no reason for them to be waiting at that spot for the deceased. Examination of the subsequent police investigation revealed that the officers had not taken steps to preserve the fingerprints on the pistol allegedly recovered from him, raising doubts whether Fawda had actually fired at the officers, or indeed whether it was in his possession at all. Though several rounds were allegedly fired, only two empties were recovered from the spot, and none from the vehicle whose windshield was supposedly shattered

---

[6] A political party that purports to promote interests of the Muslim community, but which does not have a very strong support base in the state of Maharashtra or in Mumbai.

by one of the shots fired by Fawda. The windshield itself had been replaced and the car put to use without facts having been recorded satisfactorily. The vehicle in which Fawda was said to have arrived was allowed to get away despite the fact that the police had prior information and its description. The most damaging fact for the police case, however, was the absence of blood stains or pool or blood at the scene of offence where the injured and profusely bleeding Fawda was lying and also the absence of blood in the car by which the injured was taken to the hospital. There were no independent witnesses to support the police version and one of the officers involved in the incident who had a previous history of violence was described by the report as "a trigger happy cop" which lent strength to the commission's conclusion that Fawda was killed in cold blood.

The matter did not end there, shattered by the adverse finding of the Aguiar Commission, the Mumbai police then sought to appeal against this finding by applying to the High Court. A division bench of the High Court consisting of two judges not only ruled that the police *encounter* of Javed Fawda was true and genuine and took place in the exercise of the right to private defence of the officers concerned, but also criticised Judge Aguiar's earlier report and findings (*The Indian Express,* 1999). This bench felt that the police had not questioned any independent witnesses during the subsequent investigation because there could not have been anybody present as the *encounter* had taken place at midnight and at a deserted spot, to substantiate the police version. Also since a lot of blood had been found in the chest cavity and pericardium area, it was clear that the deceased had bled internally and there was very little oozing which accounted for not much blood being reported on the spot. The evidence provided by the post mortem and ballistic experts on behalf of the police was also found to be acceptable. In addition, the Judge was criticised for calling one of the officers involved, a "trigger happy cop", as the latter had been acquitted by the High Court and the appeal against the acquittal was still sub-judice in the Supreme Court.[7] The High Court bench proceeded to lay down guidelines for good practice to be followed by the police in all future instances of *encounters.* Thus, the Mumbai High Court's verdict that the Fawda *encounter* was legal served in actual fact as a signal to the police that their actions were condoned by the legal system, almost as a go-ahead for more "proactive policing" as interviews with police officers revealed.

Trial Outcome

Trials in the cases discussed in all three cities ended in a "Not guilty" verdict. In true democratic tradition, the public and the criminal justice system in all the three cities have often been severely critical of the police for their perceived abuses. However, very rarely have police officers been found guilty of killing even in cases where clearly mistakes were made.

---

[7] "HC gives police clean chit in Javed Fawda shootout case", *The Times of India,* Bombay edition, February 25, 1999.

Bumgarner et al. (2006) suggest that police use of force is prima facie presumed to be improper and excessive unless there is evidence to prove otherwise. In addition, in cases where the physical evidence appears to contradict officer accounts, the officer is rarely given the benefit of doubt, especially by the media and the public. However, judges and juries recognise the difficult choices that police officers have to make and tend to give them the benefit of the doubt (Blumberg, 1989; Geller & Scott, 1992; Pedicelli, 1998; Uldricks & van Mastrigt, 1991). In the Diallo and Fawda cases, there were very few or no witnesses to the incident. In the Bell case, the judge preferred to accept the police officers' version of events against that of the two others injured, given their criminal history and the inconsistencies in their story. Finally, even though accounts of several witnesses in the carriage to the de Menezes shooting contradicted the police story of having shouted "armed police" while entering the carriage, these were deemed to be inaccurate versions attributed to the shock of seeing the shooting by the IPCC investigation (IPCC, 2007). The jury decided to give the benefit of the doubt to the police officers, in the imminent aftermath of the July 7 bombings as the contextual background to the incident.

Public Reaction

Public reaction to police shootings is an important indicator of the robustness of democratic process in demanding police accountability. The public reaction to the Diallo and Bell shooting in New York, especially among the ethnic minority community was one of anger and protest against the court's verdict in favour of the police officers. Public demonstrations were held to protest against perceived police brutality and racism. In London, the de Menezes shooting did not provoke open demonstrations or protests but generated lively discussions and debates as reported in the media. In Mumbai, neither the shooting of Fawda, nor the adverse findings of the Inquiry Commission, nor the overturning of the same findings by the High Court, evoked any sizable public reaction. The shootings were possibly the fallout of the "moral panic" created by the war on terror and crime. It might be argued that media representations of "folk devils" (Cohen, 1972) in the guise of suspected terrorists or criminals became part of the public's "shared imagination". Thus, these police shootings did not evoke instant sympathy in the elites, the business communities, and the majority community regardless of class in the three cities, just as Breuil and Rozema's (2009) research on public acceptance of death squads in cities as diverse as Medellin (Columbia) and Davao (Philippines) indicates. However, it might just be the fact that ordinary people did not have the time or inclination to fight battles that were not their own, as interviewees in Mumbai suggested.

The immediate aftermath of the Diallo shooting in New York provoked a spate of angry protests from the black community in the Bronx. Allegations of racism were aired in protest marches and demonstrations. The jury's verdict of not guilty evoked disappointment in the family and friends of the "victim" and there were calls for the resignation of the officers involved. On the fourth anniversary of Diallo's death, the street where he lived was renamed Amadou Diallo place, a move that was welcomed by city officials as something that would help the community to heal (Hernandez, 2003). However, there was uproar in the minority community in response to the acquittal of the police officers in the trial, including days of demonstrations and arrests. Ten years down the line, public protests over the death of Diallo and the legal and disciplinary inaction against the officers responsible continue with hundreds of people still courting arrest in civil protests (Louis, 2009).

Sean Bell's shooting provoked a public response that decried the police action, but protests against the judge's decision to acquit the three main accused officers of any charges in the case were stronger nearly a year-and-a-half after the actual shooting in April/May 2008. While the state judge's acquittal of the police officers charged in this case was muted in the immediate aftermath of April 25, 2008, a larger protest demonstration was held a few days later in New York. In the largest public protest involving over 1,000 demonstrators against the acquittal of three detectives in the shooting death of Sean Bell, the police reported that 216 people were arrested as carefully orchestrated demonstrations in six locations in the city halted traffic at busy intersections in Manhattan and Brooklyn (Lueck, 2008). The protests were mainly peaceful and a form of civil disobedience in which people signed up to be arrested to protest against the court's verdict. These demonstrations in New York were mirrored by a smaller one in Atlanta to protest the verdict, although there were no arrests. A street in Queens was renamed Sean Bell Way in his memory, a move that received support from the city council but angered the police as it apparently sent a wrong message to young-sters that it is ok to behave as Bell did (Bode, 2009). Renaming streets in memory of "victims" of police killings appears to be popular in New York to demonstrate public support for those killed and keep the cause of demanding justice in their cases alive.

Public campaigns led by Harry Stanley's family led to two inquests and several investigations into his death by the Surrey police, CPS, and the IPCC. There was anger at the refusal of the CPS to charge or prosecute the officers. Vaughan-Williams (2007) traces the public reaction in the UK to the shooting of de Menezes by the Met as initially being one of public sympathy for the officers who seemed to have made a "tragic mistake" in the immediate aftermath of the July 22 bombings in London. Notably there was some concern on the part of Muslim communities who feared for their safety. There were instant calls for the Met Commissioner's resignation from some quarters and in the media, but he did not comply (Thompson, 2005). However, whatever public sympathy there was initially, did not last long and the British public's increasing dissatisfaction with the Met and the Commissioner led to collective action in the form of public vigils and demonstra-tions, especially after the Met's decision to plead not guilty to the Health and Safety charges brought against its officers (Freedland, 2006). Though the police response to the war on terror evoked debate in the media and activists in the UK, the public, by and large, were somewhat removed from protesting vociferously against the police action.

In Mumbai, the public reaction to Fawda's *encounter* was "business as usual". It was seen as another incident in a long line of similar police shootings. As we shall see in the later chapters, there was considerable public apathy towards police *encounters* and in some cases there was some public support for what was seen as justified elimination of a "hardened criminal". This particular case did not evoke a public outcry. Only one political party and some activists protested against the shooting on the grounds of religious discrimination by the police, who were accused of predominantly targeting Muslims. The media coverage of the story was just a little more in-depth than other *encounter* stories as a result of the petition filed in the High Court by one NGO (PUCL) for a judicial inquiry into 100 cases of police *encounters* by the Mumbai police. However, this interest soon fizzled out in the absence of public sympathy for the "victim".

In Mumbai and London, the war on organised crime and on terror evoked greater public sympathy for police actions despite questions being raised about the methods employed by the police. In contrast, in New York, there was considerable public agitation against the perceived racial bias in the police shooting incidents discussed.

Impact of the Shootings on the Police Forces

Experts on police firearms policy in the Diallo case gave their expert opinion that the prevailing firearms training and procedural guidelines in New York empowered police officers, who believed that their own or someone else's life was in imminent danger, to continuously shoot at the trunk of the suspect till he/she was completely immobilised. This implied that the shooting of 41 bullets by four officers into Diallo was just "a disaster waiting to happen: it was only a matter of time before three to four officers would empty their weapons by mistake" (Harring, 2000: 14). Poor training and a faulty "police firearms discharge policy" were blamed for the "accidental" shooting of Diallo. In the immediate aftermath of the Diallo shooting there appeared to be little change in the NYPD "aggressive policing tactics" under Mayor Giuliani. Other incidents of police shooting of black "suspects" provoked mass protests and the fall in Mayor Giuliani's poll ratings was perhaps indicative of the wider white community's disenchantment with his aggressive policies (Harring, 2000).

The aftermath of the Sean Bell shooting brought about calls for sweeping changes to police procedures by senators, activists, and possible mayoral candidates (Phillips, 2008). A tri-level legislative task force, a citizen-led initiative, put forward several proposals for reforming procedures in a "Report on Improving Public Confidence in Law Enforcement and our Criminal Justice System". The New York City Police Commissioner ordered an independent study of department firearms training by the Rand Corporation (*The Post Standard*, 2008). The report found that deficiencies in officer training, especially scenario-based exercises, and the unavailability of alternative weapons of force were responsible for a higher number of officer shootings than could otherwise be justified (Rostker et al., 2008). In response to the Bell case, the NYPD began to administer mandatory breath analyser tests for all officers involved in shootings and introduced expanded use of Tasers as an alternative to lethal force (Phillips, 2008). Reportedly, due to revamped police procedures, improved training and disciplined use of force after the shooting of Sean Bell, fatal police-involved shootings were reported to have plummeted even as the size of the NYPD increased (Pineda, 2009). However, the minority ethnic community and civil rights groups still remain to be convinced that the NYPD has done all it can to allay their suspicion that black young men will continue to be targets of lethal use of force. This dissatisfaction was further strengthened when the mayor claimed to increase the accountability of the NYPD by bolstering the Civilian Review Complain Board (CRCB) with the injection of $1.4 million; claims that were disputed, instead the CRCB budget was actually slashed by the Mayor, raising suspicion that there was only a token intention to discipline overly aggressive police officers (Gardiner, 2008).

Policing in the UK has traditionally been by consent and minimum use of force. However, even though the official Firearms Manual is available on-line, the prevailing perception is that "police rules of engagement" are secret and unpublished to prevent giving unfair advantage to assailants (Kennison & Loumansky, 2007). To contain the aftermath of the Stockwell shooting, the police published a public information document on Operation Kratos on the internet to justify their use of force (Kennison & Loumansky, 2007). Following the Stockwell shooting, Home Secretary Clarke did not accept that a "shoot-to-kill" policy existed, but maintained that the police had to right to use lethal force to prevent a serious crime being committed (Home Affairs Select Committee, 2005). The police "shoot-to-kill" policy, nevertheless, came under greater criticism and scrutiny especially from the civil libertarians, some sections of the public and the media. However, the exact impact of the de Menezes shooting on policing organisational policy has not been made public.

Year on year growth in *encounters* since 1993 ground to a halt in 1998, when the Aguiar Commission's enquiry into the Fawda case ruled that Mumbai police officers involved were guilty and that the *encounter* was faked. The research revealed that the entire department was under tremendous stress and anxiety as the actions of some of their officers were under scrutiny. The judicial inquiry created considerable controversy and led to a temporary hiatus in police *encounters*. The Mumbai police later appealed against the conclusions of this inquiry to the Mumbai High Court, which returned a verdict in favour of the police. The High Court's ruling in late 1999 that Fawda's death was not a false *encounter* was like a signal to the Mumbai police that it was all right to continue conducting *encounters*, provided procedural inadequacies identified by the High Court were rectified in future cases. The High Court had laid down guidelines for police actions in *encounters* that have been used ever since as a checklist by the police to ensure that at least the paperwork conforms to them. As will be shown later, cleared of the charges of conducting false *encounters*, the Mumbai police appeared to have been given a free hand to conduct *encounters* and indulged in a spree eliminating alleged criminals in larger numbers in the immediate years following the High Court verdict (Zaidi, 1999).

Summary

Police shootings in three different cities by police forces with wide-ranging differences in ethos, operational procedures, and firearms policies, occurring under very different circumstances and situations, are compared in this chapter. Despite several differences there were nevertheless identifiable strands of similarities that bound these various stories together. In all the cases discussed, there were allegations of mistaken identity and mistaken assumptions by the police (some of which were substantiated) and there was suspicion of systemic attempts by the police organisation to protect the officers involved. There were several discrepancies in the official police stories, giving rise to the allegation that these were constructed post hoc in order to justify the shooting. Many of these discrepancies could be attributed to hindsight bias or the stressful situations under which officers acted in such incidents. These incidents were perceived to be the result of police stereotypes and prejudices that targeted ethnic minority victims.

All the incidents evoked some form of public protest: big public demonstrations, populist media campaigns, civil liberty activists agitating for "justice for the victims" and sometimes politicians condemning police actions. Despite this, in all the cases, police officers involved were let off without charges or acquitted when prosecuted, regardless of whether the trial was by jury, judge, or a bench of judges. This does not in any way reflect on what actually happened in those police shooting incidents, but emphasises the process of negotiation and political struggle for how stories and accounts are constructed, interpreted, and sometimes reconstructed and re-interpreted by the media and the legal system but with a presumption of good faith on the part of the police officers involved. There may be public protests against perceived police violence and excess use of force and calls for greater police accountability in the aftermath of such shooting incidents but there is still appears to be a reluctance to convict police officers of criminal charges in these cases, perhaps justifiably so given the nature of the difficult decisions to be taken by officers under extremely stressful conditions.

Finally, a comparative analysis of particular cases of police shooting incidents across New York, UK, and India emphasising the universal themes that bind them together serves to underscore the point that sometimes abuses can occur in developed and developing democracies which enjoy a free press and an independent judiciary. Dismissing cases of police excesses as confined exclusively to third world underdeveloped countries or to dictatorial or military regimes is a mistake that one can scarcely afford to make. A universal policing culture of secrecy which protects officers behind "blue walls of silence", the rhetoric of "war on crime or terror", combined with public reluctance to prosecute police officers, demonstrably can allow excess use of deadly force to recur almost anywhere.

In the next chapter, moving from the universal to the particular the focus will shift to police use of deadly force in one particular city, Mumbai, in an attempt to understand what makes the police in a free and vibrant democratic society use deadly force with apparent impunity.

Chapter 3
Policing and Organised Crime in Mumbai

Introduction: Mumbai

The city of Mumbai has a unique socio-economic status in India. It was originally an archipelago of seven islands on the West coast of India, mainly inhabited by tribal fishermen. In the sixteenth century Portugal invaded India and seized control of the deep natural harbour "Bom Bahia" (Good Bay). In 1661, the island of Bombay was given over to King Charles II of England in the dowry of the King of Portugal's sister Catherine of Braganza. From 1675, when the British East India Company moved its headquarters to Bombay, it became an important port and trading centre. With the introduction of the railways in the nineteenth century and the growth of the textile industry, Bombay also became an important industrial and financial centre. Since then, the city has generated immense wealth and has rapidly expanded, with migrants moving to the city in the thousands every day to seek their fortune. The population of Greater Mumbai is estimated to be around 18 million.[1] The city was officially renamed Mumbai (as it was always known in Marathi, the local language of the state) in 1995, a political move to "return to their roots" on the part of the incumbent government. Despite the renaming, residents often refer to the city as Bombay.

Today, Mumbai is the financial hub of India and also the base for India's leading companies, its largest banks, financial institutions, and the National Stock Exchange. The textile industry as the engine of growth has given way to financial services, calls centres, other business outsourcing services, information technology, and entertainment companies, and is home to the largest film industry in the world ("Bollywood"). The construction boom has created a new skyline of high-rise buildings, shopping complexes, office complexes, and hotels.[2] However, rapid expansion of the city has brought in its wake, "blatant contrasts" in housing and living standards and severely inadequate infrastructure, creating a situation of

---

[1] Source: The National Geographic Web site http://www3.nationalgeographic.com/places/cities/city_mumbai.html.

[2] See cities guide at http://www.economist.com/cities, Harris (1995).

J. Belur, *Permission to Shoot? Police Use of Deadly Force in Democracies*,   45
DOI 10.1007/978-1-4419-0975-6_3, © Springer Science+Business Media, LLC 2010

"acute urban crisis" worsened by the "sordid nature of the city's civic politics" (Patel, 1995: xii). Against this backdrop organised crime thrived and came to dominate public consciousness in the city.

Rapid growth in Mumbai was accompanied by a burgeoning in organised and other kinds of crime. Organised crime's pervasive grip on life in the city in the mid- to late 1990s appeared to be such that everyday life decisions such as the scale and opulence of wedding celebrations, purchasing a new flat, a car, or even redecorating one's house were overshadowed by fears of threatening extortion calls from gangs operating in the city. Tracing the growth of organised crime in Mumbai and the police response to combat it since the early 1980s paves the way for understanding how *encounters* as a way of dealing with organised crime seem to be accepted in Mumbai.

Policing in India

Early reference to the police in India is contained in "The Laws of Manu" (about 2000 BC), and through subsequent centuries in philosophical and economic treatises, travellers' accounts, plays, classical texts, and records maintained by ministers of Moghul rulers (in the sixteenth century) and administrators of the British East India Company (Nigam, 1963). Indigenous policing throughout Indian history has displayed two distinct systems: a rural village-based system organised on the basis of land tenure, and a more elaborate system for the towns and cities closely associated with the successive imperial powers that dominated. Rural village-based policing, where responsibility lay primarily with the headman, assisted by a watchman and sometimes by a police helper, continued unchanged by "the tides of conquest, consolidation, and anarchy that have swept over India in the past millennia" (Bayley, 1969). City policing was headed by the *kotwal*, responsible for raising and maintaining a police force as well as carrying out all policing activities such as patrolling, surveillance, arrests, controlling prostitution, gambling, alcohol consumption, etc.[3] (Cox n.d).

Research on the modern (i.e. post-independence[4]) Indian police begins with Bayley's (1969) pioneering work that looks at the relationship between the police and political development in India. Its insights are largely valid even today and inform my research in mapping out the structure and role of the police organisation in India. Since Bayley's study, there has been little rigorous academic research on the Indian police, especially on the use of force. Many books written on the Indian police are either personal accounts of senior and retired police officers about their own experiences (e.g. Bedi, 1998, 2003; Khan, 2004; Nath, 1981; Rajagopalan, 2000; Rebeiro, 1998; Singh, 1999; Subramanium, 2000; Vaikunth, 2000) or mainly descriptive

---

[3] The clearest description of city policing can be found in the *Ain-e-Akbari* (Diary of Akbar, 1556–1605), though it was a system that dated back many centuries (Bayley, 1969).

[4] India gained Independence from British colonial rule on 15 August 1947 and became a Republic on 26 January 1950.

studies or work located within the structural–functional theoretical school written by public administration scholars and criminologists (Mukhopadhyaya, 1997). Most discussions on the police appear to be armchair theorizing, that may be valuable but lack empirical grounding and there is very little written about the police from a critical sociological viewpoint (Verma, 2005). While there have been no studies directly related to the police use of force or deadly force, the studies referred to above and other studies identify problems with the Indian police (Mehra, 1985; Ghosh, 1993).

One of the most systematic and authoritative analysis in the field of policing and human rights is Krishnamurthy's (1996) study. Although his focus is mainly on the rights of the accused in pre-trial processes, he identifies some of the factors that are commonly used to "explain" abuses of police power in India, many of which would apply to the abuse of deadly force too. Nonetheless, after identifying these serious institutional and organisational problems, Krishnamurthy then dismisses them as being no justification for "lawless actions". However, some of the points raised by him recurred in interviews with police officers and were part of their discourse on justifications for the use of deadly force.

Bayley (1969) traces the impact of British rule on Indian policing, dividing the history of its administrative development into two periods 1757–1858 (under the East India Company) and 1858–1947 (as a colony of the British Empire). According to Bayley, the first 100-year period was one of experimentation, with successive attempts to find a solution to the twin problems of law and order and revenue collection that enjoyed limited success. However, the Indian Mutiny of 1857 jolted the British government into enacting the great Indian legal codes (The Code of Civil Procedure 1859, The Indian Penal Code (IPC) in 1860 and the Code of Criminal Procedure in 1861), and the creation of a police commission to study the policing needs of the country for the British government in 1860. The result of the Commission's deliberations was the Indian Police Act of (1861), which reorganised the police and introduced a uniform system throughout India and is the basis of the structure of the Indian police today (Nigam, 1963).

Recognizing that city policing had its own special requirements, a policing model influenced by the Royal Ulster Constabulary, was introduced in the three presidency towns of Madras, Bombay, and Calcutta (Bayley, 1969). This "Commissioner System of Policing" was different from policing in rural districts, in that – the Commissioner of Police combined for law and order purposes the powers of the district magistrate (the administrative head of a district) and the superintendent of police. These police forces were independent and the Commissioner reported to the provincial government directly, not through the Inspector General of Police of the state or province.

After independence from British rule in 1947, India became a democracy with a parliamentary form of government with federal features. The Minister for Home Affairs at the centre and the minister in charge of the Home Department of each of the 28 different states that comprise the federation are responsible for police affairs.[5]

---

[5] There is no national police force but there are several central police agencies, such as the Border Security Force, the Regional Armed Forces, the Central Bureau of Investigation, the Intelligence Bureau, Central Industrial Security Force, and the Indo-Tibetian Border Police. These are under the purview of the Ministry of Home Affairs at the Centre.

The Commissioner of Police is accountable to the minister holding the Home Department portfolio and ultimately to the chief minister of the state.

Bayley (1969) highlights three distinguishing features of the Indian police system: Firstly, since they are "organised, maintained, and directed" into fairly large forces by individual states of the Indian federation, they avoid the fragmentation of police under a system of local control into a number of tiny local units (e.g. the USA) and the rigidity of a national police force (e.g. continental police forces in France or Germany).

Secondly, the Indian police are "horizontally stratified", which affects not only the organisation of ranks and the distribution of power among them but also determines the relation between the state and central government with respect to police administration. Entry to the police service is at three levels – as a Constable, as a Sub-Inspector, and as deputy and assistant superintendent of police (via competitive civil services exams at the state and national level, respectively). Indian Police Service officers are selected via national level competitive exams and are recruited, organised, trained, and disciplined according to national legislation and subject to central government authority for matters other than operational control when on duty. Movement within ranks is restricted and promotions are time-bound not merit oriented. Thus, police officers can generally be promoted only to a certain level depending upon the rank they enter the system. Top ranks are reserved mainly for officers of the prestigious Indian Police Service.

Thirdly, each state police are divided vertically into an armed and an unarmed branch. The unarmed branch or the civil police are responsible for day-to-day policing and the armed branch assists the civil police in maintaining peace. Each state police also has battalions of armed paramilitary forces primarily to assist in law and order duties.[6] However, all officers above the rank of Sub-Inspector are trained in the use of and are entitled to carry firearms.

Bayley (1969: 50–51) suggests that apart from leaving behind the colonial legacy of the structure of the police forces, the British also "bequeathed a concept of the role police should play in Indian society. That is 'proper' police duties today are very much what were considered 'proper' police duties under the British". Presumably this could imply that the ethos driving modern policing in India is the same as that of the erstwhile colonial force, whose primary concern was with suppression of the "natives". Dhillon (2005: 23) describes the Indian police as being "tied irrevocably with long pre-colonial and colonial traditions of servility to the rulers and oppressive behaviour towards the masses" and suggests that because the Indian police have been unable to re-invent itself or keep in step with the pace of societal changes, they are faced with a "credibility gap and a performance crisis... creating a serious mismatch between police practices and people's expectations" (Dhillon, 2005: 26). Since independence there is a general perception in India that the civil

---

[6] These have different names in different states, e.g. the paramilitary police in Maharashtra is called the State Reserve Police, but is called the Provincial Armed Constabulary in my cadre state of Uttar Pradesh and Uttaranchal.

administration (of which the police are a part) consists of "brown sahibs" replacing "white sahibs", where "the IPS are the inheritors of the baton passed down by their British predecessors and the gulf between the 'rulers' and the ruled continues" (Verma, 2005: 48). Thus a feeling of "us" (police) vs. "them" (all others) appears to dominate administrative and policy decision-making.

There have been a number of National and State Police Commissions set up since the early 1960s looking into the question of police reforms. The reports of the National Police Commission (1978–1981) identify numerous structural and organisational problems faced by the police and have made recommendations to improve working practices and service conditions, including training, administration, and accountability structures. Even though the recommended reforms are comprehensive, Verma (2005) is critical of the recommendations of the National Police Commission for not proposing change incrementally, but because they advocated overhauling the entire system. The result would have tilted the balance of power away from the politicians and bureaucrats and in favour of the police and this, naturally met with severe resistance from the government machinery. Also, despite its sweeping mandate, the National Police Commission did not open its discussions to social scientists, other external consultants, and activists; did not involve the media or initiate a public discussion and also did not take into account sweeping changes in policing around the world, failing to go beyond *managerial* changes (Verma). Recommendations of subsequent committees, the Rebeiro Committee (1997), the Padmanabhaiah Committee (2000), the Soli Sorabjee Committee (2006), and various other proposals of expert bodies, outcomes of seminars, conferences, police workshops, and State Police Commissions have all remained exercises in futility (Dhillon, 2005), because they mainly recommend operational and administrative independence from political control. As a result, there has been little or no attempt made by any of the governments since 1947 to introduce legal and administrative reforms, or training improvements, that are long overdue.

Organisation of the Mumbai Police

The Commissioner system of policing was introduced in Bombay in 1861. After Independence from British colonial rule the Indian Police Act (1861) was adopted as the structural basis for the police in independent India and the Bombay Police Act (1951) reaffirmed the organisational and structural configuration of the Police Commissioner system in the city of Bombay.

The total strength of the Mumbai police force in 2009 was 43,242 officers responsible for the safety and security of over 14 million people. Table 3.1 shows that the number of women officers at all ranks is very low and like policing worldwide, Mumbai police is a male-dominated organisation.

Eighty-three police stations, grouped into 39 divisions and 5 policing zones manage day-to-day operational policing in Mumbai. The average police station has one Senior Police Inspector in charge of the station, 4 Police Inspectors,

Table 3.1 Rank structure of the Mumbai Police

Rank	Male officers	Women officers	Total in 2002	Total in 2009	Percentage of total (%)
CP[7]	1	–	1	1	0.002
Joint CP	4	1	5	5	0.01
Additional CP	12	–	12	13	0.03
Deputy CP	37	1	38	40	0.1
Assistant CP	121	3	124	139	0.3
Inspector	966	11	977	1,031	2
Assistant Inspector	743	13	756	985	2
Sub-Inspector	2,751	99	2,850	2,972	7
Assistant Sub-Inspector	3,324	5	3,329	3,601	8
Head Constable	8,018	128	8,146	8,426	20
Constable	23,944	785	24,729	26,029	60
Total	39,921	1,046	40,967	43,242	100

Source: Crime Branch Mumbai Police; Mumbai Police Web site[8]

6–9 Assistant Police Inspectors, approximately 20 Sub-Inspectors, 10 Assistant Sub-Inspectors, and approximately 300 Head Constables and Constables (Interview with Police Inspector, T1). There are also 15 special units, including the Anti Terrorist Squad and the Crime Branch. Figure 3.1 depicts the chain of command that facilitates day-to-day policing.

In comparison, the London Metropolitan Police (the Met) employs 48,000 police officers, staff, traffic wardens and community support officers to police an area of 620 square miles and a population of 7.2 million people. The basic street-level policing of London is carried out by 138 police stations grouped into 32 London boroughs, and one operational unit at Heathrow Airport. They have 23 listed specialist branches and departments.[9]

The New York Police Department, on the other hand, had a scheduled strength of 37,838 police officers and 4,500 auxiliary police officers in 2007 to police an area of 469 square miles and a population of 8.3 million people. Basic policing is carried out by 76 precincts grouped into 8 boroughs, 12 transit districts, and 9 Housing Police Service Areas. They have 18 specialist units and branches.[10]

---

[7] Commissioner of Police.

[8] http://www.mumbaipolice.org/right_of_information/Right_of_Information.pdf (accessed on 23 July 2009).

[9] Source: London Metropolitan Police Web site http://www.met.police.uk (accessed on 23 July 2009).

[10] Source: New York Police Department Web site http://www.nyc.gov/html/nypd/html/home/home.shtml (accessed on 23 July 2009).

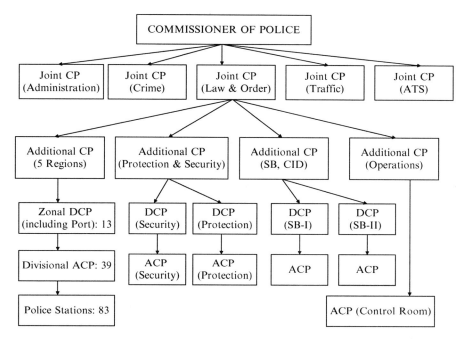

Fig. 3.1 Mumbai police – chain of command. Adapted from source: Mumbai police Web site: http://www.mumbaipolice.org/special/ (*ATS* Anti Terrorist Squad; *SB, CID* Special Branch, Criminal Investigation Department)

The Crime Branch

The Crime Branch's motto is "Excellence in crime prevention, detection, and investigation". It is headed by the Deputy Commissioner of Police (DCP) (detection) and is under the jurisdiction of the Joint Commissioner of Police (Jt. CP) (crime). There are six Assistant Commissioners of Police (ACP) in charge of various regions (south, central, east, west, north) and a special ACP in charge of various units: extortion, Maharashtra Control of Organised Crime Act (MCOCA), central intelligence, property, computer, statistics, and anti-robbery/dacoity.[11] Each regional Assistant Commissioner of Police is in charge of two or three units individually headed by an officer of the rank of Inspector. The Crime Branch, headed by the Jt. CP (crime) is the hub of the crime fighting activities of the Mumbai police (see Fig. 3.2). The DCP (detection) is in overall charge of detection of crime, monitoring the investigation of serious crime and for formulating new strategies for combating organised crime. Inspectors head the various units and cells. Some of these officers along with their Sub-Inspectors were responsible for the majority of *encounters* conducted by the Crime Branch and have been labelled "encounter specialists" by the media and the public.

---

[11] Dacoity is armed robbery committed by five or more persons.

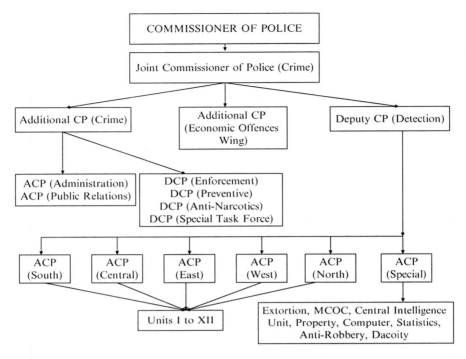

Fig. 3.2 Crime Branch – chain of command. *Source*: Official Web site of the Mumbai Police: http://www.mumbaipolice.org/

Despite similarities, interviews with police officers revealed that these cells were not styled along the lines of "death squads" that emerged in as many as ten states in Latin America (Sluka, 2000), but were mainly involved in intelligence collection, surveillance, and monitoring organised gang activities. Characteristically, death squads operate clandestinely with logistic support from state authorities; can include current and former members of the police and also outsiders; engage in torture, rape, abductions; often ensure their victims "disappear"; and leave abandoned unclaimed (often) tortured bodies (Campbell, 2000; Warren, 2000). While involved in *encounters* especially in the decade between 1993 and 2003, these cells in Mumbai did not just specialize in killing criminals but operated largely as intelligence gathering and crime-fighting units.

Relationship Between Crime and *Encounters*

In Mumbai crimes are registered under the provisions of the IPC, as well as under special local laws such as Arms Act, Gambling Act, Excise Act, Indian Railways Act, Narcotic Drugs and Psychotropic Substances Act, Prevention of Immoral Traffic Act, Scheduled Caste and Scheduled Tribes (Prevention of Atrocities) Act. For example in the year 2002 crimes registered under the special local laws accounted for 67.8% of all crimes as against 32.2% registered under the IPC in India (Crime in India, 2002).

Table 3.2 outlines the crime figures recorded under the provisions of the IPC for Mumbai between 1993 and 2003.

Table 3.2 suggests that overall the number of crimes registered under the IPC peaked in 1995, and thereafter have been steadily declining – a fact that has not been adequately explained or discussed either in sociological or criminological terms in Mumbai.

Since the police consider crime fighting to be their prime task (Reiner, 2000a; Waddington, 1999a), and dealing with extraordinary rise in organised crime was cited a primary reason for *encounters*, crime statistics for Mumbai are compared with London and New York. The annual crime figures for the year 2001 recorded by the NYPD and the MPS reveals that there are wide discrepancies in the number of crimes registered by the three police forces. Even taking into account that the figure for total IPC crimes registered in Mumbai is only a portion (assuming it is only 32.2% of the total crimes registered) of all crimes registered, the discrepancy between the crime statistics of the three cities is remarkable (Table 3.3).

Table 3.2 Annual crime statistics for Mumbai city – 1993–2003

Year	Murder	Robbery	Burglary	Theft	Rape	Extortion	All IPC crimes
1993	687	759	2,852	9,773	131	Unavailable	35,687
1994	354	718	2,707	9,927	150	Unavailable	35,375
1995	357	704	2,955	11,611	210	535	40,289
1996	327	584	2,554	9,924	153	333	32,484
1997	288	495	2,602	10,033	130	230	32,609
1998	365	470	2,472	8,020	118	341	29,869
1999	340	501	2,761	7,641	141	297	29,354
2000	311	569	2,838	7,561	124	309	29,238
2001	295	406	2,861	7,535	127	269	25,686
2002	252	291	2,596	6,181	128	175	26,275
2003	242	239	2,542	5,919	133	142	25,686

Source: Mumbai Police Web site and Crime Branch, Mumbai; Crime in India

Table 3.3 Comparative annual crime statistics of three cities for the year 2001

Crimes	Mumbai	New York[12]	London[13]
Murder	295	960	190
Robbery	406	36,555	53,547
Burglary	2,861	80,400	1,16,027
All theft[14]	7,535	3,77,603	4,43,572
Rape	127	3,546	2,498
Extortion	269	Not available	Not available
Total crimes	25,686	5,56,025	1,057,360

[12] Source: http://www.prsearch.com/crime/new_york (accessed 23 July 2009).

[13] Source: http://maps.met.police.uk/tables.htm (accessed 23 July 2009).

[14] Recorded as larceny plus vehicle larceny in New York.

Making any judgements about crime, its overall incidence, patterns and trends based on the official crime figures is fraught with problems, even within one police jurisdiction. Cross-country comparisons are even more difficult given that the recording of crime occurs in several different contexts: social, political, organisational, and situational (Coleman & Moynihan, 1996). Factors such as citizen willingness to report crimes, police decisions as to which kinds of offences to include in the official statistics, what counting rules apply, and police discretion about whether or how to record crimes contribute to the construction of official crime statistics (Farrington & Dowds, 1985; Maguire, 2002). To illustrate, the column showing figures for murder in Mumbai in Table 3.2 does not include *encounter* killings, which are not recorded as murder, but are generally registered as a crime under various other sections of the IPC and the Arms Act. The first information report (FIR) on any *encounter* case is filed on behalf of the police officer involved in the *encounter* against the alleged criminals who are accused of attempting to murder the officer (section 307 IPC); assaulting or using criminal force to deter a public servant from discharge of his duty (arresting the criminal: section 353 IPC); and acting in furtherance of common intention (conspiracy to commit crime: section 34 IPC), as well as illegal possession and use of unregistered firearms under various sections of the Arms Act.[15] Thus no criminal case is lodged against the police officers involved in *encounter* deaths in the first instance, rather the dead "criminal" is accused of attacking with the intention to kill a police officer fulfilling his official duty. Another problem, especially in the Indian context, identified by Verma (2005: 93) is the practice of *correcting* statistics at a later date, upon the receipt of new information (changing "attempt to murder" to murder) is rarely undertaken in most police organisations, but can minimize crime and distort the picture.

Official police crime figures do not include those crimes recorded by other agencies and are sometimes "cuffed" to avoid work or improve the overall clear-up rates (Maguire, 2002). Other practical techniques such as "creating", "keepy-backs" "juggling", "fiddling", "bending" (Young, 1991), what is known as "burking" in India (Raghavan, 2004) are adopted while recording crime statistics. However, in keeping with Bottomley and Pease's findings (1986) the general public's understanding of crime even in Mumbai was not so much influenced by the "hard" data derived from governmental statistical sources, rather it was moulded and maybe distorted by the powerful messages sent out by the news media and political rhetoric, as well as by personal experience, anecdote, gossip, and fictional representation in books and films (Maguire, 2002). Certainly in Mumbai, the film industry's representations of crime drive public perception of crime, criminals, police, and the criminal justice system to the extent that "reality" is considerably linked to the cinematic universe (Rao, 2006).

Crime trends have been declining in the past few years in New York, London, and Mumbai. The Bureau of Justice Statistics reports a substantial drop in both violent and property crime rates (17.7 and 19.5%, respectively) in the USA between

---

[15] Source: Mumbai Police Crime Branch.

1998 and 2007.[16] Factors such as police force size, incarceration rates, state of the economy, drug use and market activity, and changing age composition of the population are among some of the explanations put forward by academics to account for this drop in the crime trend. However, there has been little empirical research to identify the size and impact of these factors either individually or in conjunction to account for the fall in the crime rate in the USA (Baumer, 2008). Alternatively, Zimring (2007) suggests that half of the decline in crime rate in New York could be attributed to a natural cyclical downturn, and the other half to three major changes in policing. These include increase in police numbers, change in police tactics to focus on public order, and reorganization in police administration and management.

The Metropolitan Police Web site suggests that in 2007 for the fourth year in a row, overall crime was down.[17] The British Crime Survey 2005–2006 shows that crime is stabilising after long periods of reduction. Police crime figures show a 1% reduction in crime figures recorded during 2005–2006 following increases after the introduction the National Crime Recording Standards in 2002 and taking a more victim-oriented approach to crime recording (Simmons, Legg, & Hosking, 2003). However, these surveys report changing trends but do not explain why crime has been falling in England and Wales. The Home Office Web site suggests that focussing on specific problem areas such as drugs and alcohol-related crimes, gun crime, and youth crime via a multi-agency approach and by taking measures to improve community safety has led to crime reduction.[18]

In contrast, there appears to be no official coherent policy or multi-agency approach in Mumbai to account for declining crime figures. When asked about declining crime figures in Mumbai, police officers felt it was the result of their efficient work and effective crime control measures. Ironically, while officers explained a rise in organised crime by referring to wider socio-economic factors, almost none of the officers expressed any awareness that these might account for declining crime trends as well.

Organised Crime

In the USA and in popular discourse the term organised crime is "generally applied to describe a group of people who act together on a long-term basis to commit crimes for gain using the threat of violence" (Levi, 2002). However, as Levi (2002: 879) recognizes, it is problematic to discuss organised crime as if it were "a coherent common noun describing a well-understood set of arrangements to commit crimes" because it covers many different kinds of arrangements: a hierarchical organisation;

---

[16] Source: Bureau of Justice Statistics Web site http://www.ojp.usdoj.gov/bjs/cvict.htm (accessed on 24 July 2009).

[17] http://www.met.police.uk/crimestatistics.

[18] Source: Home Office Web site; http://www.homeoffice.gov.uk/crime-victims (accessed 26 June 2007).

an oligarchy of firms competing in action but in tandem; or, a network of arrangements to commit certain kinds of crime for gain. The form organised crime takes in the USA is different from that in the UK, Italy, Germany or the Netherlands, Russia, and other countries around the world (Albanese, Das, & Verma, 2003; Fijnaut, 1991; Hobbs, 2004; Levi, 2002; Rawlinson, 1998).

Hobbs (2004: 421) suggests that traditional organised crime networks in the UK were "deeply entrenched in the locations, working practices, occupational cultures and very occasionally, oppositional strategies of the industrial working class" (citing Samuel, 1981). However, Hobbs (2004: 421) suggests that the impact of de-industrialisation in the UK has led to the disintegration of this community, with the result that "contemporary organised crime has become located within ad hoc trade-based loose collectivities" that are unstable and even self destructive, but could be said to be anchored in local social systems that are not feudalistic. Though empirical evidence suggests that the traditional family firm has adapted to the contemporary cultural, economic, and geographic terrain, Hobbs (2004) suggests that the success of organised crime depends on the connectivity established between groups and individuals rather than the traditional familial or corporate connectedness that ensured success in the early 1950s and 1960s.

In the USA, organised crime was traditionally mainly associated with an Italian-American crime syndicate called the Mafia, La Cosa Nostra, or Cosa Nostra, and was defined by Jacobs and Panarella (1998: 160) as referring "not to the conduct but to a crime syndicate: a type of criminal formation with an organisational structure, rules, history, division of labour, reputation, capacity for ruthless violence, capacity to corrupt law enforcement and the political system, and the power to infiltrate labour unions and legitimate business" as well as "the ability to become a significant political force through control of grassroots party organisation and campaign contributions". While a version of the alien conspiracy theory originally considered organised crime to be an un-American phenomenon, confined to immigrants and outsiders (Block & Chambliss, 1981; Hobbs, 1997; Ianni & Reuss-Ianni, 1972), since the 1970s, studies have demonstrated that organised crime fits completely into the American social, political, and economic structures (Fijnaut, 1991).

Though organised crime does not necessarily exhibit identical features across the world (Fijnaut, 1991), the definition employed by Jacobs and Panarella (1998) to describe the American Cosa Nostra could apply to organised crime gangs known as "companies" in Mumbai. Kelly (1986: 25) suggests that indigenous groups similar to the Sicilian mafia that emerged in the rural, oppressed regions of southern Italy have been identified in other countries and states, "where the processes of economic development and modernization have produced socially and culturally chaotic conditions for sizeable segments of the population". He identifies conditions that provide ideal breeding ground for "mafias" to proliferate such as: "the expansion of the economy; the criminalization of some of its products; and improvements in the technological base of the society which contribute to the efficient organisation of criminal enterprises" (Kelly, 1986: 26).

Similar conditions prevailed in Mumbai, which continues to be a rapidly expanding city, with a daily influx of migrants, deepening divisions within society, liberalisation of the economy, combined with improved means of communication. These have provided fertile ground for organised crime groups to develop and flourish. Besides, of the various factors that characterize organised crime in any country according to Bovenkerk (1991), the first three identified by him apply to the Indian context in general and pave the way for organised crime groups. These factors are as follows: the political system (one that emphasizes personalized election campaigns and ethnic group affiliations); the role of violence in society (spirit of vigilantism; unwillingness to cooperate with local authorities and resort to violence at the slightest pretext); and the appreciation of prominent crime figures (mafia dons and master criminals glorified and romanticized by the media and films).

Deuskar (1999: 7) defines organised crime in India as "a business or an industry dealing in the supply of goods and services which are barred by law. The crime part is a by-product which is necessary to carry on the business profitably. The main aim of the business is to earn the maximum profits in the shortest possible time span". In the 1960s and 1970s goods smuggled into India were gold, illicit liquor, and electronic items; and organised gangs provided services such as illegal evictions, protection rackets, money laundering, and loan sharking. Deuskar (1999) suggests that organised crime is associated with terror, violence, and brutality, and he sees these as cornerstones of any effective organised gang. The success and survival of a gang depends on its efficiency and ability to deliver the goods without failure. It is by employing terror that gangs are able to maintain control over their own men, deter competitors, and ensure compliance from their victims.

Verma and Tiwari (2003: 243) further suggest that, "organised crime in India may be defined as a group of criminals that are closely aligned with legitimate business, corrupt bureaucracy, and political leadership and are designed to make money or achieve power through violence, illegal means, bribery and/or extortion". This definition introduces the political element in organised crime. The MCOCA (1999) defines organised crime as any continuing unlawful activity by an individual, singly or jointly, either as a member of an organised crime syndicate or on behalf of such a syndicate by use of violence or threat of violence or intimidation or coercion, or other unlawful means with the objective of gaining primary benefits or gaining undue economic or other advantage for himself or any other person promoting insurgency. This definition includes insurgency and terrorist activities within the purview of organised crime.

Hobbs (2000) highlights the difficulties of conducting research on serious and organised crime. He describes how "archive data, police and judicial reports, economic evidence, pamphlets, diaries and biographies" were used by historians to study the origins, growth and development of organised crime. However, as he acknowledges such evidence presents one side of the story and may be biased in favour of the dominant narrative of the control agencies. Despite these difficulties the mentioned sources are major secondary sources for studying the rise of organised crime. Ethnographic work with criminals, let alone organised criminals, is generally difficult and in some cases impractical, involving issues of access, objectivity, and anonymity and confidentiality (Ianni & Reuss-Ianni, 1972). Kelly (1986: 13) suggests research on organised crime groups is also made more difficult because police and law enforcers are inhibited by the law (especially if cases are sub-judice) and necessities of operational requirements that makes them reluctant to disseminate information; and the fact that organised crime groups are not easily penetrable. The fact also remains that what is known by the police, as a reactive institution, will always lag behind what is happening on the streets.

There is little official information about the nature and extent of organised crime groups in Mumbai (Verma & Tiwari, 2003). However, newspaper reports, police stories, reminiscences of retired police officers, films, fiction and non-fiction accounts, and police records and statistics (which were not as detailed and informative as ideal) help trace the history and development of organised crime groups. Bollywood films, a popular source of information about gangs and gangsters have proliferated myths, but also attempted to treat the subject with some degree of seriousness, which doesn't necessarily make them accurate, but useful, nonetheless. Since there are very few in-depth studies of the subject (Deuskar, 1999; Saraf, 1999; Sarkar & Tiwari, 2002; Verma & Tiwari, 2003), there is little to cross check the "authenticity" of these filmed depictions. However, since most of the popular representations of organised gangs in the media, via interviews with gang leaders, non-fictional and fictional accounts are roughly similar, and to a large extent reflect official perspectives on the topic, they can only be cautiously accepted as "reality".

On the other hand, close nexus between gangsters and the film industry (Treverton et al., 2009) implies that Bollywood films may have an element of authenticity in presenting the story of organised crime in Mumbai (Thevar, 2006). The film *Company* (2002), traces the rise and growth of a gang in Mumbai and the genesis of the term "company" that came to characterize an organised criminal group or mafia gang, essentially because it allegedly operates like a company – demanding loyalty of its "employees", possessing a hierarchical order, organised on the principles of division of labour, and having protection policies (good legal representation) and compensation (for the families) for its "employees" should they be injured, arrested, or sentenced in the course of "company" business. Mehta (2005) in his non-fiction study of the city of Mumbai has also recorded the recognizably "corporate" nature of these gangs and the fact that there are specialists storing weapons, supplying them, threatening witnesses, an elaborate support structure for gang members in jail, and the fact that there are "doctors, lawyers, sympathizers, foot soldiers, scouts and people who run safe houses" (Mehta, 2005: 155). However, the bottom line is that there simply is no reliable information about "organised" crime: only varying accounts of it, all of problematic accuracy.

Composition of Organised Criminal Gangs in Mumbai

Membership of organised crime groups implies a potential vulnerability to becoming a "victim" of police use of deadly force. In one of the very few studies on the composition of Mumbai gangs, Saraf (1999: cited in Sarkar & Tiwari, 2002: 10) traces the origin of organised criminal gangs in the city, their criminal activities and the inter-gang warfare and composes a profile of organised criminal gangs. Two-thirds of the gangsters in his sample were in the age group 19–28 years and only 6.5% were above 40 years of age. While a third had received primary education, less than half had received secondary schooling, and 5% were university educated. A majority of the gangsters were migrants to Mumbai.

More importantly, the research identified that in the 1970s and 1980s gangs were not based on region or religion, but after the 1993 serial bomb blasts in Mumbai, gangs have tended to be organised around religious affiliations. The gang leader has a caring attitude towards members and their families are well looked after when members are in jail or killed. The leadership style is supposed to be quite democratic and while there are no initiation ceremonies, gangsters are expected to display unflinching loyalty to the boss or be punished with death. Gangs are organised in a loose confederation, with a smaller gang sometimes merging with a bigger one, but not losing its identity altogether. The small gang is also free to operate independently as long as its activities do not clash with the interests of the bigger gang. Gang members have different roles: sharp shooters, money collectors, and liaison agents who deal with criminal justice agents. Auxiliary members provide shelter, safeguard weapons, and facilitate operations in other ways.

Pendse (2003) discusses the film *Satya* (truth), which deals with the induction of a young man into the world of organised crime in Mumbai in the 1990s, where,

> An unorganised, unemployed insecure mass of youth in an ethical vacuum and cultural confusion constantly lured by consumerist glitter caught in the trap of a speculative economy is an explosive force. A vague discontent, a well-obscured system, indirect exploitation, and unfocused anger provide a congenial atmosphere for ideologies and movements of violence, direct action, spurious identity politics, and fundamental social irresponsibility. Communalisation[19] of society and politics then becomes quite easy in Indian conditions,…The Hindutva[20] of the communalised sections…is a socio-political position that seeks easy and visible (though imaginary) enemies and targets as an outlet for its envy.

(Pendse, 2003: 326)

The 1990s saw a large number of unemployed and unorganized young men who were attracted to a life of crime. The film subtly illustrates almost all the factors that encourage criminality and how they came together in Mumbai to create a cocktail of circumstances that were fertile breeding ground for organised crime groups to flourish.

---

[19] Communalisation: a term used to mean deepening divisions based on religions – especially between Hindus and Muslims.

[20] The concept of Hindutva as elucidated by Savarkar (1969) stands for the quality of being a Hindu and is contrasted to *Hinduism* which is interpreted to mean Hindu *dharma* and as relating to Vedic *dharma*, the latter being a limited, sectarian term representing religious dogma (Lele, 1995: 92). Lele (1995: xix) suggests that the modern project of *hindutva* is based on successfully persuading people to believe in two main premises: "(a) the anxiety and uncertainty that engulf their lives today …is the product of a conspiracy of subtle and overt enemy forces which have been at work internally, regionally and globally and (b) that these forces have emerged not just in the recent past, but have been active for centuries, and against which the Hindu nation has waged heroic battles through its many heroes".

The Rise of Organised Crime in Mumbai

Hobbs (2004) suggests that organised crime is a "wraithlike entity" that exists mainly as a loose conglomeration of criminals that sometimes operate in isolation and at others co-operatively. While this characterisation may be partially representative of the organised crime groups in Mumbai, the popular perception is one of individual "dons" around whom gangs have evolved, who are a law unto themselves, and have certain distinct styles of operation and areas of domination. Thus, while smaller groups might be involved in independent operations, they owe allegiance (and perhaps a share in the spoils) to one or other of the larger organised crime groups and to whom they can appeal to for succour and support in case of trouble.

The growth of organised gangster operations in Mumbai began in the 1970s dominated by a few "dons" who were involved in bootlegging activities and large-scale smuggling operations, mainly gold, electronic items, and drugs (Blom Hansen, 2001; Ghosh, 1991; Singh, 2000). Since the 1980s Mumbai witnessed the growth and proliferation of various gangs emanating from and branching out of these original organised criminal groups. Between 1993 and 2003 six major gangs were in operation in Mumbai. Most gangs were known by the names of their gang leader. These were the Dawood Ibrahim gang (D Company), the Chota Rajan gang (Nana[21] Company), the Arun Gawli gang ("Chaddi"[22] Company), the Amar Naik gang, and the Manchhekar gang. In the late 1990s and early 2000, factions of the Dawood gang, led by Chhota Shakeel and Abu Salem became more active.

In the early 1980s Dawood Ibrahim Kaskar, the son of a Head Constable in the Criminal Investigation Department (CID) of the Bombay police, mobilised a group of mainly Muslim youth to carry on activities of the older generation of mafia leaders such as smuggling, bootlegging, and protection rackets (Nair, 2002). In their interviews, police officers suggested that his background did not give Dawood any special status or power, apart from perhaps insider knowledge of police working practices. The gang emerged as the most dreaded in the city with Chota Shakeel and Chota Rajan as its lieutenants. In 1984 Dawood, pursued by rival gangs and charged with serious offences, fled the country when it became apparent that the police threat to his life and safety was significant. He continued to direct his operations in Mumbai from Dubai (Sarkar & Tiwari, 2002), and was shortly joined by his lieutenants Chota Rajan and Chota Shakeel in directing gang operations from there. Subsequently they continued masterminding operations via remote control from destinations as varied as Malaysia, Singapore, and Karachi. According to police and popular perception it was the fear of police *encounters* that prompted these gang leaders to flee Mumbai.

---

[21] So called because Chhota Rajan is "nana" or elder brother to his troops (Mehta, 2005: 144).

[22] Meaning either underpants or shorts; the gang is called so because of their preference for wearing shorts (Mehta, 2005: 153).

The nature of organised crime changed from the early 1990s onwards when the Indian economy was liberalised. With gold and electronic items no longer subject to import restrictions, the black market dwindled and ceased to be profitable for gangs. Smuggling drugs and arms and ammunition became the new sources of revenue. Extortion (*hafta vasooli*), kidnapping for ransom and contract killings (*supari* killings) spiralled. Increased gang activity in protection rackets, gambling, money laundering (*hawala*), and upscale prostitution, along with involvement in the construction and film industries became the primary profit earners for gangs, deprived of their traditional sources of profit (Ghosh, 1991; Mehta, 2005; Weinstein, 2008).

Around the early 1990s events in Mumbai and elsewhere in India had a profound impact on life in the city and the nature of organised crime. The demolition of the Babri masjid on the 6 December 1992 in Ayodhya[23] by a crowd of Hindu activists and the subsequent waves of religious violence and riots in December 1992 and January 1993 shocked Mumbai and left hundreds dead and several hundred others injured.[24] This event caused a clear divide between the Hindu and Muslim communities who had hitherto lived in relative harmony. Police action during these riots was perceived by many to be biased against the minority Muslim community (Blom Hansen, 2001; Mehta, 2005; Punwani, 2003) with not only police control room communication recorded as clear proof of their contempt for and their unwillingness to provide adequate protection to Muslims (Agnes, 1996) but also 31 officers (including some very senior officers) were indicted by the Srikrishna Commission that was established subsequently to conduct an Inquiry into the riots, "for killing innocent people, acting in a communal manner,[25] being negligent, or rioting themselves" (Mehta, 2005: 117).

In fact, the Commission found that "Shiv Sainiks and Hindu rioters had acted with the collusion and participation of officers in the Bombay and state police. This included police murders of Muslims" (Srikrishna Commission Report: Sect. 1.30). The city police force remains overwhelmingly dominated by Hindu officers (Blom Hansen, 2001), a mere 4.2% of the Maharashtra state police (including Mumbai police), and only 3.65% of IPS officers were Muslim in 2002 (Khalidi, 2003, also citing Rai, 1998). Referring to the Mumbai police, the Srikrishna report confirmed "an alarming pattern of police indifference to, collusion with and active participation during Hindutva attacks on Muslim (and latterly Christian) communities"

---

[23] The masjid or mosque was allegedly built by the Moghul ruler Babar by demolishing an earlier temple which marked the birthplace of Lord Rama (Hindu deity) in Ayodhya, and was subsequently under dispute since 1850. The Bharatiya Janata Party and the Rashtriya Swayamsevak Sangh, following their Hindutva agenda reclaimed what they considered to be a holy birthplace and revived the controversy by beginning the construction of the Ramjanmabhoomi temple in 1990 (Engineer, 1995). This set off a wave of religious riots and disturbances in various parts of the country in the period leading up to and culminating in the massive riots that followed the demolition of the mosque in December 1992.

[24] Official figures reported 900 people dead and 2,036 injured in the riots (Srikrishna Commission Report, Chap. 1, para. 1.24).

[25] In India religious violence or religious riots are referred to as "communal" violence or "communal" riots and usually refer to tensions between Hindu and Muslim communities.

(Bhatt, 2001: 196–197). Whether as a result of the "politics of discreditability" and/ or because the Mumbai police were indicted for being partisan in the communal conflicts that occurred in 1992–1993, this image tainted the media's perception of subsequent police actions against organised gangs.

On 12 March 1993 a series of bombs went off in Mumbai, killing 317 people in the city, in revenge for the anti-Muslim "pogroms" that had taken place a few months earlier. The police subsequently charged Dawood's Muslim criminal syndicate of masterminding and carrying out this deed with the help of Pakistan's Inter Services Intelligence Agency. Punwani (2003: 253) who recorded the voices of those affected by the riots and bomb blasts suggests that Muslims in the city felt vindicated after the blasts, because "even the most communal Hindu began to realize that the Muslims cannot be beaten indefinitely". Punwani suggests the police and the state reacted with vengeance and retaliated with arrests, clampdown on all illegal and unlicensed businesses (mostly small Muslim businessmen) allegedly engaged in custodial torture, and there were large-scale seizures of illegal arms and weapons. It is not certain whether police actions in all these cases were justified or necessary, but they were certainly perceived as being retributive and retaliatory by members of the Muslim community.

From then on the organisation of various gangs began to be drawn around religious lines and the underworld, which was perceived to be completely secular until then, was said to become communalised after the blasts. However, though many of the large gangs had Muslim leaders, they still did not appear to be organised around religious communities, but rather on "criminal talent and ability" (Masselos, 1996: 119).

In the early 1990s apart from concentrating on criminal activities for economic gains, gang activities extended into financing, arming, and facilitating terrorist attacks in Mumbai and other parts of the country, thus fanning communal hatred and inciting violence and reprisals. Masselos (1996: 121) reports evidence suggesting Dawood and others planned a number of killings to provoke a communal reaction, and that the Shiv Sena (a Hindu political party) by responding in like to these killings unknowingly played into the hands of the provocateurs. Masselos (1996: 121) suggests, "the evidence seems to be sufficient to justify the idea of an extensive criminal gang conspiracy although support for the Pakistan connection is far less compelling". The theory behind this allegation was that in the early 1990s Dawood was forced to flee Dubai and seek shelter in Karachi. Beholden to the Pakistani government Dawood presumably engaged in anti-Indian acts because it was essential for receiving continued shelter in Pakistan and also because it was financially profitable. He is said to have used his local contacts and knowledge of the city to mastermind the terrorist attack on the Bombay stock exchange and other important locations in the city in March 1993. Allegedly backed by the Pakistani ISI agency, the Dawood gang was believed to be responsible by the investigating authority[26] for planning and executing the bombings and supplying arms and ammunition that

---

[26] The Bombay blast cases were investigated by the Central Bureau of Investigation (CBI), the premier investigative agency in the country.

caused the destruction to avenge the demolition of the disputed Babri Mosque[27] (Deuskar, 1999; Nair, 2002).

Another explanation for the involvement of organised crime gangs in the riots related to the structures of power that operated with respect to unauthorised land ownership of shanties and slums throughout Mumbai. Masselos (1996) suggests that legal landowners and developers employed organised gangs to set fire to shanty settlements during the riots when the law and order machinery had broken down in order to gain possession of such lands. While in some cases, the attacks were directed against particular religious groups by means of selective targeting of their dwellings, in other cases clearing occurred regardless of the religion of the occupants. The picture is unclear because there were several loci of power in these slums with interests that colluded or collided at times: the Sena branches, other politicised or active groups, slum landlords and bosses, the gangs, and the developers. Masselos (1996: 120) suggests that "when the attacks occurred there was not necessarily any clear communal antagonism at work, rather the communal situation was manipulated for ends that were not communal but economic". Weinstein (2008) goes so far as to suggest that the mafia did not just act on behalf of landowners and builders in the 1990s, but given the soaring land prices, they became a "central figure in Mumbai's land development politics", aided and abetted by corrupt politicians, bureaucrats, and the police. This explanation puts the intervention of organised gangs in the communal riots in a different perspective by adding another economic dimension to their alleged communal activities.

Around 1994 Chota Rajan, a Hindu drug dealer and contract killer, broke away from the Dawood gang and created his own faction. He allegedly joined with the Hindu Arun Gawli gang and was said to be responsible for many retaliatory killings of Dawood's chief men involved in the blasts. The Arun Gawli gang was organised by his predecessor Ramya Naik (Hindu) – who primarily amalgamated several smaller gangs with similar interests that were in opposition to the Dawood gang. The gang was composed predominantly of local Maharashtrian boys and its stronghold was concentrated locally around a particular area in Mumbai. Even after the arrest of Arun Gawli, the activities of the gang continued unabated, and in fact after the police *encounter* of Amar Naik (Hindu), his gang was also absorbed into the Gawli gang.

Another lieutenant of the Dawood gang, Abu Salem (Muslim), who went on to create his own gang, was considered a prime suspect for the Bombay blasts of 1993, and was wanted in more than 60 cases of murder, attempted murder, extortion, and abduction. When he broke up with the Dawood gang over sharing the underworld earnings from the Mumbai film industry in the mid-1990s, he fled from Dubai to the USA and then later to Lisbon (Portugal). From there he continued to conduct his extortion campaign in the Mumbai film industry. His group was said to have been responsible for the murders of several film personalities and was a source of

---

[27] See for example, "1993 Mumbai Blasts: Four Memons convicted", *The Times of India*, Mumbai edition, 12 September 2006.

terror and fear in the film world (Katakam, 2005). Salem's involvement in financing and distribution of films and his virtual presence in the film industry continued to be a source of threat and impediment to the autonomy of several filmmakers. He was also allegedly involved in the killing of several Shiv Sena and Bharatiya Janata Party (BJP, both Hindu parties) leaders (IPCS, 2005; Ketkar, 2004). Suspected of being a part of the Al Qaeda network by Indian agencies as well as the FBI, Abu Salem was extradited from Lisbon in 2005 and was brought to India for questioning and prosecution (Katakam, 2005). Around this period the Chhota Shakeel (Muslim) gang, that used to be a wing of D Company, was operating independently, though not in dispute with the bigger gang.

Apart from these major players, there were a host of other small, local gangs who specialized in terrorizing local residents, extorting money, and settling disputes by brute force who were constantly engaged in power tussles to protect their "turf" from other gangs. As interviews with police officers and "claimsmakers" revealed, most of the extortion demands or threats were made via the telephone, with the "gangster" often claiming to be part of some larger organised gang. Ordinary residents could in no way ascertain whether the threat posed to them was by an actual organised gang or a small time operator. It appeared to the public as if there was an open season for anyone who wished to reap the benefits of society's fear of organised crime groups. This was how not just the rich and famous, but even ordinary, middle class people felt the widespread impact of organised crime.

Political Involvement in Organised Crime

As in many other cities beset with organised crime groups (see, e.g. Anechiarico, 1991), it can at least be surmised that these could not have existed, flourished, and operated relatively unhindered without some co-operation from the law enforcement agencies and political patronage. Verma and Tiwari (2003) describe the relationship between business, the bureaucracy, and politicians in India as being one of reciprocity and mutual benefit: business people provide the capital in return for enhanced profits; bureaucrats misuse their authority in favour of racketeers, neutralize or enfeeble authority of official agents, and accept part of the profits as bribes; politicians, whose major motive is capturing power, act as godfathers diverting attention from the criminal activities of these gangs and ensure that arrested gangsters are treated leniently by the state. "The results of such a powerful combination are deadly: the state stands compromised, the official agencies are demoralized and made ineffective, and the public exchequer is looted of huge sums of money" (Verma & Tiwari, 2003: 243).

The connection between politics and crime is reciprocal – on the one hand, criminals are associated (overt participation and covert support via funds or muscle power) in the business of politics; and on the other, politics influences criminological discourse, affecting both perception of the "crime problem", and the techniques developed to control it (Cohen, 1996). The "criminalization of politics" and "politicization of crime" in this sense were in evidence in Mumbai.

The political location of organised crime in Mumbai was influenced by what Cohen (1996: 8) describes as "the actual incidence, severity and risk of criminal victimization...the public perception of the seriousness of the crime problem...and the rhetorical manipulation of the crime problem and public anxiety in media and political discourse". Embedding the crime problem into political discourse in Mumbai became more pronounced from the late 1980s when organised crime began to soar and its impact was perceived to be more widely felt. Power struggles between the major political parties in Mumbai may have been responsible for this development.

Indian multi-party democracy has given rise to a proliferation of parties at the national, regional and local levels. In Maharashtra, the Congress Party was the dominant political force till the mid-1990s. Factions of this party jostled for power at the state level. This party calls itself secular but has had to defend itself against general allegations that it appeased Muslim voters. Since the formation of the State of Maharashtra in 1960, the Congress Party, or one of its factions has been in power at the State level except when it was out of power for the brief period between 1995 and 2000 when the Shiv Sena and BJP won the State elections (Purandare, 1999). However, it returned to power in 2004.

The other major political party was the Shiv Sena ("Army of Shiva"), set up in 1966 by Balasaheb Thackeray to promote local and regional interests. It also promised to wipe out gangsters and tried to gain sympathy from the middle classes. Lele (1995: 3) suggests that by the 1960s "while publicly attacking the underworld, it [the Shiv Sena] managed to create within itself a strong and dedicated following that gave the organisation its muscle power and in return gave those in the underworld the benefit of its organisation and discipline". Thus the roots of their association with organised crime were sown in the slums and "bastis"[28] of Mumbai where scores of dedicated young men formed the cadres of the Sainiks, as it gave them a sense of power and masculinity (Mehta, 2005). The Shiv Sena joined the Hindutva brigade (comprising of the Jan Sangh, the Rashtriya Swayamsevak Sangh, and the BJP) in 1984, at a time when its popularity was waning and its regional appeal had dramatically weakened. This led the Shiv Sena to look upon militant Hinduism as a possible alternate ideology to win back popularity with the masses (Lele, 1995). Its association with Hindu-dominated gangs meant that rival Muslim gangs were kept under check, especially in the years the Sena was in power.

Political involvement in gang wars appeared to be communal, with the Hindu Shiv Sena Party providing open support to the Arun Gawli gang in the early part of the 1990s. However, when Gawli floated his own political party in 1997, posing a threat to the Sena, it is said that Thackeray directed the police to come down hard on Gawli (Mehta, 2005). A closer examination of the break-up of *encounters* in Table 3.4 shows that in the years after the BJP–Shiv Sena government went out of power in 2000, the number of members of the Dawood gang who died in police *encounters* dwindled drastically.

---

[28] Shanty towns.

Table 3.4 Gang affiliation of criminals killed in *encounters* – 1993–2003

Year	Dawood Ibrahim	Chota Rajan	Chota Shakil	Arun Gawli	Ashwin Naik	Others
1993	15	0	0	0	1	21
1994	7	0	0	5	12	6
1995	3	0	0	1	2	1
1996	15	11	0	5	6	21
1997	20	22	0	12	3	11
1998	13	16	0	4	6	9
1999	35	7	0	10	12	19
2000	36	5	0	5	2	13
2001	0	44	20	0	7	23
2002	1	21	7	0	1	17
2003 (31.07.03)	0	14	2	3	0	18

Source: Crime Branch, Mumbai Police

It appears that while in the years when the Sena government was in power there were many more casualties in Muslim-dominated gangs. Since then the focus of police *encounters* has perhaps shifted to rival gangs since 2000. However, drawing conclusions on the basis of these figures is not without skepticism, for there are no independent methods to confirm or verify police statistics concerning gang affiliations. Mehta (2005) reports a conversation with Chhota Shakeel, where the latter alleged that the police reported that all Muslim criminals killed or arrested belonged to Dawood's gang, regardless of their actual affiliation with any gang. Furthermore, the police have not made public the religious affiliations of the "criminals" killed by them, it cannot be assumed that all those *encountered* and said to belong to a Muslim gang were actually Muslims themselves and vice versa. It is unclear whether the police maintain such records internally, but these are not public records.

In the USA it was earlier thought that ethnic or racial identity were key factors in determining organised group membership, but empirical research had shown that "although preference may be given to kinship in some crime organisations, recruitment of and interaction with 'outgroup' criminals is based primarily on need, availability, and cost effectiveness" (Potter, 1994: 16). Similarly, in Mumbai organised group affiliations were perceived by the public to be based on communal grounds (not ethnicity or race). But there was a noticeable absence of such a discourse in either the police or criminal milieu. In fact, leaders of organised gangs have asserted that their organisations did not make distinctions between Hindu and Muslim members in interviews given to the media. For example, Chhota Shakeel was reported denying that gangs are formed along communal lines, "'Many Hindu boys are with us', he says, putting the ratio as high as fifty–fifty… 'Our motto', he declares, 'is insaniyat'[29]" (Mehta, 2005: 265).

---

[29] Ironically – insaniyat means humanity or humanism.

One of the main reasons why criminal organisations might emphasize the "secular" nature of their gang would be to disassociate themselves from accusations of terrorism, which they realized would be less tolerated than their criminal activities. In fact, one gang leader reportedly claimed in a newspaper interview that they were gangsters, and not terrorists, and that Dawood or his gang had no involvement in the bomb blasts either in 1993 or in July 2006 (Balakrishnan, 2006). On the other hand, the police alleged that they had evidence of definite involvement of criminal organised gangs in the terror attacks, and clearly felt that "Muslim" gangs had aided and abetted the terrorists. However, police officers in their interviews and in public statements maintained that their war was against criminals and organised crime in general, not against members of particular communities. A few officers who referred to the communal aspect seemed to suggest that if it appeared that stricter action was being taken against some gangs (which happen to be dominated by "Muslims") as opposed to others, it was because of the heightened activities of Islamic terrorism that had threatened the democratic world since 2001. It was interesting to note that the rhetoric against war on organised crime had changed to the rhetoric justifying war on terrorism, with the defining lines between the two becoming blurred in the process. There were two aspects to differentiating between gangs based on religion: the first was to link certain gangs (Muslim) with anti-national activities; and the second was to underscore the speculation that some gangs with a majority of their members belonging to one particular community received political patronage from particular political parties. Thus, it appeared as if the gangs that supported the party in power enjoyed some form of limited immunity from police actions.

The increasing inclusion of the "crime problem" in political discourse meant that successive governments as social control agents tried to come down hard on these organised crime groups (by encouraging *encounters*) or at least appeared to do so. While criminological discourse has recognized that crime control is beyond the state (Garland, 1996) in Mumbai (as in other places) there was no acceptance of this "well-known" fact in either police or government circles. In fact, Cohen (1996) recognized "the short-term political costs of admitting the futility of these [crime control] methods are unacceptable", as a result, governments continued to persist in devising newer, more punitive sanctions against criminals, which, in Mumbai included *encounters*. Rustamji (1992) comments that traditionally in India the wrong tests are applied to policing – if crime figures rise, it is not as a result of good registration practices, but because the police are ineffective; if a few murders occur, crime is said to be out of control and police are urged to stop it with stern measures; if an officer wants to use legal methods only, he is considered weak and inefficient. Denying the state's systemic inability to control crime, especially more complex organised crime, political and media discourse hailed police efforts as being masterful and effective in the "war on crime", even if as a result "we [Indians] have come to believe is that the country needs a police force that is dreaded by the people, with officers on the top who have been selected for their ability to wink at brutality and corruption" (Rustamji, 1992: 48). This formal crime control oriented discourse is just as evident in media and political discussions here and elsewhere.

Cohen's (1996: 8) question whether, "Is this public discourse really 'about' crime or rather a metaphor for expressing a wider sense of social dislocation and disorder?" appears apposite in Mumbai.

Political machinations in Mumbai were not restricted to the politicization of crime, that is political patronage to criminal activities, but the trend was increasingly changing towards criminalization of politics. The democratic process has turned violent where virtually every political party has encouraged an active role of known "mafia dons" and criminals with long police records in the elected offices of the state. Also elections to municipal bodies, state assemblies, even the parliament have been marred by "booth capturing"[30] and intimidation of voters by every political party. The criminalization of politics has been recognized but "none of this information gets officially recorded in any systematic manner" (Verma & Tiwari, 2003: 246). Gangsters such as Arun Gawli have contested and won local elections, creating a unique dilemma for the police, who were then obliged to provide security for the very man they were hunting. Ironically, the greatest threat Gawli allegedly faced was from police *encounters*![31] Other reputed criminals such as Pappu Kalani (who is said to lead his own mafia group) and Ibrahim Kaskar (Dawood's brother) have also contested elections, sometimes while incarcerated.[32] This caused considerable pressure on the police and the criminal justice system as the very elements they were supposed to control could potentially become their political masters and to whom they would be accountable.

Policing Organised Crime in Mumbai

Policing a large city like Mumbai is challenging, but dealing with large-scale organised crime groups involved in terrorism along with a host of other criminal activities, adds another dimension of difficulty to this task. Levi and Maguire (2004) have identified that the lack of "systematic before-and-after comparisons-based studies" makes it difficult to draw any conclusions about the impact of law enforcement measures on organised crime even in Europe. In Mumbai, the task of measuring the efficacy of policing organised crime is made even more difficult given the lack of officially published coherent government policies to tackle the problem as well as lack of official statistics on the impact of strategies other than *encounters* (even if ad hoc) adopted by the police.

Law enforcement rather than prevention has dominated crime reduction strategies and practical responses of the Mumbai police. A paradigm shift for law enforcement

---

[30] This refers to the process whereby thugs acting on behalf of a political party actually take over an entire election centre and forcibly stamp all the ballot papers in favour of their own party or destroy ballot boxes if they feel the majority of voters might have voted against their party.

[31] *The Times of India*: (2004), "Arun Gawli shoots down encounter fears", 19 October 2004.

[32] See, for example *The Times of India*: (2004), "City gangs enter political fray", 21 September 2004; and *The Times of India*: (2004), "Dawood brother to fight polls", 21 September 2004.

from a "reactive and repressive approach towards long-term preventative strategies" is still "work in progress" in Europe (Levi & Maguire, 2004: 457), but has some way to go in Mumbai, where the police, it would appear, preferred short-cut, instant solutions to the problem of organised crime.

The following account of policing organised crime in Mumbai is based on print media reports, interviews conducted during the research, memoirs of police officers (Khan, 2004) and other secondary sources (Charles, 2001; Mehta, 2005; Virani, 1999).

In the early 1970s and 1980s, the police had to deal with gangsters who used knives and daggers as their weapons of choice and police officers interviewed said deadly force was not that common, (relevant statistics were not maintained or are unavailable). Officers mentioned that the first officially recognized *encounter* occurred in 1982. However, the entry of smuggled sophisticated weapons especially since the early 1990s changed the scenario dramatically. Table 3.5, for example, shows the number of arms recovered by the police after the bomb blasts in 1993. Not only were arms smuggled illegally in the country in large quantities, but the types of weapons used by organised groups became more sophisticated and dangerous and posed a greater threat than before.

Comparative statistics for weapons and ammunition recovered for earlier years are not available, but police officers assured me that this haul was the largest recovered in Mumbai. It could be the case that prior to the bomb blasts, the extent of the terrorist threat, and the stock-piling of weapons and arsenal had escaped intelligence analysts and was not a police priority. Since 1993 the Mumbai police have recovered large quantities of firearms from "criminals", for example, over a 3-year period (1998–2000) the police seized 1,662 illegal weapons (Sarkar & Tiwari, 2002). The influx of sophisticated arms made the task of policing organised crime groups far more difficult and dangerous according to the officers interviewed. It was their opinion that emboldened by the possession of better weapons, "criminals" were more likely to attack police officers or shoot their way out of a tight corner when confronted with the possibility of being arrested. However, the official statistics in Table 3.6 do not support this contention. The fact that so few police personnel are killed or even injured in raids or by criminals does raise a few questions about police assertions that the job has become more dangerous over the years.

According to the police version, *encounters* were occurring regularly in Mumbai by 1993 mainly in self-defence. Officers felt they were already overburdened with

Table 3.5 Arms recovered by the police in the immediate aftermath of the Mumbai bomb blasts of 1993

Types of arms	Amount
RDX (explosive)	3.5 tonnes
Hand grenades	459
AK 56 rifles	63
9 mm Pistols	12
Detonators	1,150
Delay Switch No. 10	03
Ammunition	49,000 rounds

Source: Crime Branch, Mumbai Police, cited in Sarkar and Tiwari (2002: 16)

Table 3.6 Police personnel killed on duty in Mumbai

Year	In dacoity operations or other raids	By riotous mob	By other criminals	On border duties	In accidents	Total
1993	1	0	0	0	2	3
1994	0	1	0	0	1	2
1995	0	0	0	0	3	3
1996	0	0	2	0	0	2
1997	2	0	0	0	1	3
1998	0	0	3	0	3	6
1999	0	0	0	0	0	0
2000	0	0	0	0	0	0

Source: Crime in India (1993, 1994, 1995, 1996, 1997, 1998, 1999, 2000).
From 2001 onwards figures were not reported for individual cities

everyday policing activities, including narcotics, anti-piracy, protection of very important persons and sensitive installations, crowd management, ensuring peace during numerous religious festivals and processions, and were working 12-h shifts without regular days off. A senior police officer writes, "no western country places such a tall order or expects so much from its police force" (Khan, 2004: 108). The criminal justice system was also dangerously overloaded. In 2001 nearly 5,117,864 cases were pending trial in the higher courts, amounting nearly 82.3% of the total caseload for the country (Crime in India, 2001). As crimes committed by organised gangs allegedly rose sharply, the procedures for processing "gangsters" through the criminal justice system: arrest, investigation, charging the accused under appropriate sections of the law, prosecution and finally sentencing, began to be by-passed more often in favour of quick and instant "disposals" in the form of *encounters*. There were no ostensible public protests or demands for accountability and the media appeared to applaud and encourage these police actions. There were even public calls for felicitation of "encounter specialists" on occasions.

How did such a situation arise? The answer could lie in the fact that crimes purportedly committed by organised gangs were spiralling rapidly upwards, and people were feeling increasingly insecure. The number of registered crimes committed by organised gangs (apart from smuggling of arms and ammunition that are registered separately under the Arms Act), extortion (*hafta* or protection money), shootouts as part of contract killings, and kidnapping for ransom reveal an interesting story (Table 3.7).

Statistics show that organised gangs were very active in 1993, the beginning of the period of research. Thereafter, crimes committed by these gangs steadily declined because, as officers explained, *encounters*, the main weapon in their arsenal, were effective. However, these figures and trends are based on police recorded statistics, which carry all the attendant problems associated with them. Table 3.8 shows that there was a steady increase in *encounters* between 1993 and 1997. In 1998 there was a sudden drop in the number of *encounters*, followed by a sharp rise in their numbers in 1999, 2000, and 2001, when they reached a pinnacle and

Table 3.7 Registered Indian penal code crimes suspected to be the work of organised gangs

Year	Shootouts	Extortion	Kidnapping for ransom	Total
1993	34	728	Not available	762
1994	28	588	Not available	616
1995	24	535	16	575
1996	48	333	17	398
1997	38	230	10	278
1998	93	341	16	450
1999	41	297	11	349
2000	24	309	25	358
2001	18	269	25	312
2002	13	175	14	202
2003	10	142	12	164
Total	371	3,947	146	4,464

Source: Crime Branch, Mumbai Police

Table 3.8 Official figures for police encounters

Year	Number of incidents	Police stations	Crime Branch	Number of criminals killed
1993	28	Not available	Not available	37
1994	26	Not available	Not available	30
1995	10	Not available	Not available	07
1996	45	34	11	58
1997	49	21	28	72
1998	39	25	14	48
1999	65	35	30	83
2000	59	23	36	73
2001	70	09	61	94
2002	35	04	31	47
2003	27	07	20	40
Total	453	158	231	589

Source: Crime Branch, Mumbai Police

the police acknowledged killing 94 criminals in 1 year. Since then the figures have declined.

Encounters in which officers posted in police stations were engaged are distinguished from those involving Crime Branch officers to highlight the point that *encounters* were not only done by specialist units (death squads), but emerged out of a more widespread practice within the organisation. However, it is interesting that officers involved in *encounters* had at some point in their career been associated with or posted in the Crime Branch. Thus, while *encounter* squads or "special operations" squads did not have a monopoly on using deadly force in *encounter* situations, the Crime Branch played a major role in these incidents. While the number of *encounters* by officers posted in regular police stations generally declined over the period of study, the number of Crime Branch *encounters* increased, with the exception of 1998, when a judicial enquiry into two *encounter* cases found Crime Branch officers responsible for fake *encounters*. At that time, the entire department was under tremendous stress and anxiety as the actions of some of their officers were under scrutiny. The judicial inquiry into two separate *encounters* (involving Javed Fawda in one case, and Vijay Tandel and Sada Pawle in another) in 1998 created considerable controversy and led to a temporary hiatus in police *encounters*. The Mumbai police later appealed against the conclusions of this inquiry to the High Court, which returned a verdict in favour of the police.

The reduction in police *encounters* in 1998, according to officers, caused a sudden and sharp rise in organised crime activities. Emboldened by the self-imposed shackles on the Mumbai police, the number of shootouts (non-police involved shootings) and other crimes increased dramatically,[33] creating a panic situation in Mumbai. Media accounts suggested increased feelings of insecurity among public and industry alike. Faced with growing pressure, the government and the police appeared to be under tremendous strain to take drastic measures in controlling sensational crimes.

Innes and Jones (2006) suggest that certain "signal crimes" and "signal disorders" like violent muggings or vandalism of public property are indicative of presence of other risks and threats which have a particular potent impact on local perceptions of neighbourhood security, and generate feelings of insecurity about people, places, and events. Their research on "Neighbourhood security and urban change" in the UK found "signal crimes" aroused fear and alarm even amongst those who were unlikely to be their victims. Similarly, in Mumbai extortion threats, shootings, and kidnapping for ransom could be considered "signal crimes" indicative of the presence of the increased threat and risk posed by organised criminal gangs. Innes and Jones (2006: vii) suggest that "perceptions and beliefs about disorder and crime may be as important as actual crime and disorder rates in terms of how they function as risk factors". Therefore managing people's perception about such "signal crimes", as well as actually trying to control them became a priority for social control agents and the government in Mumbai.

In 1997–1998, there was increasing pressure to change the law to enable the police to tackle organised crime more effectively. New legislation, the MCOCA was passed by the State Legislature in 1999. This act provided for special courts; speedy trials of those charged with offences related to organised crime syndicates, special public prosecutors to try these cases, and more stringent powers to the prosecuting agency under the law. Additionally, whereas under the Indian Evidence Act (1872) confessions to a police officer are not admissible in a court of law, under the MCOCA confessions made before an officer of the rank of DCP were made admissible as evidence. Other special rules of evidence such as authorized interception of wire,

---

[33] Figures range from the official figure of 93 cases (see Table 3.6) to 150 people killed in shootouts as reported in the media. See, for example Shrivastava (1998). There is no way of estimating which figures are closer to the "truth", and the discrepancy in reported figures only adds to the controversial perception of *encounters*.

Table 3.9 Cases registered and gangsters arrested under MCOCA 1999

Year	Total cases registered	Dawood	Chota Rajan	Arun Gawli	Ashwin Naik	Others	Total
1999	19	33	13	6	0	12	64
2000	14	54	4	0	0	7	65
2001	20	51	18	0	4	11	84
Total	53	138	35	6	4	30	213

Source: Crime Branch, Mumbai Police

electronic, or oral communications were also made admissible as evidence. Provision for forfeiture of property of the accused in case of conviction was another feature of this act. In their interviews, police officers said they approved of this new act as it addressed some of the original problems officers faced when trying to process "organised criminals" through the usual channels of the criminal justice system.

Statistics reveal that the MCOCA may have been effective to a certain extent in enabling more criminals to be tried and for speedier disposals than through the regular channels of the criminal justice process (Table 3.9).

Between 1999 and 2001, 53 cases were registered against 213 "criminals" and over half of these, that is 27 cases were finally disposed of by the special courts within this period, a remarkable achievement, considering that if these cases had been tried in the regular courts they would have been under trial for anywhere up to 12 years. It is interesting however, that 84 "criminals" were charged and tried under the MCOCA in 2001, but 94 were killed in police *encounters*, perhaps implying that the police preferred a speedier version of justice than the special courts.

Speedier justice of the kind the police preferred was facilitated by the High Court's ruling in late 1999 that Javed Fawda's death was not a false *encounter*, but there were procedural inadequacies. The High Court laid down guidelines for police actions in *encounters* that have been used ever since as a checklist by the police to ensure that at least the paperwork conforms to them. Cleared of the charges of conducting false *encounters*, the Mumbai police appeared to have been given a free hand to conduct *encounters* and indulged in a spree eliminating alleged criminals in larger numbers than ever before (Zaidi, 1999). Since 2003, the number of *encounter* cases and media reports sensationalising them, have dwindled. Perhaps the disenchantment with *encounters* was linked to the influence of new police leadership on the use of deadly force as a policy objective.

Summary

Understanding the nature of Mumbai, the history and organisation of its police force, the socio-political milieu, and the growth and interplay of various organised criminal groups and how the police sought to tackle organised crime over the decade between 1993 and 2003 is vital in understanding police perspectives on *encounters*.

The emerging picture of Mumbai was that of a prosperous megapolis, where the pace of life was hectic, where people were drawn in thousands every year to make their fortune, and which was a rapidly expanding financial and infotainment growth centre. The growth of various organised crime syndicates and their inter-rivalry for supremacy as well as their criminal activities spread panic and insecurity through different sections of society. The growing menace of organised crime syndicates provided one of the biggest challenges for the police force, which sought to counter it with the use or abuse of deadly force in the form of *encounters* of alleged hardened criminals, as one form of rough and ready justice. However, the story was just not a simple case of cops-and-robbers. The injection of the politics of Hindutva, growing communalism, terrorism and associated violence, and alleged interference from outside forces into Mumbai's socio-political landscape, combined with an already overburdened criminal justice system to make the task of policing organised crime groups far more complicated.

Chapter 4
Defining *Encounters*

Introduction

Use of deadly force in scenarios described as *encounters* became an accepted crime fighting tool in the Mumbai police repertoire. However, the term *encounter* itself needs some unpacking in order to understand the layers of meanings hidden by the various ways in which it is understood and used by the police, the public, and the media. *Encounter* was clearly a euphemism for something much more that what was being ordinarily portrayed as police shooting of "hardcore" criminals for self-defence. Subtle distinctions between *encounters* and "fake" *encounters* was articulated not only in the interviews, but by Pettigrew (2000: 205) who defines a false *encounter* as, "a fictitious armed engagement as a cover up for police killing of a detainee".

This chapter investigates the varied aspects and perceptions of the phenomenon from three angles:

- Police officers' perception of what *encounters* are and the differences between "genuine" and "fake" *encounters*.
- Officers' perception of how the public understands this difference.
- Perception of members of the public, which includes the media and other "claimsmakers".

Although the meaning of the term *encounter* is somewhat negatively loaded, addition of the label "genuine" or "fake" appended routinely to these incidents by people, implies a value judgement about whether a particular *encounter* is considered justified or not. It is the label then that demands a positive or negative response to the act – a "genuine" *encounter* is to be lauded and a "fake" one is to be criticised. As with deviance generally, "genuineness" is not a quality that lies in the act itself, but in the interaction between those who commit the act and those who respond to it (Becker, 1963: 14).

Perception of *encounters* differs subtly when described with the terms "justified" or "legitimate". While these are generally used interchangeably, here they convey slightly different meanings – a "justified" *encounter* is one that is acceptable to the person making the judgement, and involves subjective interpretation of the situation,

J. Belur, *Permission to Shoot? Police Use of Deadly Force in Democracies*,
DOI 10.1007/978-1-4419-0975-6_4, © Springer Science+Business Media, LLC 2010

which may have legal and or moral referents. On the other hand, the term "legitimate" means that the *encounter* is acceptable on objective criteria, which include both legal and moral elements in it.

My own perception, which incorporates the legal, human rights and ethical viewpoints of what is justified and legitimate police use of deadly force needs to be articulated; the construction of an "ideal type", invoking Max Weber's argument that such "purely mental constructs" enhance our "conceptual precision" (Whimster, 2004: 305). Articulating the specific point of view from which social reality is being interpreted and making one's standpoint explicit helps the reader interpret the arguments presented in the light of it (Weber, 1904, reprinted 2004: 381).

There are incidents where the police have actually fired in self-defence resulting in the death of an alleged criminal. This is a "bona fide" *encounter*, as distinct from the terms "genuine" or "real" that are in common usage. Thus a "bona fide" *encounter* is an "ideal type" where police use of deadly force is, in some abstract and impersonal sense, legitimate. However, even "bona fide" *encounters* are deeply problematic because those incidents, which in my perception and/or in an abstract, pure sense (what accords with law, ethics and human rights) are "bona fide", may not be universally regarded as such. Even more acutely police and others often see as "genuine", *encounters* that are not "bona fide" in the sense explained.

Possibly an incident which is "bona fide" (in my perception) may be perceived as being "genuine" by both public and police; or it may be perceived as being "genuine" by the police but "fake" by the public; or vice versa; or both the public and the police might perceive it to be "fake". The secrecy, lack of credible information and misinformation surrounding *encounters* makes it difficult to predict how particular incidents might be perceived by different audiences. The secrecy normally surrounding police work was taken to an extreme in cases of *encounters* especially since it aimed at self-protection. By keeping the public at a distance to maintain their power, the police aimed to retain the "mystification" that sustains "respect and awe" (Manning, 1997: 125) for *encounters* by strictly controlling the flow of information.

"Bona Fide" *Encounters*

A "bona fide" *encounter* is encapsulated in one police officer's definition:

> Police encounter means – when the criminal has come in order to commit a crime and police get definite information – and on this definite information, police lay a trap and then we try as far as possible to arrest him. But while arresting, the criminal fires in the direction of the police, to avoid his arrest, and with the intention of killing the police. At that time for our own defence, even after giving him a warning the criminal does not heed it, then there is cross firing and he gets injured and dies in the hospital, or even before that. (T 20: Inspector)

This definition includes all the requirements of a legitimate *encounter* in both the legal and moral senses, covering all aspects that could be questioned or examined in an inquiry or by a court of law. It is therefore, "bona fide" and incorporates the following features:

- The "criminal" had every intention of committing a crime at the point of contact.
- The police had authentic and reliable information about the activities of the "criminal" to counteract any accusations of mistaken identity.
- The police laid a trap with the sole intention of arresting the "criminal".
- The attack was initiated by the "criminal" with the twin intentions of escaping and killing the police.
- The police gave due warning to the "criminal", which was not heeded and the police were forced to fire back in self-defence.[1]
- The person died in the resulting cross fire.
- The "criminal" was injured and died either on the spot, or on the way to the hospital, though the police made every effort to provide immediate medical assistance.

This "textbook version" of a bona fide *encounter* may or may not coincide with what officers or "claimsmakers" regard as "genuine".

"Fake" and "Genuine" *Encounters*

The term "genuine" *encounter* could be analysed through three interpretive frameworks. According to the Human Rights interpretation, an *encounter* is "genuine" if enacted in self-defence, as a last resort, and without impinging arbitrarily on the Right to Life of the "criminal". This essentialist viewpoint considers the actual circumstances of an *encounter* situation and comes closest to a "bona fide" *encounter*.

From a legalistic interpretation, a "genuine" *encounter* would be one that was presented as having fulfilled all the legal requirements to justify the use of deadly force by the police; and/or met the exacting standards of required paperwork; and/or which had been adjudicated as being genuine in a court of law. However, since this study is not based on observation of actual *encounters* but on perceptions of them, it adopts a formalistic legal perspective, whereby the interpretative framework limits itself to an examination of whether the formal records show that the *encounter* was conducted in compliance with the law.

The final interpretive framework adopts a more subjective, individualistic value judgement of whether the *encounter* is justifiable, and therefore "genuine". This framework suggests that individuals perceive a particular incident as a "genuine" *encounter*, based on subjective criteria that are relevant to the individual making the evaluation. For example, some may consider "necessary evil" a rational justification for a "genuine" *encounter*, but others may not.

The three approaches outlined above use different criteria for establishing whether an *encounter* is evaluated as being "genuine". What may be a "genuine" *encounter* in Human Rights framework may not be considered to be legally

---

[1] The police are thus protected under section 100 of the Indian Penal Code, which refers to "the right of private defence of the body extends to causing death".

"genuine" if there are shortcomings in the paperwork or procedural formalities. An individual applying subjective criterion may not perceive an *encounter* as being "genuine" if the *encountered* person did not have an established criminal record. The research was concerned with understanding police and other people's perceptions (individually and collectively) of what constitutes an *encounter*, and how they distinguish between a "genuine" and "fake" *encounter*; and does not try to ascertain whether they are actually "genuine" or not.

Officers' Definitions of *Encounters*

Officers' responses to the question "What do you understand by the term *encounter*?" can be classified into four broad types of definitions.

Standard Definition

A "standard" definition is the classic, textbook definition. One officer, for example said, "Encounter means we go to catch him, he fires, and in self-defence we kill him" (T 26: Upper Middle Management). On being asked what they understood by the term *encounter*, a majority of officers (28 of the 38 officers) responded by giving the standard, almost textbook definition. These officers stressed that self-defence was the main factor for legally justifying *encounters*. Some officers further elaborated their standard definition in different ways, either by distinguishing between fake and genuine *encounters* or by narrating particular incidents.

The stories given out to the press, and the First Information Reports (FIR) lodged at the police station, largely followed this standard format of police firing in self-defence. In Mumbai, it appeared as if the repetitive *encounter* story had become part of police lore, to be accepted uncritically by all officers. Holdaway (1983: 138–139) describes "folk narratives" and "keeping the tradition alive", and adds that although the stories are frequently "exaggerated, highly dramatic and probably inaccurate, their power is considerable". He cites Hannerz (1969: 111) – "An individual's vision of reality is often a precarious thing; we can find comfort in the knowledge that it is shared by others, thus acquiring social anchoring in an objective truth", which explains how the *encounter* story became "official" in Mumbai.

Incident Specific Definition

An "incident specific" definition sought to explain what an *encounter* was by describing a particular incident or experience. One officer said:

Encounter means – I had gone to investigate a murder. I learned that somebody has killed a person and left the dead body in a certain place. When I went there, the people who had killed him had come there to take the body for disposal. They did not know that the police were going to come there and suddenly it all happened. Then they attacked us, we did cross firing, in which I killed two [people]... It was my first experience... That time (XYZ)[2] was the Commissioner, he was very much pleased. Then we recovered bombs from there, recovered the dead body, one accused escaped. We had no idea how to conduct the case. Now *encounters* have become very regular – there is a standard procedure to be followed. That time, I did not know much, no experience, not many had any experience, but we somehow got through it. Then the CP[3] was very pleased, he said put this up for a medal... that is how I got my first Gallantry medal. (T 7: Lower Middle Management)

This story gives the first hint that with increased experience, the police from the latter half of the 1980s onwards arranged events and appearances so that they could be represented as completely justified *encounters*. The minority of officers who used stories to explain an *encounter*, lend strength to Shearing and Ericson's (1991: 321) contention that "police references to 'experience' as the source of their knowledge, and their persistent story-telling, appear as glosses that arise from their inability to identify and articulate the rules that generate their actions". Perhaps this indicates that either there are no fixed rules or that the rules are very crude, or officers do not think the rules and principles that actually guide police actions in *encounters* are legally or morally acceptable, or that the rules are such that they are either unable or unwilling to articulate them.[4] It could also be the case that these officers could not distance themselves from the phenomenon and think nomothetically in terms of patterns but were able to only focus on individual cases and offer ideographic descriptions. On the other hand, these officers might have used stories from personal experience as illustrations to explain what *encounters* were.

Alternatively, officers may have described their own experience in response to questions about *encounters* as a safe way out of answering what they perceived as a tricky question. Their stories almost always involved a "genuine" *encounter* that occurred in the pursuance of self-defence by the officer. By telling a "thrilling" story of their chase and hunt of a "wanted" criminal, they relived an exciting moment in their career and also, by restricting their answers to personal experience, they sought to avoid speaking about *encounters* in general terms.

Unusual Definition

Yet there were six officers who deviated from this general pattern and defined *encounters*, in "unusual" ways – mainly without invoking self-defence as a

---

[2] The name of the Commissioner is deliberately anonymised.

[3] The Commissioner of Police is generally referred to as CP by officers and citizens alike.

[4] Indications that there are corrupt and unethical reasons why some officers are more prone to "doing"*encounters* were evident in many interviews (see Chap. 5).

justifying factor. This indicates that there wasn't total connivance on the part of all officers to cite the standard story, but officers did improvise, and in some cases, openly discussed what actually happened in *encounters*. These officers gave creative answers to the question. Examples of unusual definitions were, "Aborted Arrest" (T 28: Inspector), indicating that it occurred as a result of a failed arrest operation. Another example that was reminiscent of the "Dirty Harry" talk was:

> That criminal, who has been committing as many crimes as possible by using the loopholes in the law, if he is not stopped now or jailed now, then he will become a great burden on society. To act against him, whatever steps we take are known as encounters. (T 14: Lower Middle Management)

Definition Based on Distinction Between Fake and Genuine

Finally, a few officers defined *encounters* by distinguishing between "genuine" and "fake" or "false" *encounters*. As one senior officer explained:

> This word encounter has taken a big, devious meaning. Encounter is – it is an encounter between you and me today, ok? The way it is printed in newspapers, and the way the public also began thinking [that an] encounter is where a person is lifted, brought and shot, and put somewhere. I call that a fake encounter. An encounter is one where we go for a search or a raid on a place or premises – they attack us, they fire at us, and we fire back at them. In the process, the chances are we can get injured or they can get injured. (T 24: Senior Management)

Most interviewees distinguished between "fake" and "genuine" *encounters* at some point. Officers were certain that their perception of what constituted a "genuine" (and by corollary, "fake") *encounter* was different from what they thought was the general public's perception of a "genuine" *encounter*.

According to the officers, a "genuine" *encounter* had the following features:

- It involved "hardcore" criminals with long history of recorded offences. Officers used th is term without recognizing or appearing to acknowledge that a person is only "allegedly" a criminal, unless he has been convicted in a court of law of the crimes he is accused of or charged with. The police description of someone as a hardcore criminal was deemed to be accepted as uncontroversial and no officer even exhibited awareness that the use of the term was problematic.
- Occurred in the presence of witnesses or in a very public place. This was regardless of the actual extent and seriousness of the threat posed to the lives of officers or others, whether proportionate force was used by the police and whether firing was the only or last resort.
- Occurred while chasing a dangerous criminal, or while responding to an actual crime in progress. There was a lack of awareness that the use of force would be justified only if it was necessary or employed in order to save lives.

Officers explained, use of force decisions depended on whether officers genuinely believed they or others were under threat at the time, and not on how reasonable this belief was when examined in hindsight. Thus, it is hard for courts, tribunals, or anyone else to second-guess and find officers guilty of abuse.

- If an *encounter* was "well-managed", that is if the legal requirements were fulfilled, the paperwork was in order and no messy incriminating evidence was left unaccounted for, then the *encounter* was to be counted as "genuine" (even if they knew it wasn't). Thus a "good story" (Chatterton, 1979: 94) even if the person offering an account may not himself regard it as true, will be accepted by colleagues and supervisors, because it is what "everyone knows" and has accepted (Scott & Lyman, 1968).
- An act committed in good faith, with good intentions, and in the interests of society, that involved controlling criminals, was legitimate. Therefore an *encounter* "done" in with good intentions was "genuine". Delattre (2002: 201) echoes a similar sentiment when he claims that even if officers have employed illegal methods in "hard" or "Dirty Harry" situations, they are neither morally tainted nor necessarily to be condemned in any subsequent legal proceedings.

Officers were almost unanimous in what constituted "fake" *encounters*; they possessed one or many of the following characteristics:

- Involved a person with no criminal history.
- Resulted from a mistaken identification of the person killed.
- Employed blatantly excessive use of force.
- Emerged from a "catch-and-kill" policy – this involved the suggestion that the police place a target (the "criminal") under surveillance, follow him for a few weeks or months, and build up a criminal case against him. He is then picked up by a unit of plain clothes officers, kept in a safe place overnight or for a few days, and after questioning, is taken to a lonely spot, late at night, and executed.
- Resulted from bad faith or malice on the part of the officer concerned. There were suggestions of corruption, that some officers were acting like "hired" killers. It was alleged that some "encounter specialists" specialised in eliminating members of certain gangs.[5] It was also suggested that under the guise of *encounters* some officers eliminated people against whom they had a personal grudge or for revenge.[6]

---

[5] This allegation was refuted by other officers, who explained that officers acted on the information of informants and sources, certain officers had links or contacts in certain gangs, which meant that their "operations" were limited to taking action against those particular gang members only.

[6] There was no proof to back this allegation, but there were hints of corruption in the narratives of a few officers.

- Involved personal gain for the officer, for example ego gratification, anticipation of gallantry medals, promotions,[7] or enhanced status within the department and socially.

Despite their personal feelings and moral compunctions about illegalities and wrongdoings, officers generally agreed that if an *encounter* was well-managed and/ or was committed in good faith for noble ends, then even if it did not fulfil any of the other conditions, it would be treated as a "genuine" *encounter*. Officers tended to obfuscate the borders between what they personally considered "genuine" incidents and what as an organisation, or in their official capacity, they would accept as "genuine" incidents. For example one officer gave the standard definition of what an *encounter* was and then added, "That is what is said in the FIR (First Information Report) in these cases. And experts in this area will tell you that this is the only way you can justify an *encounter*" (T 33: Upper Middle Management). Regardless of what actually happens in an *encounter* he felt, "That is what the FIR says happened and that is what is relevant. However, in real life many times even the basic procedures are not followed". Since the FIR is legally a very important document, and the information contained in it is treated as sacrosanct by the courts in India, the police tend to be very careful while drafting it.

The above comment of the officer suggests that while he personally did not think that most cases were "genuine" *encounters*, but for the organisation, good paper-work would satisfy the criteria for being one. Good paperwork included, among other things, the fact that the official police story, its timing, and other details are corroborated by all the relevant police documents and wireless messages. It also ensures that there are no discrepancies in the "stories" told by officers and "independent witnesses" (if any). A good paper trail would ensure that all the relevant procedures and follow-up reports were filed on time and without flaws or unexplained gaps. The point was reinforced by another officer:

---

[7] Some state police forces follow a policy of one *encounter* – one rank promotion. For example, in Punjab during the heydays of terrorism (in the 1980s and early 1990s) the government announced such a policy. As a result some officers had risen from the rank of Sub-Inspector to Deputy Inspector General of Police (something that is impossible under the usual scheme of promotions) depending upon the number of *encounters* they had "conducted". States like Uttar Pradesh still follow this policy, though this has been much more restricted in recent years. The Government, however, still presents gallantry medals to officers who have been involved in acts of bravery, above and beyond the call of duty. Incidentally, a proposal for a gallantry medal has to be put forward by the department and goes through to the Government for its approval. Significantly, none of the *encounters* done by the officers of the Crime Branch in Mumbai are ever put up for medals and so far only those *encounters* that were done in public presence or during an unplanned interface with criminals have been approved by the department for gallantry medals. This probably is tacit acknowledgement that the "operations" conducted by the Crime Branch are considered suspect even by the department and thus not deemed to be acts of bravery above and beyond the call of duty.

> The basic point is not what actually takes place in an encounter situation – what is important is how it is represented on paper, because all the inquiries and courts are going to examine the documentary evidence and the paperwork done by the police. If you are careful then anything can be managed. (T 35: Senior Management)

It was clear that these officers were more interested in the "recipe rules" guiding a police officer on "how to get the job done in ways that will appear acceptable to the organisation ... how to avoid supervisors and various organisational checks, and when it is necessary to produce 'paper' regarding an incident or complaint" (Ericson, 1982, reprinted in 2005: 224).

Claimsmakers' Definitions of *Encounters*

Eighteen claimsmakers' definition of *encounters* could be categorised into three distinct types.

Naive

Three "naïve" responses suggested that *encounters* were police shooting hardened criminals in self-defence, leaving no room for the possibility of "fake" *encounters*. One naïve response displayed touching faith in the police and their intentions to control crime:

> You have to empower them [the police], to give them the power to use their own discretion. You have to believe and you have to have faith in the police official. I mean, out of a hundred, maybe one or two may be misusing it [their power], but overall I would like to believe that the person who is appointed by the government is a person we can believe in, who we can have faith in. So if he does something like that [talking about excess use of deadly force] I think it would be for the general good. (I 10, Public Relations Officer, Industrial Association)

One interpretation of this response could be that it was a cultural denial of the danger that police's excess use of force could pose to the common man. It might be an example of the manufacture of "convenient truths" (that the police cannot misuse power, except in very few and rare cases), similar to that adopted by German Jews in the 1930s, who despite evidence to the contrary, did not believe the state to be capable of heinous acts. Primo Levi's explanation in the German adage, "Things whose existence is not morally possible cannot exist" (cited in Cohen, 2001: 141), applied to this naïve approach.

Another naïve response to the same question was:

> Encounters, actually, when police get information that a particular gang is there or particular gang members are there, then they search for and you can say, lay a trap for them. Once they find them, then they actually fire and in most cases they kill them.

When asked what fake *encounters* were, this person's response was:

> Fake encounters have not come to light. Fake encounters means they are running away and you kill them... So I don't think there are fake encounters, at least no fake encounters have

come to light here in Bombay…When I was studying the problem of dacoity in Chambal valley[8] I found there were a number of fake encounters, and those fake encounters were done because the police were paid [by rival claimants] for the rifles that were left on the scene [by the dead "dacoits"]. (I 15, Academic)

The interviewee stated that the police killed criminals on finding them (without mentioning self-defence) and yet staunchly went on to maintain that there were no fake *encounters* in Mumbai, because none had come to light. In this he presumably took a formalistic legal perspective, that is if no incident was proved to be a fake *encounter*, then the latter could not exist. It could also be that he had a formed a notion of what fake *encounters* were, based on his experience with a rural police force in another part of the country. The context and playing out of *encounters* in Mumbai would have been very different and perhaps the police had managed to maintain a tighter grip on the information flow making it difficult for this researcher to come across instances of blatant misuse of deadly force that his previous experience might have exposed him to. This individual was the only interviewee who steadfastly refused to accept any wrongdoing on the part of the Mumbai police and maintained that the police acted entirely within the bounds of law. He justified his faith with the claim, "For the last thirty or forty years I am working with the police and I know what the situation is". Being closely associated with the police had perhaps imbued this individual with a sense of responsibility to adhere to the official police story. The other explanation could be that the boundaries of the term "fake" *encounter* are fluid enough to be adapted to suit the occasion.

The third naïve response was from a politician belonging to the party in power, who presumably felt compelled to stress that all *encounters* were "genuine", since any other response would reflect negatively on his government as being openly supportive of illegal executions:

Fake encounter – people call it that conveniently – say that the police caught him and then did this and that – they make up stories, but no one has till now spoken of fake encounters. Yes, sometimes in one or two places, there have been cases of mistaken identity. For example, in Bihar,[9] there have been mistakes on the part of the police, that happens, it is part of their job. But I don't believe in the talk that it is a fake encounter. If the person who dies is a saintly person, if a decent person is caught and killed then you can say fake encounter, that he was killed. Who is the person who dies – there was something to him, wasn't there? Otherwise why was he killed? Why don't the police kill ordinary people? (I 7, Politician)

Not only was the interviewee refuting that the Mumbai police were capable of making mistakes in *encounters*, but was also strongly justifying police use of deadly force against "those who deserve it". Strictly speaking, his response could not be called naïve, but wilfully naïve in order to be politically opportune and selective.

---

[8] Dacoit infested ravines in the heartland of India, the state of Madhya Pradesh.

[9] The state with arguably one of the worst crime situations in India.

Realistic

There were nine "realists" who, on the other hand, accepted that there were some "genuine" cases where the police really did shoot in self-defence and in order to protect life or property, but that there was a preponderance of others where some measure of wrongdoing or excess use of force was involved. A typical realist response was:

> Genuine encounters? I think they are very few and far between. They take place in the mofussils,[10] where the police are usually out in villages where they will not find a single supporter, they are terribly outnumbered and in those situations encounters take place and I would say that those are more or less justified. But in places like Bombay there are small localities, the persons wanted may number anything from one to ten, if you come with a police force numbering twenty or twenty five, there is hardly any reason to take recourse to firearms. (I 3, Retired Judge)

Realists exhibited awareness of some amount of police wrongdoing, but were inclined to think that it was not blatant or rampant misuse. They acknowledged that perhaps excess force was used, or that those killed were somewhat culpable by being connected to organised crime groups.

Cynical

The "cynics" (six of them), were convinced that all *encounters* were staged events and that the police managed to control the narrative and the evidence to suit their story in every instance. All the journalists and activists interviewed were cynical about *encounters*. One of them described *encounters* as:

> They are rackets. There are no encounters, they are police killings... A criminal is caught and when the police know that this man is likely to get bail or the court will not book him, then why take it up to court – eliminate, kill him. (I 5, Journalist)

Another person explained:

> Encounter is defined by the police... It is a definition given by the perpetrator, which everybody including the judiciary has accepted. It is a stereotyped definition...We go there – we challenge him – he fires – we fire back in self defence – he falls – we take him to the hospital – declared dead! The entire sequence and chronology, clubbed together as a package is called an encounter. (I 2, Activist)

This interviewee used the concept of "interpretive packages" (Beckett, 1997) to describe a police *encounter*, either intuitively or knowingly acknowledging the fact that this particular "package" results from the use of particular frames by the media to make sense of the *encounter* story. A process in which, "media output may simply reflect the frames of the most powerful actors with little independent contribution from journalists" (Gamson & Wolfsfeld, 1993: 119). At the centre of the package

---

[10] Rural areas are known as mofussils in India (Oxford English Dictionary).

is a core frame and a central organizing idea that gives meaning to a series of events or phenomena related to the social issue, and while Beckett (1997) feels that such "culturally available" descriptive packages (she uses the example of "crime and drug issue") typically do not appear in the media in their entirety, in Mumbai we find that they are repeatedly being used to describe and define *encounters*.

This interviewee made some interesting observations regarding the absolute control on the narrative and discourse on *encounters* by the police, who as institutional "primary definers" (Hall, Critcher, Jefferson, Clarke, & Roberts, 1981) have managed to make their version of events in an *encounter* the definitive and authoritative account, accepted by all others, including the judiciary. The cynics were convinced that the police misuse of deadly force was authoritarian, politically motivated, and not always in the interests of crime control.

Officer Involvement in *Encounters*

The extent to which officers admitted and/or were aware of serious issues concerning the legality of *encounters* depended upon the exact nature of their involvement in *encounters*, rank, and gender. Officers had three types of engagement with *encounters*, as active participants; facilitators and/or supervisors; and non-participants. Huggins, Haritos-Fatouros, and Zimbardo (2002: 1) have similarly categorised police officers interviewed as "*direct perpetrators*" (active participants) and "*atrocity facilitators*" (facilitators and/or supervisors) in their attempt to "reconstruct social memory about state-sanctioned violence in Brazil". However, they did not have the third category of officers (non-participants) who had no connection to "violence work" in their sample of interviewees.

Active Participants

Fifteen of the 38 officers interviewed had been active participants in *encounters*. They had "done" *encounters* and grappled with the legal, moral, and ethical issues involved. Nine of the 15 active participants were posted at that time of interview, or previously, to the Crime Branch. Only some of the active participants belonged to the select group of self-styled "encounter specialists" who had made *encounters* the mainstay of their policing career; others had had limited experience and involvement in these operations. One of the "specialists" said he had used firearms in over 50 *encounters*, most of them fatal, as casually as if he were discussing trips to the supermarket. Active participants were concentrated in the Inspector rank (eight), while some belonged to Lower (two), and Upper Middle Management ranks (two), the remaining (three) were of the rank of Sub-Inspector. Lower Middle Management officers had participated in *encounters* prior to promotion, that is while they were still Inspectors or even Sub-Inspectors. This is the cutting-edge operational rank at which officers actually carry out *encounters*. Active participants in the Upper Middle Management ranks had been part of *encounter* operations, mainly outside Mumbai, in areas affected by left wing extremism.

Facilitators and/or Supervisors

Ten officers, including all the Senior Management officers, had at some point been involved directly or indirectly in the planning or aftermath of *encounters*, ensuring they were conducted with efficiency and minimum disruption to "normal" policing. Five facilitators and supervisors were connected to the Crime Branch either in the past or were posted there at the time of the research. One officer (T 34: Inspector) described his facilitation as training police officers in the police stations by making them aware of the procedural formalities and necessary paper-work to be completed in an *encounter* case. He was considered an expert on the paperwork in *encounters* and said he was consulted, particularly in complicated cases to ensure that all the requisite formalities were completed (at least on paper), and no mistakes were made.

Possibly the officer was implying that regardless of the actual facts of the case, his job was to ensure the paperwork reflected that all the proper procedures had been followed by the police. This manipulation of the "paper reality" (Goffman, 1961) is almost a universal feature of police work, which Manning (1997: 166) describes as, "writing the proper paper in order the construct the appearances". The officer went on to describe similar sorts of vertical and horizontal situational negotiations and collusions with supervisory officers and colleagues in order to manipulate written records to protect oneself from superiors and legal proceedings that Manning describes in his work and which is part of the audit trail that officers have to ensure as protection from punishment.

Non-participants

Thirteen officers were "non-participants", with no involvement in *encounter* situations (all five women officers interviewed belonged to this category). The significance of gender was primarily in the fact that all actors involved in *encounters* (police and "criminals") were male. Women officers were not part of "specialist" teams in the Crime Branch or police stations. This may be partially explained by the universal dominant male attitude towards women officers that they are less likely to be suitable for certain types of policing tasks, especially involving violence. Informal practices such as discouraging women candidates from applying for specialist positions and misplaced gallantry in protecting them (Boni, 1998) could be part of the explanation for why women officers did not play a significant role in *encounters* in Mumbai. Previous studies in western countries have suggested that women officers do engage in more ethical behaviour and one of the reasons for this could be "because male officers do not accept them – hence they are not incorporated into the male 'brotherhood' of officers" (Brown & Heidensohn, 2000: 102, citing Miller and Braswell, 1992).[11] Either hypothesis remains untested in Mumbai.

The majority of the group of non-participants were Sub-Inspectors and Lower Middle Management. Typically a non-participant's attitude was, "I'm lucky, I've not had to use my weapon. Without firearms, I could control difficult situations, and arrest many criminals with just a warning". (T 3: Lower Middle Management). The officer's comment gives rise to the notion that non-participation could be a matter of choice or opportunity. Some officers may have deliberately chosen not to participate in *encounters*; others may just never have been in a position where they would have to resort to the use of firearms. The sample was skewed towards officers who had experience of *encounters*. However, non-participants represent the bulk of the police force having little or no contact with *encounters*. They only possessed second hand knowledge about *encounters*. Many among these said they had no information about what actually happens in an *encounter* and refused to speculate or admit that there could be any "wrong doing" involved.

The Crime Branch

Of the 38 officers interviewed, 15 (all male) had connections with the Crime Branch and were at the time of the research, or had been in the past, active participants, facilitators, or supervisors. Four officers were "encounter specialists" who openly acknowledged their special status. There were different versions of what these officers said happened in *encounters* depending on their different roles, and in relation to the amount of trust and rapport I developed with them. There was often a difference between what officers initially said in response to the question – "what do you understand by the term *encounter*" – and how they subsequently talked about it during the course of the interview about what they thought actually happened in such cases.

When formally defining the term, officers used language carefully, constructing the story in a way that could withstand scrutiny in any inquiry. Some active participants and facilitators admitted that in most *encounter* situations the police ensured there were no witnesses to contradict their account. A majority of *encounters* were committed in lonely spots, in the early hours of the morning, with only two parties, the police and criminals, involved. Police controlled the narrative by ensuring that "criminals" involved in *encounters* did not live to tell their side of the story. "Low visibility" of police work combined with high levels of discretion vested in the cop on the street allows for opportunities for the police to control and transform

---

[11] Other studies contradict these findings where women officers were found to be no more virtuous than their male counterparts in the countries observed (Brown & Heidensohn, 2000).

the nature of any incident and its official accounts (Holdaway, 1983; Manning, 1977; Skolnick, 1994).

Officers were asked whether they thought the official story in the documents and in the press reflected actual events. Why was the same story being repeatedly recycled with just the names, places and times changing in each incident? There were a range of responses from "there can be no other story"; to "that is what actually happens"; "how could there be any change since it is what happens every time"; and finally "it is a standard formulaic story, carefully constructed and checked by experts to see that all the requirements and formalities are completed to satisfy the Courts and the Human Rights Commission". However, the degree and extent to which officers were willing to admit that there was more to *encounters* than appeared on the surface, was largely dependent on their role in *encounters*, and their rank.

Officer Attitude Towards Legality of *Encounters*

An *encounter* has two components – the act itself, and the motivation (or moral force) behind the act. Whether a particular *encounter* is considered "genuine" will depend on perception of either the nature of the act (its legality) or the motivation behind the act (its morality). Illegalities in *encounters* range from: excess use of force, "catch-and-kill operations", mistaken identity, and fudging official records and papers. Immorality of the act would refer to the intention behind the *encounter*. Thus, *encounters* that result from – corruption (killing for a price), killing for the sake of personal advancement, ego gratification, or simply excess use of force – are not only immoral, but also involve illegal or extra-legal actions on the part of the police.

A majority of officers (25 out of 38) were willing to concede the illegality of the act, but some among them were not willing to concede the immorality of the act. These officers might accept that an *encounter* was "fake" in the legal sense, but justified it as being "genuine" in the moral sense. Officers tended to merge themes of illegality with immorality and separating the two was quite an analytical challenge. When officers talked of acceptance of wrongdoing, they really meant acceptance of the illegality of the act. In many cases this might or might not have involved acceptance of the immorality of the act. Officers were inclined to justify the appropriateness of *encounters* as a crime response putting forward one or more of several arguments discussed in Chap. 7, obfuscating the degree to which they accepted police wrongdoing.

There were four basic types of responses to the question of police "illegalities" in *encounters*: direct admission, indirect admission, denial, and evasion. The picture, however, is not quite as definitive, because apart from a few offices who took up entrenched positions of direct admission or direct denial, the vast majority of officers vacillated between admitting illegalities at one point and denying them at another. This confusion arose due to officers not drawing clear boundaries for themselves, between "bona fide" *encounters* and what they considered "justified" *encounters*.

Officers tended to veer inconsistently between adopting various frameworks while talking about *encounters*, showing that their feelings on such a complex subject could scarcely be unambiguous and compartmentalized into neat categories. Most *encounters* in the accounts fell into an intermediate grey zone – transcending, crossing and recrossing moral, ethical, and legal boundaries.

Direct Admission

Fourteen officers said they thought there were illegalities in police *encounters*. For example, one officer said, "Last year alone, we killed nine people in my area. We got them, we picked them. They were wanted criminals – we shot them" (T 1: Inspector, Active Participant). Another officer said that almost none of the *encounters* were genuine. In every case the "criminal" was watched, his movements observed for many days, even months. The police then picked him up when it was safe to do so, that is no witnesses or other obstacles are present. Usually the "criminal" was taken to a chosen secluded place late at night and killed. The officer added,

> Otherwise why would you find such a big criminal hanging around in these lonely places in the middle of the night, and many times, alone? In such cases the places are also fixed, every officer ["encounter specialist"] has his own favourite spot in a favourable police station area. They have the whole system set up – they have their "setting" with the doctors in the hospital where the post mortem will be conducted. Some of these officers have a lot of money to spread around – they can "manage" virtually anything. (T 34: Inspector, Crime Branch Facilitator, from verbatim notes[12])

As a police officer, I was aware of this behaviour within the police organisation, which did not come as a huge surprise; even so, actually hearing another officer openly declare how these operations were conducted was uncomfortable, especially since the admission was rather matter-of-fact.

Indirect Admission

Ten officers indirectly admitted to illegalities in *encounters*, for example a senior officer said:

> After all why give a weapon in the hands of the police? You want that in certain situations the police should use it that is why you have given the weapon. I am not endorsing a police act of catching and killing – that is very bad and very dangerous. But, let me tell you why

---

[12] This officer clearly said at the beginning of the interview that if I wanted to hear the truth, I should not record the interview; otherwise he would give me standard, officially approved answers, which, he felt, would not help the research. The officer however, was happy for me to take extensive notes as he spoke.

it has become necessary for the police to become proactive and aggressive – you may call it just a euphemism… But this would not have been necessary if our legal system had worked effectively and was seen to be punishing wrong doers. (T 31: Senior Management)

The officer went on to list a number of reasons why the police needed to be "proactive and aggressive". These included the negative impact of rising crime on the economic and social well-being of Mumbai; rising insecurity and fear of crime that was said to have gripped its citizens; pressures on the political party in power to remedy the situation, who in turn demanded an effective police response to organised crime. It was clear that the officer was acknowledging excess use of force and other illegalities, while trying to minimise the negative import of the words by justifying aggressive policing.

Denial

Twelve officers denied that there was any wrongdoing, but only three officers maintained denial right through the interview. Officers' denial of any "wrongdoing" could be partially attributed to "cop's code", whereby part of the street cop culture is "don't give up another cop" (Reuss-Ianni and Ianni, 1983), and partly attributed to other key cultural characteristics of the organisation, secrecy, solidarity and the "operational code" which enshrines the "rule of silence" (Punch, 1985; Reiner, 2000a; van Maanen, 1978; Westley, 1970).

A majority of these officers initially denied "wrongdoing" strenuously. They later modified their position saying though there were illegalities, these were "minor" or mere technicalities (e.g. use of excessive force), but that they did not consider these to be anything serious. One officer said:

Every person is not encountered. If only he attacks us too much or fires on us, only then an encounter happens. And normally if you feel that if a person can be subdued then he is arrested. But if you know that this person has a weapon and will use it, then we kill him. (T 19: Sub-Inspector, Active Participant)

The officer did not specify which "criminals" can be arrested and who "have to be killed". This talk is redolent of the notion of "victim precipitation" or "victim blaming" that was invoked not only in incidents of homicide and rape (Amir, 1971; Wolfgang, 1959) but a form of early "proto-victimology" literature that discussed the functional responsibility of the victim (Rock, 2002). In order to shift responsibility onto others, the officer's suggestion that certain criminals "had to be killed", implied that it was their own conduct that precipitated elimination rather than arrest.

In effect, this officer denied that the intention of the police was to inevitably kill criminals, but that arresting them was a viable and vigorous option exercised. However, the same officer subsequently said:

Really hard core criminal who are constantly committing crimes and are not reforming, then finishing them is the best. There is no point in keeping them around. It unnecessarily wastes the government's time, court's time and our time… As a result there is a sort of terror of the police and the others do not have the guts to commit such crimes. So it is in the society's interests to finish them. (T 19: Sub-Inspector, Active participant)

Here the officer does not mention the possibility of arresting "hardcore" criminals, instead, clearly shows his preference for extermination in the social interest. The contradiction and complexity of denial comes through in these two quotes, where initially the officer denies that killing criminals is the primary aim of the police, but later goes on to extol the virtues of a "policy" of *encounters*. While this officer does not exemplify denial in the literal sense of the word, the justifications and arguments put forward by him fit into the wider denial framework (Cohen, 2001) discussed in Chap. 7.

Evasion

Two officers evaded giving any kind of direct answer to the question on police wrongdoing in *encounters*. These officers were uncomfortable in committing to any clear position. Perhaps they thought there actually were illegalities involved, but just did not want to accept it, nor did they want to blatantly or self-delusionally say that all *encounters* were above board. There is also the possibility that an evasive response might be an artefact of the interview situation. People often deal with morally difficult or incriminating issues by not talking about them. One officer gave an answer so as to neither deny nor acknowledge questionable conduct on the part of the police thus,

> Just because nobody questions, one would think that there would be a sort of a free situation of people getting knocked out, I haven't got the statistics offhand with me – but we have had less number of shootouts and encounters – which means obviously we are not talking about it as a policy – that we must kill so many this month and so many in the next. No, not at all. The reduction in the number of both [shootouts and encounters] itself shows that the problem has been contained. (T 30: Senior Management)

This officer did not directly answer the question whether he thought there was police wrongdoing in *encounters*, but appeared to say that the police were not going berserk, killing "criminals" randomly. The officer seemed to suggest that since *encounters* were declining, it showed that the police were not killing for the sake of it (implying that there was no "wrongdoing"), but were doing so in response to crime trends, which vindicated any kind of "wrongdoing" (if any) that might have occurred. Thus he did not answer the question of whether there was any wrongdoing in his opinion, but evaded commenting on it by saying that since they were effective crime control measures, *encounters* were justified.

Claimsmakers' Attitudes Towards Legality of *Encounters*

Within even the small sample of claimsmakers interviewed, there was no clear consensus about what *encounters* were and while only a few expressed the belief that *encounters* were chance occurrences, a majority of those interviewed were sceptical of the official police version of events. They acknowledged that there was lack of clear evidence about police wrongdoing, but various factors were put forward as indicative of police malpractice. These included:

> We have heard reports of police officers talking amongst themselves, constables and others and they say today we have to go for an encounter – so that means it is pre-planned (I 8, Activist and Lawyer)

– Indicating that these were not chance occurrences.

> Only once or twice I think a police constable is killed, but otherwise why is nobody even injured? Do you think that those criminals who otherwise shoot point blank, who are sharp shooters, they cannot hit even one police officer? So the criminal is caught, made to stand, and fired at! (I 5, Journalist)

– Implying that the lack of police injuries showed there was no cross shooting, but that it was a clear case of execution.

> They had killed this peanut vendor in an encounter saying that he is a criminal. I went to his house, I mean, he lived in a shanty in Bandra, where there is absolute poverty. Now how could he afford [the weapons allegedly found on him], he was selling peanuts. It was a case of mistaken identity (I 1, Journalist)

– Circumstantial evidence and the fact that the "victim" was too poor to have been the "hardcore" gangster he was alleged to be, was cited as being proof of mistaken identity.

> From the spot where he [the "criminal"] has done rampant firing with an automated weapon, which can fire up to 30 shots a minute, I mean, how can they not find empty cartridges in any of these instances? Why is the spot report not made that 40 cartridges were found? (I 2, Activist)

– Highlights awareness that there was inadequate ballistic and forensic evidence to prove that the police were under attack at the time.

> More often than not, the information that so and so is coming here, is given by the rival gang [to the police]. So you have connivance somewhere. If one gang gives you information about the other gang, then you are doing that man's job, and not your legal duty. So it has started becoming political (I 4, Director Cultural Centre, Retd. Senior Management); and
> Those big people who are abroad [referring to gang leaders who have fled to other countries], when people break away from their gangs, instead of killing them [the leavers] themselves, they [the latter] are killed by the police... The police do encounters on behalf of some or the other gang or group. (I 17, Politician)

– Evidence of politicisation and criminalisation of the force, and an acknowledgement of rampant police corruption led credence to the viewpoint that the police were acting as hit men for rival gangs and politicians.

Similar doubts have been raised in other public discourses (such as media reports, fiction and numerous films) but somehow the overriding perception of *encounters* appeared to be that of the realist, who despite being aware that there were police wrongdoings involved in *encounters*, was willing to accept these as "collateral damage" in the "war" on crime.

Discussion

The research uncovered that the role an officer played in *encounters*, which in turn was dependent on the rank a person held in the organisation, determined to a large extent what sort of attitude officers would have towards illegality of *encounters*. Table 4.1 shows the relationship between active participants, facilitators and supervisors, and non-participants and those who admitted either directly or indirectly to illegal *encounters*, and denied or evaded the question of illegal *encounters*.

It is significant that around half the active participants (mainly from the rank of Inspectors) did not have any problems with making a direct admission and together with those who indirectly admitted to illegality on their part, constituted close to two-thirds of the total group. On the other hand a majority of the non-participants (Sub-inspectors, and Lower Middle Management) opted for denial or evasion as a response. The majority of supervisors and facilitators were inclined to indirectly admit to transgressions.

It was surprising that almost half the active participants openly accepted wrongdoing, but perhaps it showed their confidence in the "correctness" of their actions. A strong element of moral rectitude allowed officers to have no qualms about accepting that there was overuse of deadly force because they were convinced it was done to promote social good. They felt that there were many limitations placed on them by the requirements of the law, their general lack of faith in the criminal justice system, and the sheer lack of resources, infrastructure and manpower to tackle large-scale organised crime. The "active" active participants did not show much remorse or regret for the actions taken by them, which seemed logical considering their motivation to pursue this course of action was ongoing. By comparison, a small majority of the "dormant"[13] active participants, it seemed, had had more time to reflect on the implications of their actions and were more questioning of the "policy" of *encounters*.

Some of the active participants did not see why either their motives or actions should be questioned as they were perfectly justifiable – from their viewpoint. Organised crime could not be controlled through the legal means available to them; however, the police were expected by society at large to deal with it effectively, regardless of the means adopted to do so. Foster (2003: 205) cites Hunt and

Table 4.1 Officer involvement and attitude towards "Wrongdoing" in *encounters*

	Active participants	Facilitators/ supervisors	Non-participants	Total
Direct admission	7	3	4	14
Indirect admission	2	6	2	10
Denial/evasion	6	1	7	14
Total	15	10	13	38

---

[13] "Active" participants were those who were then still actively doing *encounters* around the time of the interviews as opposed to the "dormant" ones, who had ceased such activity for the past few years.

Manning's (1991) study which found, "police lying and how the nature of police work, and officers' responses to it, opens up a moral and practical minefield and, in so doing, creates the backdrop for a range of illegitimate behaviour and abuse of the rule of law". Thus powerful forces that motivated officers in Mumbai to adopt illegal means to do what they perceived was their job, resonate in other policing contexts.

Studies in the UK revealed similar pressures on the police, especially the lower ranks to adopt whatever measures they felt they needed, even illegal ones to do their job (Chatterton, 1979; James, 1979; Settle, 1990). Officers in Mumbai were remarkably confident that nothing could ever go wrong, that they could never make a mistake that they would get the "right" man every time. They had spent so much time and energy on covert surveillance, collecting intelligence and keeping track of a particular individual that there were very little chances of any mistakes occurring. Also their confidence in controlling information about *encounters*, meant they did not feel threatened by media exposures or scandals.

The reasons why officers tended to deny any "wrongdoing" were more straight-forward. There must have been some amount of distrust not only of the researcher, but also of the purpose of the research and what the research material would be used for. Part of police culture is to be suspicious and distrustful of others (Reiner, 2000a: 91). This was especially understandable because the topic under discussion was so sensitive and any misuse of the information could have drastic consequences for the individual and the organisation.

Officers who denied illegality preferred to stick to the official police version of *encounters* as a matter of policy. This made them feel safe and they probably were not interested in introspecting or a detailed discussing of the topic because either it was too sensitive for them or they experienced guilt. Guilt on the part of the active participants borne out of the recognition that despite all their bluster and justifica-tions, what they were doing was illegal and tantamount to murder.

Possibly non-participants suffered feelings of guilt that they themselves were incapable or unable to take this decisive action, and they did not want to "rat" on others who did. Some non-participants might have denied any knowledge of wrong-doing because of lack of adequate and reliable knowledge about what actually happens in these situations. Facilitators and supervisors may themselves be complicit in some "wrongdoing", or may just have turned a blind eye to knowledge of some "wrongdoing" involved in *encounters*. For this reason they may be unwilling to admit to any illegality.

Police sub-cultural values of secrecy and loyalty to colleagues are "central to controlling the flow of potentially explosive material and hence each other" (Brogden, Jefferson, & Walklate, 1988: 39). The sub-culture also fosters a group solidarity that punishes whistle blowing with a "cold shoulder treatment", dismissal, demotion, discrimination, ostracism, even assault (Chan, 1996: 121; Kleinig, 1996: 187); and worse still, being set up in a shooting incident without back-up as alleged by officer Serpico who broke the "rule of silence" and deposed before the Knapp Commission (1972) in New York (Maas, 1974).

An element of fear might have prevented officers from accepting any wrongdoing in the interviews for fear of the repercussions. They could not be sure that the material would not be "misused" and used to implicate them in any legal or departmental action[14] as was evident in the reaction of some of the officers to their interviews being tape recorded. The same officers did not mind discussing some of these issues openly once the recorder had been switched off. Some other deniers were perhaps careful enough not to commit themselves either on tape or off it.

There certainly was evidence that loyalty towards colleagues and the department prevented officers from accepting illegalities existed. Even if they admitted illegality, they were to support the action out of a sense of loyalty. As one officer put it,

> We are still a team… We have been doing it [*encounters*] for the past 10 or 12 years and I think it is enough. But even then I will do whatever I can. I am not doing a favour to anybody – they are my colleagues – good luck to them! I am simply doing what I can to see that the department does not get a bad name. This department has given me a lot – status and respectability, and I will do whatever I can to protect the reputation of the department – not any one person or officer. (T 34: Inspector, Facilitator; from verbatim notes)

The denial mode was more in keeping with my preconceived expectations of how police officers would react because they had no reason to trust me and no obligation to do so.

When patterns of denial or admission of illegality were examined based on officer ranks, the majority of Upper Middle Management tended to directly or indirectly admit illegality. Perhaps it was easier for them to do so since they were neither ultimately responsible for formulating and directing policy, nor actually executing it. Officers at the middle managerial levels could afford to criticise and question *encounters*. It is unclear whether it was easier to accept wrongdoing when the responsibility could be passed on to others. Alternatively, it could be that Middle Management officers were more objective and had thought through the consequences of police actions as they were not directly involved in *encounters*. Finally, Upper Middle Management officers were directly recruited, young Indian Police Service officers with a more critical attitude towards the established attitudes of deference and unquestioning acceptance of "tried and tested" standard police policy decisions made by the Senior Management. They were the proverbial "piggy in the middle" (Punch, 1985: 75), sandwiched between the lower ranks and the elite senior management. In Mumbai these officers liked to think of themselves as "thinking cops" who were (at least theoretically) open to new methods and ideas about dealing with traditional problems.

Senior Management took a different stance and opted for official denial of illegalities, but diluted it with indirect acknowledgement of some transgressions. It is incontrovertible that as facilitators, if Senior Management had not been complicit in the actions or decisions taken by the lower ranks, or had not given directions to that effect in the first place, numerous *encounters* could not have taken place, without

---

[14] These last two factors are surmises and I don't really have concrete evidence from the interviews. However, it would seem plausible that fear and guilt would be some of the reasons for their refusal to discuss this issue openly.

serious consequences for the active participants. However as facilitators (either directly, or indirectly by turning a deliberate blind eye) Senior Management were not in a position to openly admit any transgressions on the part of the police. The fact that they were ultimately responsible for all actions (*encounters* included) and inactions (disciplinary proceedings to discourage abuse of force) of their subordinates at a force-wide level, they could scarcely openly accept that any illegality was being condoned or encouraged by them. Additionally, being the highest authority responsible for formulating policy and taking the decision that *encounters* would be one of the measures used to combat organised crime, Senior Management could not then accept that there were any illegalities involved. The fact that a policy of *encounters* prevailed can only be inferred indirectly from the complete confidence the active participants seemed to have in the support and backing of their senior officers. There were obviously no written instructions or guidelines that openly articulated such policy.

Senior Management officers interviewed felt a compulsive need to explain that in their experience *encounters* were one of the most effective responses to combat organised crime and this justified their use as a crime control mechanism. One senior officer admitted that though some *encounters* might not have been in accordance to the law in the strictest sense; however, as a leader, he needed to take effective action against crime that had spiralled out of control. He could not afford to be known as the officer during whose regime, crime reigned uncontrolled. This senior officer was influenced by the occupational culture, which also influenced Skolnick's patrolmen and led him to observe that they had an "overwhelming concern to show themselves as competent craftsmen", and to being a "skilled worker" as opposed to "a civil servant obliged to subscribe to the law" (Skolnick, 1966: 231, 111). Senior Management needed quick and immediate results to prove their leadership capacities. As these officers had only a few months left in the job, it appeared as if they could not afford to think of the interests of the force, or society, in the long run. Several officers echoed the opinion that since "senior officers feel that during my tenure, crime should be under control" (T 22: Upper Middle Management), they favour the adoption of short cut methods like *encounters*.

Senior Management felt it incumbent upon themselves not to admit that their subordinates had been indulging in illegal actions; had abused the use of deadly force; and that they, in turn, had supported or encouraged this apparent abuse. Thus, they probably felt that as the public face representing the organisation, it would be irresponsible on their part to openly admit that the force was countenancing such gross misconduct.

Focusing on gender as the defining feature for analysing officer responses to this question, there were no significant changes in the pattern of acceptance or denial. Of the five women officers – three opted for direct admission of, one indirectly admitted to, whereas one officer staunchly denied illegalities on the part of the police. There were also no significant patterns created across ranks of female officers, in terms of their opinion. However, admittedly the number of women officers in the sample was very low and thus was inadequate to make any kind of generalised extension of gendered patterns.

Summary

This chapter describes the complicated network of terms associated with the core term *encounters*, and the interrelationships that exist between them. Unpacking the different interpretive frameworks through which *encounters* can be perceived and analysing the different ways in which police officers and claimsmakers defined the term is indicative of the complex nature of the phenomenon that is more grey than black or white. Police officers had four different types of definitions and claimsmakers exhibited three different approaches towards *encounters*. Clearly everyone interviewed was aware that the term *encounter* had dubious connotations and there was universal recognition that there were "genuine" *encounters* and "fake" *encounters*; however, these terms were used by the police and the claimsmakers in more nuanced ways than one would have expected. There were different situations and conditions under which particular incidents would be seen as acceptable or not by the officers and by the public. The research shows that police officers' perceived the difference between "genuine" and "fake" *encounters* differently from what they thought was the public understanding of the terms.

Officers had different views on whether they thought there were any "wrong-doings" involved in *encounters*. Whether officers would directly or indirectly admit to or deny illegalities in *encounters* depended upon the extent of their participation in *encounters*, their rank in the organisation, as well as how they responded to the interview situation. Claimsmakers, on the other hand were also aware that there were illegalities involved but were unsure of the extent and nature of the wrongdoing.

The next chapter explores questions around the efficacy of *encounters* as a crime fighting tool and the police understanding of their role and expectations of the society they serve.

Chapter 5
Are *Encounters* Effective? Police Role and Police Image

Introduction

The strongest argument put forward by Mumbai police officers to explain the continued employment of *encounters* as a crime control tactic was rooted in their unanimous perception that they were very effective. In comparison, claimsmakers were not as convinced of the overall utility of *encounters*. The other argument that empowers police officers to use every means at their disposal to stop criminals is the police organisational and general social belief that crime control is the sole responsibility of the police. The officers' image of themselves and their role to "serve society" appeared to have given them an innate conviction that adoption of any means, fair or foul, to promote social well-being was legitimate and unquestionable. On the other hand, claimsmakers were more objective in their assessment of what the police have and can achieve.

Comparing and contrasting officers' viewpoint with the perspective of claimsmakers yields interesting shades of opinion that serve to build up the picture of a society that to all appearances is complicit in a state crime, but actually reveals that the situation is more complicated than that.

Are *Encounters* Effective?

Police Officers

Despite any reservations police officers had about the legality and morality of *encounters*, or "genuine" and "fake" *encounters*, every single officer interviewed agreed that *encounters* were effective. There were no significant differences across either ranks, gender, or officer involvement on this aspect of *encounters*. There were however, different criteria by which effectiveness was construed.

J. Belur, *Permission to Shoot? Police Use of Deadly Force in Democracies*,
DOI 10.1007/978-1-4419-0975-6_5, © Springer Science+Business Media, LLC 2010

Crime Control

It was universally held that *encounters* had a dramatic and instant impact on gangs operating in the city. One officer explained the effect thus,

> If a criminal is killed, then his followers or those crimes which he would have committed in the future, those would definitely be reduced... So many criminals have fled away from this Bombay city, they now have shifted their headquarters. Otherwise in Mumbai there would have been a great deal of unrest – gangsterism, extrortionists, kidnappers. A lot of serious offences have gone down. (T 17: Inspector; Non-Active participant)

Newspaper accounts of the crime statistics for 2003 presented by the Police Commissioner to the media in January 2004 report "Murders dropped from 365 in 1998 to 242 last year, shootouts declined from 101 in 1998 to 10 in 2003 and extortion complaints came down from 987 in 1998 to 273 last year".[1]

Impact on Gang Activities

Officers were convinced that *encounters* had a knock-on impact on recruitment of new, as well as, mobility of established gang members within the city. One officer explained,

> In one encounter, for example, of the Abu Salem gang, we killed four people. Now for the next six months there will be no activities of that gang – because basically that Abu Salem is from Azamgarh (in Uttar Pradesh) and he mainly uses shooters from there... for some days people will not get recruited to that gang. And for some days he [the leader] will have to provide money to their families. In this a few days will pass, then he will recruit and train new people – that takes time. (T 27: Inspector; Active participant)

This is a very brutal form of disruption of gang activities. However, there is little independent evidence to support the officer's opinion, which, in all fairness, was probably based on insider knowledge.

Establishing Supremacy of the Police

Officers felt that *encounters* had the power to create and establish the ultimate superiority of law enforcement over organised crime. This was expressed by one officer,

> It is my opinion that criminals, he could be a pickpocket or an organised criminal, or top gangster, criminals are not worried about courts – they are not worried about the system, or cases against them. They are worried only about the police and bullets. What hammering

---

[1] *The Times of India* (2004a, 2004b, 2004c, 2004d), "I want more cops to be nabbed by ACB: Pasricha", January 15, 2004.

they get from the police and their bullets – they are only worried about those two things.
(T 1: Inspector; Active participant)

The conviction that criminals are only afraid of the police and not of the courts or the criminal justice system was widespread among the officers interviewed and also officers I have interacted with over my own police career.

Reassuring the Public and Warning Criminals

Officers felt that *encounters* sent a clear warning and an unambiguous message to the public and criminals that the police was taking "proactive and aggressive" action to prevent "trademark" crimes of organised gangs in Mumbai. One officer said, "the police send a message that if you do anything wrong there is no escape. You will be subject to the bullet" (T 7: Lower Middle Management). This ostensibly was meant to reassure the public that the police were actively tackling crime.

Immediate Impact

Officers believed *encounters* were an effective shortcut method to get immediate visible results for the public. In the words of one officer,

> Yes, it has an impact on crime. The only thing that the criminals fear is an encounter. They know that if they are caught, they can get the best lawyers, they can get bail, they can try to manipulate the system, they can even jump bail. But they are really scared of encounters, so it does have an impact. (T 33: Upper Middle Management)

Officers' opinions differed on the extent to which they thought *encounters* were effective and the time span for which it would prove to have a beneficial impact. Most Upper Middle Management officers were unsure of the long-term effects on crime control and whether it would prove effective in the long-term. They were also unsure of the consequences of such a policy, given the changing human rights climate in India. They did seem willing and able to reflect on the effects and consequences of a policy that was considered by all others as being very effective. Upper Middle Management, as future leaders of the force, were worried about the psychological impact of deliberate encouragement of *encounters* on the officers involved in particular and on the force in general. They expressed concern about the impact "out of control" officers or the "encounter specialists" could have on the general morale and reputation of the force in the years to come. These concerns were not really shared by officers of other ranks.

Claimsmakers

Claimsmakers' opinions on the success of *encounters* were grounded in their opinions about the nature of crime in general and the incidence of organised crime in particular.

A majority of interviewees thought that the crime situation in Mumbai had improved over the years, especially that organised crime had been brought under control. Interviewees' perception of effectiveness of *encounters* roughly correlated to their perception of the crime trend in general. Those who thought that *encounters* were effective felt that crime was going down, especially organised crime. However, those who thought they were ineffective said they thought crime was on the rise over the past 10 years.

In contrast to police officers, "claimsmakers" were more divided on the issue of efficacy of *encounters*. Ten of the 18 interviewees felt that *encounters* achieved their intended effect of controlling crime; two thought they were effective only in the short run, whereas six felt they were ineffective. One interviewee articulated the reasons for their ineffectiveness:

> It is an admission of the failure of our professionalism. As a policeman everyone is trained to bring an offender to justice. And there is a legal system to do that. When we resort to the technique of encounter, apart from whatever it does to our psyche, it is also an admission that we have not been able to practice our profession properly... The question is, have we been able to put an end to the underworld and organised crime by resorting to encounters? The answer is no... and in the process you have dehumanised so many police officers. It is a pity that even politicians have said that this should be done... When the elected representative, who is also a Cabinet Minister says this is the only way we can deal with them – I think something has gone wrong with us. No government, much less a democracy can ever give a licence to anyone to kill, because this licence to kill can be very costly... The moment you give somebody the licence to kill, he can go and kill anyone for selfish purposes. [Also] in spite of encounters the underworld exists, we have not been able to eliminate it. You kill two people, there are four available to do the same job, because really speaking, you are killing menials. You are not attacking the source, no harm has been done to Dawood Ibrahim or Chhota Rajan. If they get killed, they will be killed by each other. Gangs after gangs after gangs... lots of gangs have come and gone, but other gangs have come up. So how do we say that this policy has succeeded? If it is a policy, even an unannounced policy, or a tacit understanding. The very fact that the problem exists is an indication of the failure of this policy". (I 4, Director Cultural Centre, retd. Senior Management)

The interviewee (possibly on account of being a retired police officer) identified almost all the problems resulting from unaccountable police use of deadly force. Themes identified by the interviewee included: unprofessional police practices; misuse of political and police powers; erosion of democratic values; adverse effects on individual officers and on the force; ineffectual culling of lower (and powerless) ranks of the gangs; inability to curb the real gang leaders; and finally, historical evidence showing that gang activities continued despite existence of tacit policy of *encounters*.

Claimsmakers who disapproved of them, felt that the "tacit policy of *encounters*" had failed. Again this was in contrast to police officers who, regardless of their personal opinion about *encounters* as a policy, nevertheless thought they were very effective, at least in the short run. This discrepancy arose perhaps because officers' perception was influenced mainly by the immediate operational and practical aspects of *encounters* as opposed to long-term ethical considerations. While admittedly, there appeared to be temporary gains in terms of their immediate impact on gang activities, apart from a few Upper Middle Management officers most police officers were unable to assimilate the wider psychological, social, and ethical impact of *encounters* extending beyond the boundaries of day-to-day policing. "Claimsmakers", not hampered by the expectations and restrictions placed upon police officers, and as outsiders, were thus able to have a better appreciation of the wider socio-psychological impact of *encounters*.

Are *Encounters* Desirable?

Police Officers

Officers were asked, what they, as individuals, thought pursuing a policy of *encounters* as an organisational goal. There were different shades of opinion on this: some approved, others disapproved, and still some others held a neutral position. Individual attitudes towards desirability of *encounters* in terms of rank or gender did not reveal any distinct patterns. Of the five women officers interviewed, two officers approved, one officer disapproved, one officer denied any need for approval of, and the remaining officer did not offer any opinion on *encounters*.

Whereas officers of all ranks broadly approved of *encounters* as an organisational goal, the five disapprovers were mainly from the ranks of Inspectors (two officers) and Upper Middle Management (three officers). Five officers who maintained a position of neutrality were actually the deniers of "wrongdoing" and were mainly from the ranks of Lower Middle Management (three officers), one Inspector and one officer from the Upper Middle Management. One Sub-Inspector and a Lower Middle Management officer did not offer any opinion on the desirability or otherwise of *encounters*.

Approval

This was the most complex emotion officers had towards *encounters*. Twenty-six officers approved of the *encounter* "policy" since they thought it was an effective method of controlling crime. However, some of them approved of *encounters* with certain reservations – i.e. they explicitly mentioned that they did not approve of "fake" *encounters* (mainly implying killing an "innocent" person). Even when officers acknowledged that some active participants might be corrupt or have ignoble intentions, they tended to approve of the action, as long as the target was a hardened "criminal". A few officers admitted that they would not like to be active participants, but that they approved of others willing to do this job.

Emotions towards *encounters* were complex. Officers often expressed contrary views, and shifted perspectives and positions. For example, one officer (a Sub-Inspector with over 25 years of service, and a non-participant) who indirectly admitted to illegalities, and who, I concluded, personally approved of *encounters*, denied agency when he said,

> Encounters are not conducted, police don't do them, they happen. Like how it is not in your hands whether it should rain or not – it is a natural phenomenon – like that whether *encounters* should be done or not is not in our hands – they occur! (T 2: Sub-Inspector)

> JB: "Sometimes *encounters* are done, aren't they?"

> T 2: "If they are done, then it is a crime". (T 2: Sub-Inspector)

The officer initially denied that *encounters* were staged and were criminal if done for any reason other than self-defence. Just a few minutes later, the same officer while lamenting the ineffectiveness of the criminal justice system and the restrictions placed by the courts, Human Rights organisations, and NGOs on the police, said:

> Nowadays the police no longer have an upper hand; there is no fear of the police. The reason for that is the increasing fear of goondas.[2] You ask me, why is this so? Because the goonda takes hold of you, breaks you hand, leg, murders you. So if a goonda demands anything, people comply. What can the police do if they pick you up? They cannot break your hands or legs, cannot do anything, cannot hit you, cannot even abuse you. He is like a bound down tiger, cannot even roar. The police are completely tied down, cannot do anything, cannot even stare intimidatingly at anyone – there will be an allegation that he was looking at me angrily! The policeman has become a blind, immobile, useless oaf – merely existing. But the goondas are not like that – they are very powerful and can do anything. In such a situation if *encounters* take place then they are good for the police and for society. It will give the bound down tiger an opportunity to strike! (T 2: Sub-Inspector; Non-Participant)

While on one hand the officer denied that the police engineered *encounters*, on the other hand he felt that *encounters* were not only effective in boosting police morale but also "good for society". Subsequently, the same officer laughingly recounted an incident where he had the opportunity and the means to shoot a dreaded criminal but had desisted. He also admitted that his supervisory officer had half seriously questioned him later, as to why he had missed such an opportunity. His explanation was that he did not believe in using unnecessary force, thus making his own moral views on the subject clear.

Though this officer said that if *encounters* were "done", it was a crime; at the same time, he also felt that *encounters* would help re-establish the superiority of the police and restore their bruised and battered self-image. One could only conclude that the officer personally approved of *encounters* but realized that they could not be officially condoned, and certainly would not want to be personally involved in one. The same officer was also aware that *encounters* were not the chance happenings they were portrayed to be but continued to maintain that they were not "done". This was just one example of the kind of complexity and different levels of approval and acceptance of wrongdoings in *encounters* exhibited by officers. Some non-participants approved of *encounters* as long as they did not have to do any "illegal" or "dirty" work. For example, one officer admitted,

> I cannot do it myself, my conscience does not permit that I should kill – but if someone else does it then it is a good thing as all the future procedures and complications are avoided – and it prevents another big criminal from being created. (T 12: Sub-Inspector, Non-Participant)

---

[2]Ruffians or gangsters.

The officer appeared to be confirming the unspoken suspicion that usually those targeted by the police were not "big" criminals, but those on their way to becoming big and whose elimination might avoid possible future problems.

Others, it appeared, approved of *encounters* as an institutional practice, without really having thought deeply about what it entailed and the seriousness of the consequences for the alleged criminal, the organisation, and the faith reposed in the criminal justice system by society. To all appearances, some supervisors and facilitators approved of *encounters* merely as an effective crime control measure, without wanting to reflect on its adverse implications on the Right to Life, or how a police organisation that wields deadly force unethically might be perceived by society. Active participants, it may be deduced, approved of *encounters* to the extent of being able to pull the trigger on more than one occasion without qualms.

Disapproval

Five officers in the sample disapproved of *encounters* on legal as well as ethical grounds, as they were unsure of the long-term impact of such a policy on the morale of the organisation and the psyche of active participants. One officer said,

> After the last case, the Fawda case, we were in so much trouble and have just escaped narrowly. It was luck or the judges' or God's will, I don't know, but we were very, very lucky. I don't think these people know how lucky we were and this is so dangerous, it could turn on us at any time. It is like sitting on a time bomb which could blow up any minute. (T 34: Inspector; Facilitator, from verbatim notes)

This particular officer had been involved with the fallout of the alleged false *encounter* case of Javed Fawda in 1997, and subsequent police efforts to contest the finding of the Augiar Commission. Two other officers closely connected with the same case mentioned the "narrow escape" the police had at that time and disapproved of continuing along this self-chosen path strewn with landmines and pitfalls – "a ticking time bomb".

It is significant to note that almost all those officers who disapproved of *encounters*, or whose conscience did not permit them to normalize these actions, were facilitators and supervisors (Inspectors and Upper Middle Management) who nevertheless said that they would continue to facilitate and provide support to the active participants out of a sense of loyalty for the department, or because they were afraid of whistle blowing, or turning traitor.

Neutral

Five officers, who strenuously denied that *encounters* were "done", continued to maintain that they "happened". Thus, they felt that it was not for them to either approve or disapprove of any policy of *encounters*, because they denied that such a policy existed in the first place. These were the actual deniers in the whole sample, and as one of the officers said,

> No police officer would like to kill a criminal because he is a criminal. Unfortunately in exchange of fire somebody dies, it is a totally different act... It is sometimes clear from the media or people talking that police are killing gangsters or police are killing criminals, but I don't think it is a permitted goal, or it is doing something for the sake of killing. (T 14: Lower Middle Management)

According to this officer, there was no question of him personally approving *encounters* as an organisational goal, because it was not deliberate police policy. Two other officers did not express an opinion on whether they approved or disapproved of *encounters*, although they accepted *encounters* happened, but did not say whether they felt them to be either desirable or not, policy goals. They just did not answer this question. One of the officers said that she did not understand the question. Rephrasing the question was just met with silence. The other officer went on to talk of something quite irrelevant to the question, thus indicating that he was unwilling to comment on it. Refusal to answer the question was thus a different response from the position of the deniers, who maintained that *encounters* were chance happenings and thus the question of whether they personally approved or disapproved of them did not have any bearing. These officers might not have wanted to comment on what they saw as a potentially controversial issue or may have felt they did not know enough about it in order to express any opinion of approval or otherwise.

Claimsmakers

When asked whether they personally approved of *encounters* as a crime control measure, 11 of the 18 claimsmakers said they did not:

> My personal impression of encounters is that it is rough justice, which police are attempting to enforce. And rough justice must, in any case, be rough, and in many cases may not be justice at all... I don't approve of them. And I am afraid that it will come around and hurt a lot of innocent people, it may already have. (I 16, Corporate Executive, Representative Industrial Association)

Though expressed somewhat obliquely five interviewees approved of *encounters*. One interviewee said,

> Well, if breaking the law occasionally is the only way of enforcing the law, then you have to break the law. Supposing a person finds that his servant is committing theft, what will be the reaction? Will you not beat him mercilessly? If he feels that the servant has stolen some jewellery or money, do you think the man is going to say – 'Oh, human rights – I will sit here and call the police?' He will first kick him, he will give him at least 10 slaps, even his wife will take the chance to beat him, which the woman would ordinarily never dare to do. But that is human reaction. Breaking the law occasionally is the only way, you know, to uphold the majesty of the law. That is why policemen do it – there is no other way. (I 13, Retired Judge)

On the other hand, two interviewees said they disapproved, but their subsequent comments suggested secret approval of *encounters* of "genuine" "hardcore" criminals:

I 3: "Desperate situations require desperate measures, but here the wrong people are getting eliminated – they are small time criminals. The real big ones are getting police protection".

J.B.: "So do you think if big timers were eliminated, it would, in a sense, be justified, given the prevailing situation?"

I 3: "Looking at the havoc they [criminals] are creating, I think it is perfectly justified". (I 3, Retired Judge)

However this same person went on to object to *encounters* on the grounds that:

If someone is eliminated today, tomorrow it will be your turn. So this [social approval] is an attitude which has been inculcated by brainwashing, brainwashing carried out by the media, by the politicians, by the so-called society leaders. That is incorrect; people should start thinking for themselves. This is a serious matter and if there is deterioration in police efficiency and integrity, it is society at large which will suffer. (I 3, Retired Judge)

There were several important themes in this statement; strikingly, the objection to *encounters* was not on the grounds of protecting human rights, but on more practical issues like the need for accountability in police actions and the danger a "trigger-happy" police force may pose to ordinary citizens. Also the interviewee condemned social approval for *encounters* arising out of a "herd" mentality, which possessed people to be blindly led by influential public opinion makers. What the interviewee criticised as "brainwashing" is similar to the structural processes described by Hall, Critcher, Jefferson, Clarke, and Roberts (1978) when they suggest that the "mutually reinforcing" relations between the primary definers (police officers, judges, politicians, spokespersons of associations) and the secondary definers (the media) reproduces and transforms controversial issues into a full blown social crisis, thus legitimising more authoritarian police actions. The interviewee felt that a lack of accountability for such police actions would ultimately have a deleterious effect on the morale and professional efficiency of the force. Though interviewees had different perceptions of *encounters*, there was a thread of consensus running through their discourse that society appeared to regard *encounters* as a defensible crime control policy for the police.

Officers' Perception of Their Role

Police officers perception of their role as a lone force saddled with the responsibility of crime reduction was central to the argument for *encounters* as a crime control policy. In Mumbai officers thought that only they, not the larger criminal justice system, were responsible for securing public safety.

Officers described aspects of their role that were grouped into three main policing concerns – crime related, keeping the peace, and service-related functions. While 31 officers mentioned crime-related functions (including crime control, investigation and detection and crime prevention) as their main role; 22 talked about keeping the peace functions (including law and order and maintenance of security) functions; and 26 talked about service-related functions (either public service or social work).

Notably, officers' conception of their role as "social workers" is not the same as what is traditionally understood by the term. Officers categorised "helping an old lady cross the road" or "preventing a bullying landlord from forcibly evicting a poor tenant from a slum hut" as "social work". One officer evocatively described this as,

> There is no other social worker like the police... If an unidentified dead body, or a beggar's body or anything is found then there is no person in society who will say that, 'Sir I will do his last rites, if it is a Hindu, then a cremation'. In the end this has to be done by the police. (T 10: Sub-Inspector)

Officers conceived of social work as an assortment of functions performed by the police that no one else could be held accountable for or volunteered to perform. Westley (1970: 19) refers to this as "dirty work" that is "exceedingly unpleasant and in some sense degrading". Officers referred to actions they thought were service functions, regardless of whether these were within their legal mandate. One officer talked about his work in the following terms:

> Police department does more than just enforce the law. I worked for the neglected and downtrodden people. I did a lot of work and helped the people and took decisions on my own which the senior officers would like... I did as much as I could, we are police officers but we are social workers. My reputation spread as one who would help the poor and not entertain all the other useless people, like fraudulent social workers and political people. (T 17: Inspector)

The mixed bag of responses was perhaps because not only is the police role so diffuse, but also because officers' answers were very much influenced by the topic under discussion just prior to the question, or the tone of the interview as a whole. Officers' answers were also clearly linked to the officer type as explained by Reiner (2000a: 102). Drawing parallels between "officer types" analysed in the works of other police researchers (Broderick, 1973; Brown, 1981; Muir, 1977; Shearing, 1981; Walsh 1977), Reiner identified four basic types of officers from his own research: the "bobby", who applies the law with discretionary common sense and is essentially a peace keeper; the "uniform carrier", a cynical and disillusioned time server; the "new centurion", a dedicated crime fighter and crusader against disorder; and the "professional", ambitious, career conscious and poised for largely public relations functions of a senior rank.

In Mumbai, the more "action-oriented types" talked mainly about crime prevention and maintenance of law and order; the more "professional" officers responded in terms of "investigation and detection of crime"; and the practical "street cop" emphasised "keeping the peace". Officers who emphasised values of care and service talked of "service" and "social work" as main functions. Only nine officers mentioned social work as their role, but nearly all officers described their work in social service terms during the course of the interview. This demonstrated the difference between service role as ideal vs. service being the reality of police work.

Observational studies in other countries have revealed similar patterns of actually how much police time is spent in service activities as compared to crime-related functions, across different contexts (Ekblom & Heal, 1982; Punch & Naylor, 1973; Shapland & Hobbs, 1989; Skogan, 1990, as cited in Bowling & Foster, 2002: 987). However police studies in the UK and the USA concluded that despite the "proportion of time spent on 'service' or order maintenance roles, these aspects of police work are devalued by the police themselves" (Bowling & Foster, 2002: 988, referring to Fielding, 1995; Holdaway, 1983; McConville & Shepherd, 1992; Waddington, 1999b). Unlike Bittner's policeman who believes that his real function is to pursue the likes of Willie Sutton, while feeling "compelled to minimize the significance of those instances of his performance in which he seems to follow the footsteps of Florence Nightingale"[3] (Bittner, 1990: 268), most officers interviewed were actually proud to emphasise the service aspect of their job. This contrasts with how service functions were perceived by officers for example, in Cain's study (Cain, 1973: 74) as "being officious" or in Bittner's study (Bittner, 1970: 42) as being "nuisance demands for service". The police in India have historically been seen as the repressive arm of the state. An image inherited as a colonial legacy that the police are desperately trying to change. As this officer said,

> From the times of the British, the police were seen as oppressors, and that image is fixed in the minds of the people. But even with today's improved and reformed police, even when officers help and co-operate with the common man, help them... the same image continues.
> (T 5: Upper Middle Management)

Reiner's (2000a: 112) conclusion that "most police work is neither social service nor law enforcement but order maintenance – the settlement of conflicts by means other than formal policing", seems apposite even in the Mumbai context. However, although as he goes on to say that this raises important ethical dilemmas in terms of accountability, equity and fairness (Reiner: 114), these did not seem to trouble the Mumbai officers, who saw no conflict between their roles as crime fighters and service providers. In fact, they tended to see their crime-fighting role (*encounters*) as contributing to their service role by providing instant justice and relief to the public.

Clearly, officers in Mumbai were passionate about their role and took their job very seriously. Reiner (2000a: 89) mentions that for the police, their work is not just another job, but a way of life, a vocation to be pursued with evangelical zeal (Mills, 1973; Reisman, 1979). The "working personality" of a policeman stems from the combination of "danger and authority" facets of policing (Skolnick, 1966). This personality coupled with constant pressure to produce results leads policemen to prefer being "efficient rather than legal when the two norms are in conflict" (Skolnick: 231). Research evidence shows that the police employ various stratagems like, "lying, perjury, undue violence, planting evidence..., altering documents, manipulation of suspects and informants, falsifying evidence, intimidation, and a battery of seamy tactics... as legitimate techniques in getting their work done" (Punch, 1985: 203, citing Ericson, 1981; Skolnick, 1975). Mumbai police officers also exhibited this pragmatic "working personality" considering that a

---

[3] Bittner (1990) explains in an endnote – "Florence Nightingale is the heroic protagonist of modern nursing; Willie Sutton... was in his day a notorious thief".

majority of the officers did not feel hampered by the restrictions placed upon their powers by the law and considered it fully justifiable that under the guise of helping people or solving problems they could go beyond their legal mandate. As one officer put it:

> People bring grievances to us of all kinds, and we have the backing of the law and the authority of the khaki uniform, that is why people are afraid and they listen and obey, even though it may not be strictly within the framework of our powers. Anything done in good faith is accepted. If there is a dispute between two brothers, it is a NC [non-cognisable] matter,[4] we can just take down a report and send them away. But the quarrel does not stop. But if I call both of them and try to make them see a few points – I can do two things, either explain or threaten – this work can be done only by the police, to solve the issue. (T 7: Lower Middle Management)

When I asked whether this approach went beyond the law, he replied:

> What is the aim of the law? [It is] to preserve peace and maintain order. I can do something to preserve peace at my level only. That is why Section 100 is included in the Indian Penal Code, which says anything done in good faith is no offence. If my intention is good and if no one has any objection to it, then why should I not do it? (T 7)

Evidently the officer had no qualms about overreaching his mandate, or taking on a role that was beyond what was officially expected of him. This officer's comments were typical of those who believed their main role was providing the public with the service they needed. It is unclear whether the officer invoked Section 100 of the Indian Penal Code (IPC) as justification for *encounters* or generally to cover any acts committed "in good faith", but he was clearly invoking the wrong section of the IPC to buttress his argument.[5] The officer had obviously (or conveniently) mixed up the wording and misunderstood the meaning of two sections of the IPC and drawn a totally erroneous conclusion that allowed him to exceed his legal powers and mandate. While police officers operate more by discretion than the letter of the law, they prefer to be seen working within the law.

Officers felt that as "reproducers of order" (Ericson, 1982) their main task was to implement the spirit of the law, which was aimed at maintaining peace and security

---

[4]The Indian Penal Code categorises most offences as "cognizable", i.e. offences that the police have to take cognizance of and act there upon; and some small, petty offences as "non-cognizable", which may be registered at the police station, but the police are not bound to take any further action.

[5]Section 100 actually refers to "When the right of private defence of the body extends to causing death", under certain conditions specified as: when there is apprehension that death, or grievous bodily hurt will be the consequence of the assailant's action; when the assault is done with the intention of committing rape; gratifying unnatural lust; kidnapping or abduction; or with the intention of wrongfully confining a person under circumstances that cause him to reasonably apprehend that he will be unable to have recourse to the public authorities for his release. The words "acting in good faith" do not appear in this section but in Section 99 of the (IPC) which deals with "Acts against which there is no right of private defence" and refers to the fact that there is no right of private defence against an act which does not reasonably cause the apprehension of death or of grievous bodily hurt, if done or attempted to be done by a public servant or under the direction of a public servant, if the latter has been acting in good faith under the colour of his office, though that act may not be strictly justifiable by law.

and solving people's problems. They believed that in the process of implementing the spirit of the law, the law itself could be infringed or set aside, and as long as the police action was in "good faith" all would be forgiven.

In the same vein, another officer saw his own role as that of an "elder brother",

> People think that the police should help them in distress. Any man in distress will look to the police for relief. Police is the protective arm of the state... how a small child looks up to his elder brother to protect him from bullies or from being beaten up, in that way the common man looks up to the police to protect them from the bad guys. (T 29: Sub-Inspector, "encounter specialist")

This attitude extended to the use of deadly force. Officers were convinced that since their main aim was to control crime, if eliminating "criminals" was the best way to do what they saw as their job, and "if no one has an objection to it, then why should I not do it?" typified their attitude. The connection between the self-image of "elder brother" and the use of deadly force was clearly visible in another "encounter specialist's" views,

> In my opinion the main job of the police in society is to protect them [the public] from people with goonda[6] tendencies. Maintaining law and order etc. is the job of higher ups. Our job is to control the dadas[7] in the slums... The main role of the police is that of a dada among these goondas. Now, I have done many encounters, more than 85, so these criminals are scared of me. If someone gets a [threatening] phone call and I go to his house, if that goonda gets to know that I had gone to this house then he will never phone that house again. (T 27: Inspector, "encounter specialist")

It was evident that this officer's self-image, of the policeman being a bigger bully than the criminal "goondas" in society, clearly influenced his decisions and actions to invoke deadly force. The officer visibly revelled in his self-image as "one who struck terror in the minds of the criminal elements", and the assumption that his mere presence in someone's home was a guarantee of protection for that person, actually gave him a sense of power. Very few officers expressed this sentiment quite so openly, but it was clear from the interviews that most officers preferred to think of themselves as being more powerful than the criminals. There were repeated references to the perception that the police were, in a sense, official "dispensers of justice" and "providers of relief" to the common man. Given the failure of the criminal justice system there was also a tacit conviction among officers that there was nothing wrong in actively pursuing a policy of *encounters* as a popular crime control measure to secure the confidence of the public. A senior police officer, A.A. Khan expresses similar sentiments when he describes the aftermath of one high-profiled *encounter* that occurred in 1992, "These [positive] reactions from grateful people more than made up for the trauma of being "on call" day and night and living from moment to moment, while conducting dangerous operations..." (Khan, 2004: 74).

It was ironic that while most officers were aware that people most affected by the rise of organised gang activities were a handful of rich, successful businessmen,

---

[6]Goonda meaning hooligan or ruffian.

[7]Dada – literal meaning: elder brother, but the term is often used colloquially as a euphemism for bullies, or a sort of "Godfather".

building magnates, film personalities, or industrialists, and not the common man, only a few of them actually acknowledged that this was the case. Officers glossed over this reality, suggesting that the common man was also affected, in that, they were the victims of extortion phone calls and threatening messages from groups of petty criminals, masquerading as the "big boys". However, officers did not attempt to make explicit the connection between how the *encounters* of a few criminals belonging to the big gangs would be reassuring for the multitudes that were far removed from the reach of these gangs. Presumably, the theory was that the atmosphere of terror and fear that *encounters* created in the minds of the criminal classes would have an adverse effect on the desire of petty criminals to boast of their (mythical or otherwise) connections with the big gangs and thus keep them under control. It was convoluted logic, but it appeared to work for this officer, who said,

> Encounters provide a good amount of terror. Everybody, in the lanes and by-lanes was wearing a white shirt and saying, "I am from the Dawood gang". That practice has stopped as a result of encounters; it is a big benefit... There is a good impact. These two or three boys, who had no work, were wandering around, wearing a white shirt, saying they were attached to this gang or that. At the local level, they used to extort from the small grocers and shopkeepers, all that has stopped. They were never attached to any gang, but just boasted about it. (T 21: Sub-Inspector)

Officers judged their own policing performance by the impact it had on the activities of criminals. It seemed that if a particular police action created panic and terror in the criminal classes, and dissuaded them from further indulging in crime, then it was considered to be particularly effective and was more valued.

While officers felt that they took a great deal of responsibility (at times beyond their remit) to serve society and control crime, claimsmakers perceived the Mumbai police in a slightly different light.

Claimsmakers' Perception of Police Image

A large majority of the claimsmakers interviewed thought that that the Mumbai police was a reasonably efficient force, significantly better than other forces in the country, and though corrupt, fairly effective in keeping Mumbai a safe city.

> Compared to the other police forces within India, they are far better, far more professionally managed, particularly at the higher levels, far more competent and diligent and sticklers for the norms. I mean, there might be rotten apples everywhere. Also it is fairly disciplined and accountable, perhaps on account of its size and the media exposure that Mumbai gets, and also on account of it being the capital city, all the ministers and bureaucrats, so lot of indirect controlling... So though it is declining very rapidly and though it is going down from bad to worse, by comparison, it is still, in my opinion, a far better police force than including that of Delhi or other places... That is in comparison, but in isolation the public feels that they are the rotten ones. They do feel that they are corrupt and hand-in-glove with the criminals... That is precisely why many of the ordinary complaints are not even taken to the

police. That is another reason why the local dons have all come up, because I will rather have them as my arbiter. They will take some money and sort out the things, rather than the policeman who will make me do chakkars (rounds) of the police station 'n' number of times and ultimately I may end up coughing out far more money and spending far more time. (I 2: Activist)

Evidently the interviewee felt that though there were many problems with the Mumbai police, still they were better as compared to police forces in other cities and states. One of the main reasons for discontent with the police was the cumbersome nature of the bureaucratic procedure that takes up time, energy, and resources (in the form of money to expedite matters in a corrupt police force) making them an unpopular "arbiter" in many disputes. People approached gang leaders for relief, and, at the same time, feared their ruthlessness. Aware of their influence and political power, it appeared as if people were secretly happy when gangsters were killed by the police, especially since there were no expectations that the courts would deliver.

More than one interviewee expressed the opinion that it was the only city in the country where women could safely travel even late at night and compared favourably with other large metros in the world in this respect. This was a source of pride to some of them. One interviewee said,

Parents find it a safe city. They say, 'My daughter comes home alone at 11 o'clock and nothing happens to her. It is because the police are effective that is why my daughter comes home safe. Why should I complain against those policemen? They are killing only goondas.[8] (I 13: Retired Judge)

A few interviewees felt that the police were better in the "golden past" but deteriorated in the past 20 years. The phenomenon of harking back to what Pearson (1983) calls "a still unlocated 'golden age'" is not unique to Mumbai but has been documented by Pearson as the "law-and-order" myth in the UK. Celebration of the "old-fashioned bobby" amidst the policing crisis showed a break from historical reality which did not take into account the fact that the police had traditionally employed "strong-arm tactics and were accused of brutality and disregard for civil liberties" over decades. Pearson suggests this form of historical mythology does not engender reform but merely a reaction that a return to the "good old days" can somehow solve all current problems and dilemmas and is not helpful.

Other issues around police image that affected public perception of police *encounters* were also discussed by claimsmakers.

---

[8] This confidence in the police has however been misplaced as there have been a few cases where policemen have been accused of rape in Mumbai in 2005. (Chadha, 2005, and "Protests over Minor's rape continue in Mumbai", *The Hindu*, April 26, 2005).

Fear of Crime

Public acceptance of *encounters* depends heavily upon how fearful society is about organised crime and how effectively the police construct their image as crime fighters in the public imagination. In Mumbai, although the discourse emphasized that organised gangs affected everyone and increased a general sense of insecurity in the populace, there was little or no discussion about actual patterns of victimization. Most "claimsmakers" acknowledged that the "ordinary common man" was rarely a direct victim of organised crime, but could potentially be indirectly affected by it, as one interviewee said,

> The sense of security is affected. Now see Sumeet Khatau[9] was killed in broad daylight on a chowk [major crossing] of the city. If unfortunately I were passing by and if even one bullet had hit me I would have been killed for no reason.... Secondly, because of the gang activity real estate prices had gone up. Builders had to pay up to these gangs and they would pass on these costs to the buyer. So the prices of flats went up tremendously. Also when I would manage to buy a flat, immediately there would be a telephone call to me saying that 'you have paid 60 lakhs,[10] now you pay me 5 lakhs'". (I 5, Journalist)

A few interviewees felt that only certain sections (builders, film-makers, businessmen, i.e. the very rich) felt the impact of organised crime most directly, via threatening phone calls, extortion demands, kidnapping for ransom, and being shot in broad daylight in case of non-compliance with their demands. On the other hand, as interviews with police officers showed, very few of the officers explicitly recognized this, instead they talked about the broad impact of organised crime and how it affected all sections of society.

Rule of Law

Indian society, according to many "claimsmakers", did not respect the rule of law and it was generally expected that rules would/should apply differentially to people depending upon their status and wealth. As one interviewee said:

> They [police] have been very, very ineffective in [upholding the rule of law]. Why do we blame the police – the society itself has no respect for the rule of law in general. So why do we expect policemen to – I mean, they have not descended from heaven in helicopters – they are the products of this very society. If journalists can park their cars wherever they want and get away with it because there is a 'press' sticker on the car, if bureaucrats and politicians feel that with my 'red light' on the car, I can park in the no-parking zone or go in the opposite direction on a one-way street, then you can't isolate the police alone, because that reflects the mentality and the mindset of the society as such". (I 2: Activist)

---

[9] A businessman who was allegedly the victim of organised gangsters (Weinstein, 2008).

[10] A lakh in the Indian numbering system equals 1,00,000.

Thus, the very idea that the rule of law does not apply equally to all, legitimises *encounters* as a crime-fighting tool against incorrigible "criminals". Additionally, it was also possible that officers bolstered by the faith that the system will treat police differently from "criminals" are emboldened to have a different set of ethical and legal standards when dealing with "hardened criminals".

Human Rights

Some interviewees deemed the Mumbai police had a better record than other forces in the country in the protection of human rights. It would not require a great leap of imagination to surmise that this made *encounters* somehow more acceptable because they were conducted by police officers who otherwise respected human rights. The majority opinion, however, summarized in the words of one interviewee was,

> Very, very poor…There is a large chunk of our citizenry who believe that human rights are of no consequence – "maaro saale ko" [beat the rascal]. They approve of that – not upholding human rights, they condone it, they say it is good thing… They know that human rights are violated left, right and centre, critics like us also know that they are violated left, right and centre but our responses are different. People like us criticize it, others, like our opponents or our critics say, "well, so what?" (I 2: Activist)

Three interviewees who defined *encounters* in naive terms also felt the police were effective in protecting human rights. Other interviewees covered the whole spectrum of opinions: the police image as one of brutality and insensitivity; a more moderate view in which the police only violated human rights of the poor and powerless; an extreme view suggesting that police were bound to protect only the human rights of the criminals, and the rights of the victims were neglected. Recompensing victims of organised crimes was one of the justifications for *encounters* for these interviewees.

Summary

The research showed that despite differing personal attitudes towards *encounters* being an approved method of crime control, there was near universal unanimity in the perception of officers that *encounters* were effective in more than one way. Despite this unanimity, officers were not in total agreement on the desirability of *encounters* being an approved organisational goal. Some officers approved of *encounters* and others disapproved of them, and still others took a neutral stance, either unwilling or unable to give an opinion. These positions were in some way linked to the ranks and roles that officers held at the time of the interviews. "Claimsmakers" on the other hand, were more divided on whether *encounters* were really as effective as claimed and their comments indicated their attitude towards *encounters* as a policy for the future, with most of them not really in favour, nonetheless not willing to take a stand against their employment as a crime-fighting tool.

Thus, looking at how officers understood their role and responsibility in general, and taking into account how they interpreted the expectations that society placed on them, specifically in dealing with organised criminal gangs, one can begin to understand the justifications the police in Mumbai put forward for the use of deadly force in *encounters*.

Chapter 6
A Culture of Complicity? Social Attitudes Towards *Encounters*

Introduction

In Mumbai there was a shared perception between police officers and claimsmakers that social reaction to *encounters* was either apathy, or in most instances, acceptance, or even in rarer cases, approval. Bayley (1996: 285) puts forward examples of countries like Argentina, Brazil and Jamaica where "police executions" of "undesirables" has been justified by officials, politicians, media, and the public generally. Consolidated public sympathy for police excesses, "creates a grim world of vengefulness in which persons accused of crime are literally outlaws, subject to execution by everyone, official or private" (Bayley, 1996 citing Chevigny, 1990: 412). Bayley's observations might apply equally to the situation in Mumbai, according to interviewees' perception of the general public attitude towards *encounters*.

An Illustrative Case

A first person account of one of the most talked about *encounter* cases in Mumbai (Khan, 2004) is illustrative of officers' perception of reaction to *encounters*. This incident, in which seven members of a gang were killed by a huge party of policemen in 1991 was also the subject of a major Bollywood film (*Shootout at Lokhandwala* 2007). Khan, a senior IPS officer was well-known in Mumbai for "the fact that 44 hardcore criminals had been slain by him, [but he] was not indicted by any commission of inquiry." (Khan, 2004: 136). According to Khan's account of the *encounter*, the police received a tip-off from a "petty-gangster-turned-informer" that Maya Dolas, alleged hit-man, extortionist, and core member of the Dawood gang, who apart from committing heinous crimes had also assaulted police officers and escaped from police custody, and his cronies were holed up in one of the flats in Lokhandwala complex [an enclave of closely spaced buildings] (Khan, 2004: 69). The police surrounded the building in the

J. Belur, *Permission to Shoot? Police Use of Deadly Force in Democracies*,
DOI 10.1007/978-1-4419-0975-6_6, © Springer Science+Business Media, LLC 2010

afternoon and began a stake-out. When adequate reinforcements were in place, they used a bullhorn to warn the "gangsters" and asked them to surrender. In response the police were attacked by a "strategically placed machine gun" and other firearms. The police fired back and after a thrillingly described exchange of fire, lasting over four-and-a-half hours, all seven members of this gang were shot down by the police. Khan then describes the "bouquets and brickbats" that followed in the aftermath of this operation:

> The initial applause was overwhelming. The Chief Minister of the State of Maharashtra, as well as a lot of political bigwigs, called to record their appreciation. We were congratulated, felicitated by the grateful residents, by the Lions, the Rotarians and several other social organisations. Warm letters poured in from unknowns, whose faith in the state machinery and its ability to bring offenders to book had been reinstated... Since the entire episode that been witnessed by hundreds of eyes, it was difficult to dismiss it as yet another staged encounter...Despite the presence of concrete proof, some accusations were hurled at us, even from within the force...jealous fangs were bared...A few of these debunkers actually implied that like Dolas or Buwa [his cohort], we too were on the don's payroll, settling scores on his behalf because some goons were getting too big for their boots, Others hinted that it was the builders' lobby which had hired us to finish off the extortionists...I requested the state government to reward my boys with some special compensation, and I am glad to report that [they received monetary rewards and bravery medals]...in spite of all the positive reactions we got from the majority of the press, the public, and even the local political party in power, we still had to undergo a trial by fire before the fingers pointing at us were finally put to rest. We had to submit our self-esteem for cross-examination by the special enquiry officer who was appointed to investigate the legitimacy of our actions...During the hearing in court however, many senior journalists testified in our favour...both cases were eventually dismissed, but... this case taught me that you are forever guilty, until you are proved innocent (Khan, 2004: 73–76)

The account alludes to several interesting themes: vilification of the "gangsters" and unquestioned acceptance of their "criminal record" by all; *encounter* as self-defence; absence of discussion around whether force used was necessary, proportionate or reasonable; overt public celebration; political approval to police *encounters*; police outrage at having to account for their actions; recognition of divisions within the organisation and envy of elite squads; accusations of police corruption; presence of several witnesses justifying it as not "another staged encounter"; and finally officers' sense of being betrayed by a system of accountability that is considered to be unnecessary and stressful. This incident is an example of how an *encounter* went well, which was then considered to go pear-shaped when criticisms were made and inquiries instituted and finally ended well.

The incident described illustrates the layers of complexity that surrounds *encounters*. Given the lack of reliable information, the dominant public perception becomes very important in determining how *encounters* will be viewed. None of the allegations and counter arguments really made any difference to the public perception in the Lokhandwala shootout case, since Dolas was a "feared" criminal there were few, if any, sympathisers to support his case.

The research revealed that police officers' conviction that this public perception will prevail each time they shoot a "criminal" gives them the confidence to persist. The following sections will explore these perceptions in some detail.

Attitude of Colleagues

Sensitivity and awareness of other officers' reaction was important because of the negotiation required with colleagues and supervisory officers while creating the written records for "situationally justifying action" (Manning, 1997: 131) in *encounter* cases where management of appearances was of vital significance. At one end of the spectrum was the belief that everyone in the organisation approved and supported *encounters*, and at the other end, that a few chosen individuals, a highly privileged and pampered group, monopolised the use of deadly force, thus gaining undeserved professional recognition and social status. The majority held the moderate position that most of their colleagues disapproved of "fake" *encounters*, but generally supported justified, even if not legitimate, *encounters*.

Crime Branch officers talked and thought about *encounters* quite differently from others. Regardless of whether they adopted the position of denial, indirect, or direct admission, officers connected to the Crime Branch were in the "know" – i.e. were aware of the exact nature and extent of the illegal and unethical practices involved in these operations. Some of these officers hinted at the murkiness beneath actions ostensibly portrayed as enhancing social good. Active participants were proud of the image created around them and encouraged the media portraying them as "cleaners of scum". One "encounter specialist" is recorded as having claimed, "Criminals are filth. And I'm the cleaner" (Perry, 2003); talk reminiscent of what Hughes (1961) has referred to as "dirty work" in policing.

Officers boasted of the number of "scalps" they had claimed; one officer described his first *encounter* thus, "That was my first. Since that day I have not stopped killing...My name is a brand today. Prisoners stick my photos on the walls of their cells" (Lakshmi, 2003). Active participants enjoyed a special status within the organisation, which was resented by some and coveted by other officers. The "specialists" had a somewhat patronising attitude towards those stuck with the banalities of everyday police station routine duties. Some of these dynamics are captured in the police literature on what is considered to be "real policing", the emphasis officers place on "action-oriented", "macho" aspects of police culture (Reiner, 2000a: 89: citing works of Holdaway, 1977, 1983; Skolnick & Fyfe, 1993; Geller & Toch, 1996; Crank, 1998) as opposed to routine and regular policing tasks that comprise of a majority of any police officer's job which is non-crime related. Morgan and Newburn (1997: 81) also suggest that studies have shown that "this 'service' work is widely regarded by the mainstream police occupational culture as 'bullshit' and very much the poor relation of 'real' police work".

A large majority of non-participants not connected with the Crime Branch, only had an inkling of the illegalities and corruption that might accompany *encounters*. They secretly envied their more flamboyant colleagues in the Crime Branch but there was also a feeling of "better them than me" doing this dirty job! One officer, a dormant active participant with no connection with the Crime Branch, and who had run into legal difficulties during two *encounters* he had been involved with, added as a post interview comment,

> However having said that [encounters are effective] I feel that it is better that encounters are left to the Crime Branch rather than the regular police. They are better trained; they have the time and resources for the planning and cultivating their sources. This is their entire job so they are the professionals and should do it. (T 38: Upper Middle Management)

A comment clearly indicating that *encounters* need much planning and management and that ordinary officers would find difficult to get away with use of deadly force under careful scrutiny.

Organisational Attitude

Officers, by and large, felt that there was general organisational approval and support for *encounters*: "Our force believe that they are into encounters, I think, irrespective of the government support. There is no alternative to control crime in an effective manner" (T 1: Inspector). However, a few officers felt that this approval could not always to be taken for granted, but was conditional upon the merits of each individual case, and in some instances, upon the personal relations of the officers involved in them. It was generally felt that if the paperwork was legally sound and there were no major procedural lapses then the organisation tended to support *encounters*. Nonetheless in case there were any problems, public protests, or inquiries ordered, officers involved would then be on their own and have to defend themselves as best as they could. The Javed Fawda case was an exception as the officers involved had full support from all elements of the hierarchy. Nevertheless, officers actually involved in that operation still faced many months of agonising uncertainty and underwent tremendous mental stress and anguish for 10 months in the year 1999. One officer said,

> When the Aguiar Commission was supposed to look into 100 cases of encounters done by the Mumbai police. The paperwork was incomplete, the formalities had not been followed and it was such a big problem. We could have been in very serious trouble, but we just managed to miss it because the High Court took a favourable view of the police action. The Fawda case was a terrible experience Mumbai police went through... (T 33: Upper Middle Management, verbatim notes from interview)

None of the officers talked about this stress openly the unspoken trauma that the officers had undergone was implicit. However, the comments of the officer indicated that Mumbai police did not seem to have learned their lessons from this experience.

Attitude of Other Related Agencies

Officers were asked whether they thought other agencies, including medical departments (who play a vital role in producing the post-mortem report[1]), forensics (who produce the ballistics report[2]), the administrative bureaucracy (responsible for conducting magisterial inquiries – mandatory in every case of custodial or unnatural death), and the courts (conducting judicial inquiries and criminal cases against the police) supported the police in *encounter* cases. It was intentionally a loaded question, obliquely implying that the police needed "extra support" to justify *encounters*. The aim was to elicit whether officers thought other agencies supported police "wrong-doings" (for either moral or corrupt purposes), making it easier for them to get away with killing alleged criminals, and indicating wider support for such actions. A few officers (mainly the Deniers), aware of the tricky nature of the question, replied that other agencies did their job according to the merit of the case – so there was no question of "support" of any kind. A typical Denier had this to say,

> There is no support as such from them. They have a very indifferent attitude. What the police have done, whether he [the victim] was a big criminal, a small criminal – they have nothing to do with that... And basically we [the team doing the *encounter*] don't keep the case with us. Immediately we have to refer it to the nearest police station. Then they have all the control, it is not under our control. (T 28: Inspector, "encounter specialist")

One Crime Branch officer felt that other agencies were not providing as much support or co-operation as extraordinary *encounter* situations demanded. He felt,

> We have difficulties with them (other agencies)...They may not be doing it intentionally but it is our expectation that – we have done this for (the country). It is a unique occasion; it is a life and death situation for the policeman, so the reaction from other agencies should also be fast. But they treat us as a normal thing, 'Let it be, leave it. Today the doctor is not there. It cannot be done today'. Magistrates ask them (encounter specialists) to line up, routine enquiries go on. This is, for the force, it is slightly demoralising. (T 26: Upper Middle Management)

This officer continued to make the extraordinary suggestion that specialist officers should be treated, "Like (in) the armed forces, where all their actions are in-house;

---

[1] The Post-mortem report is of the most vital significance in establishing the cause, mode, and time of death. Any discrepancy in this report from the official account given by the officers, can land them in serious trouble. The courts tend to hold this document sacrosanct and thus undisputable. For example, if any signs of scorching or blackening round the wound are indicated in the report, it would be damning evidence that the *encounter* was conducted at very close quarters or point blank range and raises questions on the veracity of the self defence account given by the officers. One officer recounted his personal experience where the post-mortem report indicated such black scorch marks around the bullet wound and this created endless hassles for the officer and his team to get second and third opinions on this report that contradicted the findings of the original report.

[2] Forensics have to provide the hand wash report of the criminal, providing evidence that the "criminal" had indeed attempted to fire on the police party; ballistic report on all the weapons used during the *encounter*, belonging to the "criminal" (had been recently discharged) and to the officers (matching the bullets with the weapons and the number of shots the officers claim to have discharged), etc.

in-house doctor, in-house court martial and where you have dignity as an officer. Here, you are exposed to civil agencies like doctors and magistrates – it is demoralising". Given the general opinion that these situations could be "managed" either on grounds of personal rapport between officers and other agency officials or as a result of money being exchanged, the officer wanted to take the level of management to a new dimension, where there would be no "civilian" involvement in the investigation of *encounters* thus avoiding any accountability to outside agencies. The language of militarization, and the distinction between the police and "civilians" (a term used rather disdainfully), is reminiscent of similar talk by officers in studies conducted in other countries (Chevigny, 1995; Huggins, Haritos-Fatouros, & Zimbardo, 2002).

A few officers felt that the Crime Branch had good connections and requisite resources for the purpose of "managing" the aftermath and subsequent investigation into *encounters*. Other officers felt that relevant other agencies approved of police action and thus co-operated or supported in whatever way they could. Still others, honestly admitted that money ruled – and that if the authorities concerned were paid enough, they would write a report as per your specifications. Eleven of the thirty-eight officers said that these things could be "managed", an opinion expressed unequivocally by one officer,

> They co-operate, but it all works on money. In the districts there may be a case of personal relationships and rapport making a difference but here in Mumbai only money speaks. So yes, they do help and co-operate, but it has to be managed. It has to be done by the people involved, co-operation is not assumed or automatic (T 38: Upper Middle Management)

Officers also felt that while on the whole the courts were very tough on officers in other matters, they gave more latitude to the police in *encounter* cases. The legal system's attitude towards officers involved in *encounters* of "hardened" criminals was sympathetic, much like that documented by Brinks (2008) in Latin America where blatant killings by the police do not result in convictions because judges apply their own normative standards based on who was killed. The Javed Fawda case clearly demonstrated the power of the courts and individual judges in interpreting events in favour of (or against) the police, as one officer said,

> Now if a Sessions Court convicts in a particular case, the High Court acquits, if the High Court convicts, then the Supreme Court acquits. The law is the same, the arguments are also more or less the same, they just study the papers (in the Appellate courts) and decide and give different decisions… judges have a different viewpoint and they have different interpretations for the law…they have discretion…There are some judges who have this fixed feeling that they will trouble the police, then they do cause trouble. (T 7: Lower Middle Management)

Clearly, officers were aware of the power of the courts to punish, if they failed to "manage appearances" or slipped up in creating a credible "paper trail".

"Claimsmakers" had two kinds of views about the criminal justice system. The first lamented the inadequacies of the courts to convict criminals swiftly and surely; and the other referred to the perceived inadequacies of the courts to prevent police malpractices in *encounters*.

As an integral and important part of the criminal justice procedure to control and prevent crime, the courts were seen to have failed dismally by almost all the interviewees. Echoing the sentiments of police officers, "claimsmakers" also lamented the undue delays, corruption, inefficiency, and uncertainty in the way the courts dispensed justice. That the whole system was geared to be of advantage to the criminal was the general opinion expressed, which was also reflected in the wider discourse on rights of the accused.[3]

However, one judge's explanation for this state of affairs was as follows: however effective the courts wanted to be in demanding police accountability; they were limited by the evidence that was presented before them. Since investigation of *encounter* cases was led by the police themselves, the courts did not have any say in the quality of evidence that was gathered. This limited their ability to act as a deterrent to police deviance.

Political Attitudes

Officers' perception of the political reaction to *encounters* in Mumbai was mixed. A majority of officers mainly Sub-Inspectors and Inspectors felt that while there was some interference in the matters of transfers and postings, there was no political interference in policing operational matters. This might presumably be so because at that rank they would not have been subject to political pressure in *encounters*. One officer said, "In Maharashtra there is little political interference in general... by doing encounters if activities of criminal gangs are dampened, then in Maharashtra there is no political trouble about encounters. They support the police" (T 8: Sub-Inspector). Another officer felt, "Action is supported also [by politicians] and not also. Because they have to continue ruling, so from that viewpoint they do what is suitable. There is pressure to control crime" (T 15: Sub-Inspector).

There appeared to be political support for *encounters* in Mumbai.[4] Almost all officers believed there was political support, if not open encouragement, for *encounters* to counter organised gangs. Senior officers admitted that at various points in time, especially during 1998–1999 when heightened gang activity was apparent in the city, there was a lot of political pressure on the police to be seen as being effective and proactive in the war on crime. One officer said,

> When the situation became grim and things became uncontrollable in the city. Businesses started closing, the multinationals started packing up. Capital inflow had stopped, share market had reacted, real estate collapsed, hotel industries, car purchases had stopped, then the whole thing had come to a grinding halt. Obviously society wanted some desperate help

---

[3] For example, see news analysis reports such as in *The Pioneer* (2002).

[4] See, for example Aiyar and Koppikar (1997), "Triggering Controversy", *India Today*, December 22, 1997, where the Deputy Chief Minister is reported to have "admitted that he favoured the policy of encounters".

to be rendered by the police. The state government, no-confidence motion was brought; the traders called the Chief Minister and told him that we are not going to pay you taxes… Then they said we will celebrate black Diwali,[5] instead of bursting crackers in all the houses and business establishments we will all put up black flags and protest… Then the Government of India was thinking of dismissing this government belonging to the other party and applying 356 [section of the Constitution of India] for collapse of law and order. So obviously under such circumstances, any measure which was legal, which was giving help, was all right – the press and the judiciary …would welcome any medicine given to this uncontrollable, galloping disease. (T 24: Senior Management)

The officer essentially described the state of law and order and the resulting economic and political crisis as the reasons for why the public, press, judiciary, and politicians approved of *encounters*. Officers either did not perceive it as such, or did not want to admit that they were receiving direct political directives regarding *encounters*. However, in interviews with senior members of the ruling government and the opposition, they admitted in the conversation following the interview that they had given directives to Senior Management officers to "take care of" members who were on the "wanted" list of criminals and that they would monitor police action against such persons on a regular basis. The overall impression received was that officers were at pains to convince me that while they had no political interference as such, they had political support for these actions.

One senior officer remarked-

The Law and the Constitution are like God, you cannot touch them, or see them, but they are there. The politicians are like priests and you do their bidding, that's all. We should work according to the law – but we don't – because of personal glory and somehow we feel obliged to please our political masters – that is how we are moulded or trained. (T 6: Upper Middle Management)

Following this logic it becomes clear that the police would not pursue such a potentially controversial policy if it did not have the political mandate, and one Crime Branch officer clearly admitted that they would not be able to continue operating the way they had been, if political support were withdrawn. This is manifested in the fact that the state government has the power to order magisterial or departmental inquiries into alleged misconduct of police officers. Also, according to Section 197 of the Code of Criminal Procedure, no criminal proceedings can be brought against a public servant for alleged offences committed or purported to be committed in the discharge of his/her official duty except with the sanction of the concerned Union or state government. Neither could the investigation of such cases be transferred to the Criminal Bureau of Investigation without the prior approval of the state government. Thus the political party in power wields considerable powers to either protect or prosecute police officers, making their approval for *encounters* of utmost importance.

The National Police Commission's Reports (1978–1981) have recommended that the police be freed of control by the political executive, but there has been little political movement towards accepting and implementing these recommendations.

---

[5]Diwali, the festival of lights, is celebrated all over India. A Black Diwali, that is Diwali without lights is the ultimate form of protest, signalling society-wide unhappiness and resentment.

Since Policing is a State Subject[6] implementing these recommendations is the prerogative of individual state governments. Even if the federal government at the centre were interested in implementing the recommendations of the eight National Police Commission Reports to reform and modernise the police, it cannot do so without the approval of every state government. Any such initiative to do so has met with resistance from state governments so far.

There was a near unanimous perception among the "claimsmakers" interviewed that strong political support and encouragement for *encounters* existed. One interviewee described the political attitude as "Very conniving, patronising, approving" (I 2: Activist). Another response was as follows: "They support if it suits them, if it is the opposition's gang which is being exterminated or whose numbers are being brought down, they support it. Contrarily [sic], if their interests are affected, they will criticize" (I 3: retired Judge). This raises the issue of criminalization of politics, where political leaders associated with certain gangs not only provided patronage to their favoured gang/s, but actively encouraged the police to target criminals belonging to rival gangs. However, whether political affiliations were organised around communal interests remains to be established.

There were also allegations that certain governments were predisposed to allow one or other of the major gangs to operate relatively freely, provided they did not run amok and cause political embarrassment to their patrons, an allegation refuted by a member of the ruling party in 2003,

> Our government, we say that if the police are doing it [encounters], let them. We never interfere. Some people were alleging recently that people from a particular gang are being killed less, and more from the other gang, But it is not like that, if you see our record then you will find that only criminals have been killed, not really any particular group or community (I 7: Politician)

This statement could be read as open acknowledgement of state-sanctioned *encounters*, but when asked whether "false" *encounters* occurred, the same interviewee said no incidents had occurred. Even "claimsmakers" understood and talked about *encounters* in different, inconsistent ways. On the one hand they admitted that deliberate, cold-blooded killing was forbidden, but on the other they felt that "hardcore" criminals deserved to be justifiably eliminated.

However, despite claims by the politician that they did not "interfere" in police *encounters*, public discourse supported the perception that there was political direction in the way the policy on *encounters* was formulated and executed. The growing trend of politicisation of organised criminals was also evident in the fact that organised criminals are increasingly participating in local democratic elections. Thus social awareness of the close nexus between politicians, organised criminals, and the police, who act as a liaison agent between the two was acknowledged by interviewees. This nexus between organised crime syndicates, politicians, and the

---

[6] Article 246 of the Constitution of India distributes legislative powers between the Parliament and State Legislative Assemblies, and places police in the State List, whereby the State legislatures have exclusive powers to make laws pertaining to the police.

police was demonstrated in high profile scams and scandals.[7] Almost all Bollywood films centred around the theme of organised crime unfailingly depict this nexus. Though fictional representations, films can have a considerable impact on the construction of social meanings and relations.

Some "claimsmakers" recognized that there were vested interests in maintaining the status quo, whereby the government controlled the police force. One interviewee ironically remarked, "Every political party wants an independent police force, and an independent judiciary, which will have complete liberty to decide in their favour only. This is the definition of independence!" (I 11: Retired Judge).

Media Response

The attitude of the media towards *encounters* was summarised by one officer as: "Generally they are not adverse. After about 200 encounters somebody may complain about a single case or in one or two cases they make allegations, but basically they are not against" (T 1: Inspector). Another officer felt, "Encounters make good news and that is how the media looks at them" (T 32: Inspector). While a small proportion of officers felt that the media unconditionally approved of *encounters*, a majority of others felt that media reporting displayed a mixed attitude – approval if the *encounter* was perceived to be "genuine" and criticism if the dead person was not a "hardcore" criminal.

> In the beginning 1992, '93, up to '97, they used to feel that encounters are big news. Now encounters are not that sensational. There are some press people who are directly or indirectly connected with these gangs, their viewpoint is different, so there is a mixed reaction. But overall there is less criticism, for encounters. (T 27: Inspector, Doer)

This officer recognized the "normalization" of *encounters* by the press and alleged that the media had vested interests and links with gangs, which coloured their coverage of *encounters*. While a majority of the officers maintained that the press was neither prejudiced nor biased either against or towards the police and reported facts as they saw them, the subtext implied that the media reported events only to sensationalize. It was not responsible reporting but commercialised packaging of news. From the interviews it emerged that while officers realized the importance and impact of the media on public opinion, they nevertheless did not consider the media to be of any intrinsic value. In fact there was an undercurrent of contempt for the media, their perceived irresponsibility, and lack of integrity.

Nearly 40% of the officers felt that the media was mainly interested in sensationalising the issue, and serving their own interests, as one officer said,

> There are categories in the press – you can read the same news in four different ways. Some newspapers are always publishing anti-police stories and they have a habit of printing

---

[7] For example, the Telgi Fake Stamp Paper scam involving high-ranking corrupt police officers and politicians that enveloped the city in 2003 (see, e.g. Chaturvedi, 2004).

everything negative in every matter… They have a habit of exaggerating…none of them have any professional knowledge of their job…Here the journalists are really petty and amateurish. (T 20: Inspector)

When asked about the reports of the police achieving a set target of conducting 100 *encounter* deaths in the year 2001, a very senior officer felt that it was mere speculation on the part of the press; there were a 100 or just over, *encounter* deaths in the year 2001, and the 100th person being killed on New Year's eve was a mere coincidence; however, the officer felt this was sensationalised by the press as being a target set by the organisation for itself.

Some officers felt that the reporting of an incident was largely dependent upon the reputation and personality of the officers involved and their personal relations with the reporters, in other words, "If your work is good and if you have good relations, good contacts with them then they publish favourable news." (T 31: Senior Management). Other officers implied that that the so-called encounter specialists had established good personal networks with media reporters and enjoyed a good rapport, ensuring that they did not get negative press coverage or elicit too close an inquiry into the background and circumstances of the incident.

Press have both reactions – they are against it in some cases and in favour of others. But it depends on the officers who did it, how they "managed" it. There is a group of officers, if they do it (*encounters*) then there is always a positive coverage for it, but if anyone else does it then they allege that the police picked them up and killed them. (T 11: Sub-Inspector)

However underlying all these conflicting opinions was the firm conviction that the media on the whole approved of *encounters* and that this provided a morale boost to the organisation. One officer mentioned that in the 1980s a reporter had tried to probe into an alleged "fake" *encounter* case, one of the earliest in Mumbai. His editor was flooded with angry letters from the public and it had generated a lot of public anger against the reporter who dared to question the "effective action" taken by the police! The reporter and the editor had to abandon their approach. Since then there have been articles and editorials questioning police *encounters* but on the whole these have not appealed to the masses and one can only infer that they have not made much of an impact on the general attitude towards *encounters* as there have been few serious investigations into these cases since. Officers remained secure in their knowledge that they could continue to manage appearance and ensure that there would be no danger of the media raising uncomfortable questions.

There were three kinds of local press reports on *encounters* in Mumbai: the first, was a bare description of the "facts" contained in the official police version; the second, was articles and editorials raising questions about "controversial" police shootings, and reports of demands for inquiries and probes into some incidents, and the third, was the celebration of *encounters* and "encounter specialists". This latter category is in a sense unique to Mumbai, in that it does not exist in the kinds of media reactions to incidents of police use of deadly force described by others in Western democracies (e.g. see Lawrence, 2000b; Ross, 2000b, and the media reaction to the shooting of Charles de Menezes).

Most "claimsmakers" interviewed said that initial *encounter* reports were invariably of the first kind, which followed a standard format, reflect[ing] the conventions of contemporary journalism…. the standard formulas for news writing – that is, who-what-when-where presented with the story's most important aspects first, followed by increasingly specific items as the story develops.(Best, 1999: 37)

Claimsmakers observed that apart from the media reporting *encounters* as being routine and standardized, there was very little analysis or in-depth investigation. The reports were also increasingly being relegated to the back pages as a tiny news item, perhaps because as Best (1999: 45) explains,

> Every news story runs its course: when there are no remaining facts to uncover or angles to explore, once there is nothing left to say, interest in the topic seems to die down; what once seemed novel becomes 'old news', boring; and coverage shifts to a different topic. By themselves, the media cannot and will not remain focused on a particular crime problem.

The importance and extent of the role of the print media,[8] though vital in the social construction and acceptance of the *encounter* story, was not recognized or acknowledged by the "claimsmakers" interviewed, almost all of whom, (including the representatives of the media themselves) were contemptuous of the quality and integrity of the media in the portrayal of *encounters*. Adjectives employed by the "claimsmakers" describing the media ranged from – "poor reporting", "non critical reporting", "sensationalist", "flippant", "playing a dirty role", "glorifying *encounters*" and "specialist' officers", "glamorising crime", "pathetic", "irresponsible", "populist", "disinterested", and "apathetic". Evidently the media were not held in high esteem by those interviewed. One interviewee commented: "I suspect there is a certain degree of incompetence in the Indian media, every single person in the media can be bribed. I think that is the general problem." (I 16, Corporate Executive)

Apart from incompetence, factors such as corruption and politicisation of the media led to the production of biased reports, not just by one particular newspaper mentioned by this interviewee but by almost all newspapers:

> Media, unfortunately, take a hands-off approach. Not really concerned about it, they report the event without much research into the subject as to why the elimination [encounter] has taken place, whether it was necessary or not. Once upon a time the Saamna[9] was protecting people like Arun Gawli. Now because he has picked up a hassle with Bal Thackerey, he has become an enemy. So long as he was perceived to be a friend, doing anything against him or his gang was a crime in those people's eyes. … Media, by and large, is so apathetic and our reporters are so used to handouts that they don't do any investigations… There is in fact an editorial policy that we should not get into a controversy…not get into the bad books of politicians or people who have any clout. We lose advertisements…. The better thing is to be inane and uncontroversial (I 3, Retired Judge)

The journalists, among the interview sample, acknowledged these problems, and not only recognized their own limitations but also the limited sphere of their influence.

---

[8] I will concentrate on the print media as the number of electronic and broadcasting media in India have proliferated to such an extent which makes it difficult to conduct a systematic assessment of how they report on *encounters* within the constraints of this research.

[9] Saamna – a fiercely right wing Marathi daily newspaper, considered to be the mouth piece of the Shiv Sena (fundamentalist Hindu Party) and its leader Mr Bal Thackeray, and considered to be influential in some sections of the citizenry.

"The [print] media has a limitation, given the levels of illiteracy, but maybe the electronic media may have a wider appeal and do more than the print media" (I 6: Journalist). This was recognition of what studies on the effects of media on public opinion have indicated, that is that the "hypodermic syringe" effect (Reiner, 2002: 399) rarely operates. There is little evidence to indicate that the consistently biased impression of events presented by the media has an influence "on public perceptions of, and opinions about, these phenomena" (Roshier, 1981: 51).

On the other hand, the media can also provide an "organizing frame, the narrative structure, the story line" consistently for a number of years and "hammered home the notion that crime was increasing, that criminals were… 'wicked people', and that the Government…could not protect the people" (Cavender, 2004: 346). Further, Beckett's (1997) research on the media coverage of the crime and drugs problem in America found that it could even influence policy-making independent of its potential effect on public opinion. In Mumbai too, it could be said, that the media had an impact on perpetuating the police myth of what Reiner (2003) calls "police fetishism" – the idea of police indispensability, in the absence of meaningful public discourse on alternate social and cultural changes as solutions to the crime problem. Reiner (2003) suggests that although the media highlight scandals and controversies about the police and policing, they propagate the idea that policing solutions are the only conceivable ones for the crime and disorder problem. Thus, the image of the police as protective shields ("thin khaki line") survives and is propagated by journalists in Mumbai (Blom Hansen, 2001: 185) through the acceptance of *encounters* as a policing policy in the discourse.

Journalists interviewed admitted that there was a general unwillingness to create controversy by raising uncomfortable questions or to "rock the boat", as this quote illustrates:

> [Media reaction to encounters] is generally – I would say, "passive acceptance". There is a sort of apathy also. See, in these cases, there is a lot of police co-operation. They take these journalists to the spot, show them the [encounter] scene, the weapons – two shots fired by the criminal, two bullets will be lodged in the wall somewhere. And then they also take the reporters into confidence – "Why are you asking so many questions? After all it was Amar Naik,[10] or 'so-and-so', who was killed. Leave it be". The journalist also wants to keep good police relations. He is thrilled that a senior officer is talking to him so nicely, so he also does not ask too many questions (I 5, Editor)

The intermingling of the two themes of the police ability and power to control the discourse and the necessity for crime reporters to be in the good books of police officers, demonstrates what Crandon and Dunne (1997: 91) call "symbiosis at least and vassalage [a position of subordination or subjugation] of the media at most" and has also been noted in the wider literature on policing and the media (Leishman & Mason, 2003; Reiner, Livingstone, & Allen, 2000; Ericson, 1989; Hall, Critcher, Jefferson, Clarke, & Roberts, 1981). Research has shown that news media are often hesitant to report on systemic miscarriages of justice because of their heavy reliance on the law

---

[10] A prominent gang leader, who was shot dead in an *encounter* by the Mumbai police in August 1996.

enforcement agencies for information and those papers who offer uncritical accounts of the police appear to have more inside information than others who are more questioning (Callanan, 2005). Ross (2000b, citing the research of Ericson, 1989) draws attention to the fact that academic literature points to two major types of police reporters: those in the inner circle (who work in close co-operation with the police and therefore seek stories sympathetic to the police) and those in the outer circle (who are more likely to report police deviance and use a wide variety of police sources and units). "Claimsmakers" accounts indicated crime reporters in Mumbai mainly belong to the inner circle and the few from the outer circle who raised questions about police deviance quickly found themselves marginalised (also see Blom Hansen, 2001).

Another interviewee said:

> The first thing is that the Indian media, just like the Indian people, are great believers in the state and we tend not to oppose what the state says... Also, our notion of human rights does not extend to people we see as being grey or black. Thirdly, the quality of reportage in the Indian media is pretty low. So to expect us to stitch together and make a pattern, to join the dots out of something which is evident is expecting a little too much. We tend not to attack stories, we tend to wait for them to come to us and them maybe take them to the page (I 14, Editor)

Several interesting themes were raised: comments on the nature of Indian society and its attitudes towards human rights; subservience to authority; the extent of control that people in power and authority (police officers and political leaders) have on the discourse and social construction of *encounters*.[11] Interviewees were aware of the poor quality of reporters and reporting and anecdotal evidence of how "investigative" journalism on *encounters* was not just discouraged but positively frowned upon by the authorities, and often even the public. One journalist narrated his personal experience referring to one of the earliest *encounters* in Mumbai which a police officer had talked about earlier:

> I gave a story that this was not a police encounter, but that the police killed XYZ,[12] and not even one bullet was fired by him. But he was killed point blank by the police. There was a hue and cry, there were so many letters [to the editor] against me. My readers never approved this line that the police killed him... Absolutely not, I would have been stoned to death if people knew who was writing the story...As a journalist I thought my job was over the moment I gave the story. OK, now it was my responsibility to reflect public opinion on that, which was done. There was no clarification from the police... the police did not give their version because it was true [what I had alleged]. (I 5, Editor)

The comments raise the question: how much responsibility lies with the media to inform and/or to mould public opinion? It is the classic dilemma of which theoretical model drives the media: the "market model" (giving the public what it wants) or the "manipulative model" (giving the public what the establishment thinks should be given) (Surette, 1998a). There was a general perception among those interviewed

---

[11] A situation which, as Hall et al. say "ensures that the media, effectively but 'objectively' play a key role in reproducing the dominant field of the ruling ideologies", thus they feel that the media play the subordinate role of *secondary definer*, reproducing the definitions of those who have privileged access, that is *primary definers*.

[12] Identity withheld in the interests of preserving anonymity of the interviewee.

that the media was populist, but there ought to be greater involvement of the media in raising awareness and mobilising public opinion against such illegal use of force. The media can play a crucial role through editorials, and by providing "a crucial link between the apparatus of social control and the public" (Hall et al., 1981) they can either reinforce the dominant ideology or mobilise public opinion against police actions. Bonner (2009) found that the media can play an important role in framing the discourse around police violence as unacceptable, thus acting as a form of preventive social accountability. In Mumbai, media reporting of *encounters* appeared to slant more in favour of reinforcing dominant ideology and were perhaps less inclined to mobilise public opinion against them.

However, it was recognized by the "claimsmakers" that there were other influences governing media attitudes towards *encounters*. Factors identified included – *sensationalism*, described by one interviewee as "Media is not interested in telling the whole truth, they are more interested in the news value... everybody wants to make money by showing extravagant scenes and giving extravagant messages. The very role of the media has become suspect" (I 11, retired Judge). Another factor, *populism* was defined as, "At the end of the day newspapers tend to narrate the readers' worldview more than their own" (I 14, Editor). Some suggested that perhaps *personal animosity* influenced the way *encounters* were reported, "Some people from the media play a dirty role in this...they lay the entire blame on the police, make it personal, then they talk of fake encounters" (I 7, Politician). Finally, one interviewee pointed to a *lack of journalistic integrity*, "It is just ineptitude or laziness. [For raising awareness] you would have to create the situation and the space to write it... It would require a much sharper focus on the issue that I would have. I should be doing it, it is wrong for me not to do it". (I 14, Editor).

The media in Mumbai had what Young (2003: 43) describes as an "institutionalized focus on negative news", where the fear of crime was highlighted and public opinion whipped up in favour of extraordinary powers for the police. This role played by the media was similar to that reported by Young (2003: 41) in the UK context, "given the direction of political leadership and the prevalent mass media coverage of crime, (that) public opinion is pushed in a pessimistic and vindictive direction". Perhaps, the media in Mumbai, taking their cue from political leaders, exaggerated fears of crime during the 1990s and beyond, but downplayed the abuse of deadly force by the police. One interviewee summed up what he thought the media's attitude was towards *encounters*:

> I have a very strong feeling that the media has become very flippant, has stopped doing its homework, they are the yuppie types, who have no social concerns and no social obligations. All the pages can be called Page 3 [society page]... everything is the projection of personalities. But issues are not debated or discussed... There is flippancy, also on the part of the readers... Basically we as a society are lazy to think. We want clear-cut Nescafe solutions! Put in a spoon, stir, and the brew should be ready. Nobody wants to apply his mind. (I 2: Activist)

The quote illustrates the third type of media reporting that eschews serious, balanced analysis but eulogizes officers (ab) using deadly force. One political leader interviewed proudly claimed that he had invited some "outstanding officers" to a special function to "felicitate" them on their numerous successes. The fact that the media displayed a tendency to make them into Page 3 (conventionally, the society page) heroes was acknowledged in many interviews, and considered to be an unfavourable development by some. This also raises doubts about whether the press in India is truly free and whether it is capable of in-depth analysis and assessment of the crime situation and the police response to it.

Attitude of the Public

Twenty-five of the 35 officers in the sample felt that the public attitude towards *encounters* was one of unconditional approval. Speaking of the "extraordinary" situation that prevailed during the late 1990s, and especially during the period (1998–1999) when *encounters* were at a standstill while the Mumbai police appealed to the High Court against the Augiar Commission's verdict that the Javed Fawda *encounter* was "fake", one officer said,

> When in 1998, these shootouts became on the higher side, when it started affecting the local masses... Because all these local henchmen also started extorting money from the people, there were calls in marriages, even when you purchased a new car you would get a threatening call, "I am from this gang, or from that gang, give me money". Even people have cancelled marriage celebrations, in fear of these calls... Then there were these shoot-outs, and escape from police custody... in courts also there were shootouts. People were reading that a lot of big fellows, builders and businessmen were getting shot dead, ...so after 1998, society in general, is supporting police for taking this stern action against gangsters. If there is no stern action or proactive action by the police, then questions are raised: "what are the police doing"? (T 26: Senior Management)

Describing the situation in the early 1990s, this officer felt that the general public demanded stringent police action. In fact, the officer seems to be saying that if the police had not obliged with *encounters*, it would have created widespread dissatisfaction among the public.

Ten officers interviewed felt that there was conditional approval on the part of the general public towards *encounters*, on a case-by-case basis. One officer said,

> General public don't support any kind of encounter deaths if they feel they are false or fake or that the person has been framed. But when there are genuine instances, which are 99.9% cases, they support the action by the police. (T 37: Lower Middle Management)

Officers concluded that *encounters* perceived to be "genuine" by the public were applauded. The lack of public outcry or sustained campaigns against this policy might have been the result either of public apathy or a sort of resigned acceptance of other "fake" *encounters* as "collateral damage". There occasionally were some mutterings of dissatisfaction but rarely a public call for further inquiry or investigation into the matter. Caldeira's (2000) research with residents in Sao Paulo found that the public favoured the administration of "summary justice", including executions and other illegalities, by the police as a result of a perceived failure of the "institutions of order" (the criminal justice system) to fulfil people's desire for justice and vengeance. This "implosion of the legal model" in Sao Paolo in the early 1990s (2000: 194), might not be exactly replicable in Mumbai, but officers were convinced that there was serious public demand for "affirmative" action against organised criminals in the form of *encounters*.

Three officers interviewed were convinced that the common man was indifferent to *encounters*, as it did not affect him (the common man) personally and that he was too immersed in his own problems and with daily survival. One officer said,

> They (the public) are in no way concerned. They are not interested, except the family of the person killed. It has become an everyday occurrence because, in general, the public has become insensitive towards others' problems in Mumbai. If it is my problem, it will pinch me – if it is somebody else's problem, it will not pinch me. I am not going to ponder over it because my life is so busy, I don't have time for that. Bombay life is such – even if you ask a beggar how much time he can spare from begging? He will say, 'I have very little time'. (T 1: Inspector)

Some active participants and deniers felt that the reaction of the public was immaterial since *encounters* would occur regardless. However, public approval and lack of organised opposition for *encounters* did no harm.

The only public opposition to *encounters* came from "fringe" Non Governmental Organisations (NGOs) whose credentials, integrity, and intentions were considered suspect by officers. The few Human Rights organisations and NGOs working in this area with regarded with a degree of contempt and officers thought that they did not have wide enough following or sufficient popular appeal to make any significant impact. However, they were recognized as having sufficient "nuisance value" to cause inconvenience and waste officers' time trying to justify *encounters*. One officer (T 1: Inspector) described NGOs as a "hindrance", peopled by officers who had "ample time but no knowledge of the system", and "only causing nuisance". This contempt on the part of police officers for "do-gooders" or "challengers", who offer a threat to the secrecy and interdependence of policing is reflected in wider policing literature (e.g. Reiner, 2000a; Holdaway, 1983).

For a country estimated to have over one million NGOs, there has been increasing apprehension about their reputation and effectiveness (Sooryamoorthy & Gangrade, 2001). It was generally held by almost all "claimsmakers" interviewed that NGOs in India had a history and reputation of limited success in general, and particularly in the context of *encounters*. Even activists associated with opposing or questioning police actions in *encounters* admitted that their influence was limited, primarily because NGOs were not seen as having sufficient legitimacy in the eyes of the public. NGOs were either perceived to be "fly-by-night" operators, or furthering the agenda set by their foreign sponsors. Also, NGOs themselves had failed to provide the stimulus for awakening social conscience, because they were perceived by some as having vested interests in protecting the rights of "criminals" and "mafia" dons and by others as being not committed enough to appreciate the circumstances and police compulsions that legitimize *encounters*. One activist said that NGOs and commissions had only what he termed as a "ginger effect" (meaning just spicing things up marginally),

Partly because, you know, the government and the police have become so insensitive to these things. Secondly, [the police say] 'you [the public] could keep on shouting and screaming, after all I [the police officer] am not accountable to you, nor am I accountable to anybody. So what? You keep on barking, I don't care'. They [the police] have this sort of nonchalant attitude, 'it doesn't affect me'. Thirdly, the social respectability and now the social glamour attached to such deeds neutralises all this shouting and screaming that we all do. They say for every activist and one NGO that is condemning encounters, there are 10 Rotary clubs willing to invite the encounter specialist to give talks on how to fight crime and there are three Mid Day's and Bombay Times to take his exclusive interviews. So obviously he says, 'what do I care for you?' The NGOs are not having any public support. (I 2, Activist)

Reference made by the interviewee to the "glorification" and "glamourisation" of *encounter* "specialists" led him to believe that it resulted in the demonization of NGOs and activists who demanded accountability for the actions of these "heroes".

Others felt that, "If these NGOs thought that they could get mileage out of any case they would take it up. It has to be politically motivated" (I 5: Journalist). Still others were suspicious of what they called the "foreign funding" that backed some NGOs, believing the latter to be a "money laundering kind of set-up" and not "really committed or passionate about what they are doing" (I 10: Representative Industrial Association). In fact, it appears that the term NGO itself has acquired a pejorative connotation in India, and working in the voluntary sector is considered the route to comfortable living, money, and a secure job, so much so that leaders of these organisations live in palatial houses and enjoy a jet-setting lifestyle (Sooryamoorthy & Gangrade, 2001 – citing Roy, 1994; Aiyar, 1998). The secrecy, lack of transparency, misuse, and other corruption scandals surrounding funding have been well-documented (Das, 1998; Prasannan, 1996; Shourie, 1995) lending support to the views expressed in the interviews.

A few of the interviewees agreed with the sentiments expressed by this person,

These Human Rights Commissions and all – yes, we have to fight for our rights, we are all human – but the police are also human, and victims are also human. But only the rights of the accused are protected, why? … What happens to a woman and her children after her husband is killed [by criminals]? If they open their mouth they will be harassed. What have we done to maintain these people who are bereaved? Nobody is taking up that issue. NGOs are not doing it. But one small error and they attack the police. (I 9, Lawyer)

By belittling the efforts of the commissions and NGOs working to protect the rights of *encounter* "victims", this interviewee sought to justify police actions by saying that they were not only retributive justice, but also aimed at protecting the family of the victims of organised crime who aid prosecution from harassment and intimidation. Another interviewee went to the extent of saying:

After two or three incidents [of *encounters*] have gone up to the courts, the position of the police gets upset. When some commission, either Minority Commission or Human Rights Commission they question the police in front of the public, that is the main source of all trouble to the police. Then the fear of the police is finished for the criminal. (I 8: Politician)

It was clear that this politician considered commissions and courts to be more a nuisance hindering effective police actions than actual functional accountability mechanisms.

He felt that the democratic process of calling police actions to account in a public forum would in some way emasculate and humiliate the police, so that the "fear" of the police would be lost.

Finally, officers interviewed accepted that there might be anomalies and mistakes committed, but these are largely accepted as unavoidable but inevitable by-products of human error by the public. A very senior officer summed up the attitude of the majority of officers as follows:

> There is a silent and now no longer silent, rather, vocal, acceptance of this police approach [encounters] from the public at large. In the debates in the State Assembly, the people's representatives have defended this, rather demanded it openly from the floor of the house. The media has also supported it and the public at large feel relieved that these dangerous elements are given a dose of their own medicine. (T 30: Senior Management)

Ross (2000b: 115) suggests that in Canada low level of public arousal, and reaction to events of police use of deadly force arose out of three processes, "alienation, apathy, acynicism, non-participation, political inefficiency or avoidance; ... or automatic acceptance, obedience or deference to authority; ...or the product of sublimated frustration". Similar processes operated in Mumbai according to the perceptions of "claimsmakers".

There was near unanimous consensus among "claimsmakers" interviewed of the perception that the public at large approved of *encounters* in an unquestioning, unconditional, and mostly apathetic manner. In fact, the main public reaction to *encounters* was perceived to be one of apathy. One interviewee, echoing the sentiments of some police officers said,

> People are so desperate to survive, jobs are getting scarce, employment is not amenable... In Bombay, commuting by public transport takes a sizeable portion of our time, then our family needs, the distances we have to travel, hardly leaves any time for contemplation, for reading. So how can people make up their minds [about serious issues]? They also believe that it is useless, the situation is much too powerful, the system is much too powerful and they cannot do anything. (I 3, Retired Judge)

This feeling that the system was too big, the problem too pervasive, and the judiciary too ineffective to deal with either organised crime or disciplining police deviance was expressed by most interviewees on behalf of themselves and of the common man. The latter, they believed, burdened by the business of making a living, felt it was a losing battle to demand accountability from either the police or the judiciary or even the politicians, when obviously all three appeared to have a nexus and strong vested interests in maintaining the power balance and status quo. Experience in other countries has shown that even in states where the accountability systems are well developed, rarely have the prosecutions of police officers in abuse of force cases been successful (Blumberg, 1989; Uldricks & van Mastrigt, 1991; Geller & Scott, 1992; Pedicelli, 1998).

However, not everyone felt that the public reaction to *encounters* stemmed from apathy. One interviewee felt that active agency was exercised by the people because he felt:

> We have accepted it to be a desirable or an acceptable norm. People want encounters – I'll tell you within my own family, my aunts and all...they are well meaning. Incidentally,

my aunts are devout Jains[13]...but they are all for these encounters. It is not that they are dishonest people, not that they are villains, or that they are devious people. They are God fearing, religious minded, ordinary citizens, who are not political in the sense they do not have a public profile, but who instinctively in their heart of hearts feel that this is the way of handling the issue and there is nothing wrong in it. I mean, such decent people who have neither suffered nor have to face organised crime, they feel it is good. This sends two signals – the police feel that it has got social acceptability and secondly, police feel that: 'Bloody, I handle this situation day in and out, I should know. If a person who does not even handle it feels that it is justified then I cannot say that it is less justified'. (I 2: Activist)

The quote illustrates some key structural and cultural factors that shape the public reaction to, and in turn influence police perception of *encounters*. The interviewee went on to make the point that ordinary people considered organised gangsters as "evil or wicked" or "beyond the pale of redemption". He appeared to suggest that people made the distinction between "them" and "us". Other interviews also revealed a perception reminiscent of Garland's description (2001: 184),

They [criminals] are dangerous others who threaten our safety and have no calls on our fellow feeling. The appropriate reaction for society is one of social defence we should defend ourselves against these dangerous enemies rather than concern ourselves with their welfare and prospects for rehabilitation

It could be argued that the "social defence" Garland refers to had taken the extreme form of elimination of "dangerous others" in Mumbai, which, according to the interviewee, the police feel they are justified in using, especially since it has citizen approval.

Perhaps public tolerance towards hardened criminals was reducing in Mumbai, as research in the UK and USA has found that tolerance towards crime had reduced in general, and there was a rising trend towards becoming a more punitive society "orchestrated by manipulative politicians and the media?" (Matthews, 2003: 224). Incidentally, the inclination towards greater punitive measures to deal with crime in the West resulted not just in the demand for more prisons and tougher sentences, but also sometimes in calls for "emotive and ostentatious punishments, which involved new forms of humiliation and degradation as well as public displays of remorse" (Pratt, 2001, cited in Matthews, 2003: 225). This trend, however, appeared to have gone a step further to public approval of summary executions of "hardened criminals" by the police in Mumbai.

Wider Culture

The attitudes of the "claimsmakers" towards the phenomenon of *encounters* were situated in the wider culture of Mumbai. The essence of this "wider culture" was difficult to capture, but was reflected in "claimsmakers" perception of: police image of violence and brutality, a hangover from its colonial past; media and political spin

---

[13] The basic tenets of Jainism as a religion are peace and non-violence towards all living creatures.

that exacerbated fear of crime; social attitudes towards Rule of Law; protection of Human Rights and notions of justice; and lack of a culture of accountability – aspects which had a direct bearing on the construction of attitudes towards police *encounters*, some of which discussed previously.

The intriguing question is why did the public feel *encounters* were the only solution to the problem? The answer lies in the discourse on organised crime in the public sphere in Mumbai, which revolved around what Cohen (1972) calls the construction of *Folk Devils*, and the subsequent creation of a *Moral Panic* that lends itself to adoption of extraordinary measures on the part of the authorities to deal with them. While there were no specific incident or series of incidents that sparked off a "moral panic" – the gradually deteriorating crime situation in Mumbai lent itself to a media-generated "moral panic" about organised crime and its impact on everyday life during the 1990s. This, in turn, led to moulding and sustaining public opinion against folk devils such as "hardened criminals" and in favour of *encounters*, especially amongst the middle classes, who are seldom directly affected by organised crime but have heard or read enough to fuel their fears of crime (Callanan, 2005). Fear of organised crime combined with despair and frustration resulting from the perceived failure of the criminal justice system, might have led people to condone police use of deadly force to rid society of such "folk devils" as "hardened" organised criminals.

There was overall agreement that Indian society was not egalitarian and everyone expected rules to be applied uniformly to others but not to themselves. One interviewee said, for example,

> We Indians have always felt insecure, we don't want to rub anyone on the wrong side. The instinct for self-preservation prevents us from protesting. We have lacked a public spirit, or even social ethics, because if we were strong in social ethics, this caste system would not have been perpetuated or women pushed into backwardness...It speaks of a total lack of social ethics (I 4: Director, Cultural Centre)

In essence, the interviewee was claiming that over generations, society had accepted and propagated an unequal social structure, and the desire to live non-confrontationally had over the years leached away the "public spirit" to defend social ethical principles and practices. This was a sweeping generalisation about the nature of Indian society but not necessarily invalid because of it. Another reason for why the public did not oppose police *encounters* was articulated by one interviewee,

> In India our great notion of tolerance extends to cover these things – that a few good guys getting killed with a lot of bad guys is fine – the price to be paid. The tolerance for mistakes is very high in India. We don't expect ourselves to have the same sort of efficiency as others (I 14: Journalist)

Dhillon (2005: 101) comments that because Indians are "blessed with unlimited capacity for patiently suffering indifference, callousness, and hypocrisy from their rulers, has made the task of the political and bureaucratic classes so much easier". This "capacity to endure" allows for mismanagement and inefficiency in the state machinery to proliferate relatively unchecked. It is almost as if the public expect that the police cannot possibly be as efficient or accountable as the British police, whom they held up in reverence and as a role model to aspire towards.

However policing accounts of British officers (Sillitoe, 1955; Mark, 1978) show that the police in Britain in the 1940s and 1950s also had a history of using brutal and violent measures to control "criminals"; a fact that received popular approbation in days when police accountability was not as developed as it is today and the breach of criminal's rights was not a serious issue. The change in the nature of policing in Britain did not happen overnight, but greater public awareness and activism, combined with a sense of social responsibility as well as other complex social and cultural changes engendered mechanisms to ensure that police excesses are made more accountable (Reiner, 2000a).

The other interesting question claimsmakers were asked to speculate on was society's attitude towards equality and the right to life for all. One of the difficulties of analysing claimsmakers' interviews was that often they switched between articulating their personal opinion and what they thought was the general opinion or the opinion of the common man, making it difficult to recognize whether they thought that Indian society did not recognize the right to life or whether they believed it was the generally held opinion. One interviewee said, "In India we don't have things like right to life at all. We simply just don't recognize the right to life. I mean the apathy is unbelievable" (I 6, Journalist), while another said,

> Have you read Orwell's book 'Animal Farm'? We do not believe in equality. We believe in equality on the basis of caste, creed and money. We feel that some people in this country are second class human beings therefore they can't claim equal human rights – rather they should not claim any human rights – rather they should be used for protecting our human rights at the cost of their human rights (I 11: Retired Judge)

This Orwellian concept that all human beings are equal but some are more equal than others is not restricted to Indian society. However, it was recognized by many of the interviewees that Indian society was unequal in essence, with its caste system and the hierarchical way in which society has always been organised, where all human beings were never considered equal. Hence, despite its allegiance to democratic principles and being a signatory to the Universal Declaration of Human Rights there was little acceptance on ground level that all people deserve an equal right to life. On the contrary, there was a widespread belief that criminals were fair game for the police, because the criminal justice system was ineffective.

In trying to understand what allowed the largely unquestioned existence of *encounters*, one could justifiably ask whether there were any accountability mechanisms in place to control police abuses and misconduct at all. Almost all the "claimsmakers" interviewed believed that the lack of rigorous accountability mechanisms and a lax attitude towards police accountability within the criminal justice system (including the police organisation) and more widely was responsible for excessive use of deadly force.

The current accountability structure with respect to police *encounters* in Mumbai has four levels: there is an official internal mechanism of accountability in the form of departmental and governmental enquiries into *encounters*, legal mechanism of accountability resting in the courts and the criminal justice system, social accountability in the form of a "free and independent" media, and independent accountability mechanisms in the form of National and State Human rights commissions and NGOs.

With respect to internal accountability, "claimsmakers" said that formal organisational structures set up to ensure accountability in the police use of deadly force were merely paper exercises. While few interviewees had knowledge about internal departmental police procedures and rules, most (magisterial and departmental) inquiries that followed all *encounter* incidents were seen to be a sham, in that, they said that no officer had publicly ever been found guilty of malpractice or misuse of force and they generally resulted in little more than a symbolic "slap on the wrist".

The other mechanisms of accountability, that is social (media and political leadership), legal (courts and commissions), and independent (NGOs and Human Rights Organisations) mechanisms were found to be severely deficient as views expressed by "claimsmakers" on these topics clearly indicated.

Thus "claimsmakers" realised that a combination of factors and social conditions contributed towards encouraging police abuse of force in Mumbai.

Summary

Police officer interviews revealed the conviction that they had a mandate from and had the support of the press, politicians, and the public, that is society as a whole (criminals did not matter), for *encounters*. In their perception, however flawed, they felt justified that the strategy of combating organised crime activities with *encounters* was appropriate and just.

"Claimsmakers" interviewed supported the police officers' perception that *encounters* were deemed acceptable by the public not only for the most part as passive bystanders, but were also actively encouraged by some sections of society. The interviewees displayed considerable knowledge about what they thought actually happened in *encounters*, but at the same time accepted that there was no discernible public protest against what was blatant misuse of deadly force. Factors such as media, political, and police spin which magnified the fear of organised crime; secrecy surrounding operational details; public apathy in Mumbai; despair at cumbersome and long delayed criminal justice processes; frustration with an elaborate bureaucratic machinery, which impedes more than it facilitates; a tolerant attitude born out of fatalism; the non-egalitarian nature of Indian society; and finally, inadequate accountability mechanisms were attributed for the phenomenon of *encounters* being sustained and encouraged.

Chapter 7
Justifying *Encounters*: The Theory of Denial

Introduction

The previous chapters discussed interviewees' perceptions on their understanding of the term *encounter* and its related "folk terms", their attitudes towards the effectiveness, desirability, and social acceptability of *encounters*. In this chapter, the discourse around the phenomenon is organised into a theoretical framework to provide a coherent explanation for the existence of *encounters* in Mumbai.

Examining officer justifications for *encounters* involved distinguishing between the actual and articulated reasons which required drawing upon my own personal experience and knowledge of police working and culture, and relying on relevant police literature supporting the analysis. There was always an element of speculation in this aspect of the research. Analysing how officers articulated their reasons and justified the use of deadly force against "criminals" using the Theory of Denial provided an explanation of how officers accounted for acts that were legally and ethically prohibited and also explained other social actors' response to the phenomenon.

Why *Encounters* Occur

Police decision to use deadly force is influenced by "environmental, organisational, and situational" factors (White, 2001: 131). These factors comprise the "external and internal police working environments": external factors such as crime rates, degree of danger to the police; situational factors such as citizens' demeanour, or the presence of weapons; and internal factors such as administrative policy, informal peer group norms, policies and philosophies of the chief (White, 2001: 131–132, citing Fyfe, 1987). White suggests that there are two types of police shootings – "elective and non-elective". Non-elective shootings are influenced mainly by situational and environmental factors. On the other hand, as the amount of danger that the police officer has to face decreases, the decisions to use deadly force become more elective. Internal working conditions and culture largely affect such "elective" decisions to invoke deadly force. They also affect perceptions of situational/environmental circumstances.

J. Belur, *Permission to Shoot? Police Use of Deadly Force in Democracies*,
DOI 10.1007/978-1-4419-0975-6_7, © Springer Science+Business Media, LLC 2010

Using White's (2001) terminology, reasons given by Mumbai police officers for invoking deadly force can be categorised as environmental factors (social good, crime control, police work, and faulty criminal justice system), organisational factors (organisational directives and personal responsibility), and self defence as the only situational factor mentioned invariably as part of the standard story. However, in Mumbai, officers articulated a new set of variables, what I call "moral" (or "immoral" as the case might be) factors (good intentions, Hindu philosophy, and personal gain), that influenced their decision to "electively" invoke deadly force.

Social Good

This all-encompassing phrase was the dominant theme that ran through almost all justification accounts for *encounters*. "Social good" was defined in different ways, one officer said, for example:

> Sometimes if a criminal is arrested, he is wanted for many murders and crimes and if he is not punished by the courts, or he is released early, or he kills others and though we try our best to capture him, but he escapes and runs away. In such a situation, keeping in mind the interests of society, of peoples' lives and property, then you have to do encounters. (T9: Sub Inspector, female)

This quote shows the intermixing of two themes, the inadequacy of the criminal justice system and the resulting harm to society if the police do not take decisive action (i.e. *encounters*) to remedy the situation. Most officers tended to assert that police actions in *encounters* were selfless, were motivated by the desire to achieve social good, were in public interest, and to safeguard life and property. Officers invoked the utilitarian argument that in the interests of the society, in order to engender a sense of security and reducing fear of crime in the minds of people, the death of a few men was not a large price to pay. Thus, they spoke of the necessity of eliminating "hardcore criminals" as "justified homicide" and in the process, if by accident or mishap, a few "not so deserving" people were killed, this "collateral damage" to serve the interests of the larger majority was well worth the effort. This sentiment not only relates to policing culture in India, which still follows the militaristic colonial model (Arnold, 1986, 1992; Das, 1993; Dhillon, 2005; Verma, 2005) and is based on an adversarial mode; but also reflects the social and political culture of the society within which such police actions are accepted, if not welcomed.

Another way of understanding social good was in terms of responding to the demands made by the public, the representatives of the public, and the media. Officers felt that since the public, media, and politicians approved of and asked for more *encounters* in the public discourse (media reports, the state legislative assembly, and public speeches) and in private communication with police officers, they obviously were beneficial to society as a whole. Reducing the fear of crime and boosting public confidence in the police were also considered to be contributing to social good by some officers.

Crime Control

Almost all officers interviewed were unanimous in their opinion that *encounters* were effective, that is they had a direct, visible, and substantial impact on the criminal activities of organised gangs. No statistics were offered, but officers were convinced that an increase in the number of *encounters* resulted in a proportional decrease in organised crimes. Some officers felt that since crime control was their primary role, *encounters* were justified because they helped fulfil a core police function.

Police Work

Officers defined their role rather broadly and considered themselves to be solely responsible for dealing with crime and maintaining law and order. Thus, all measures taken in the pursuit of that aim were considered to be part of their job and were legitimate police work. There were officers who mentioned that *encounters* "happened" in the course of their work but others believed they had to be "done" in order to fulfil their mandate.

Faulty Criminal Justice System

For a majority of police officers interviewed, one of the most powerful reasons for *encounters* was the inadequacy of the criminal justice system. One officer's words summarised the feeling that prevailed in the force as a whole,

> It [crime control] depends on the whole criminal justice system and is not the sole responsibility of the police. Witnesses will not come, or witnesses will turn hostile. Documentation is faulty. Whether he [the investigating officer] has collected ample evidence. There is not enough supervision...The delay between the crime and the hearing is so long that the complainant loses interest then there is no reason for the investigating officer to retain interest, because he has at least investigated 25 to 30 cases after that.. A person whose brother or husband or son has died will not feel anything about it 8 years down the line, frankly speaking. They get used to it and start living in the normal flow. So when they have to go to court after such a long time, it is more of a hassle than anything else. (T21: Sub Inspector)

Many officers provided anecdotal evidence of how witnesses were silenced, or intimidated into turning hostile, or had moved away, moved on, lost interest in, or could not recall the incident, or in some cases had died in the many years it took for the cases to come up for hearing and the final judgement be reached. It was clear that officers thought that the cumbersome processes of the criminal justice system put a severe toll on the limited resources and manpower that could be devoted to successful prosecutions of cases. Officers bemoaned the quality of the public prosecutors and the way in which many cases were prepared and presented in court.

The judiciary in India, as also in Mumbai, is heavily overburdened with an excessive backlog of pending cases, which runs into tens of thousands as Table 7.1 shows.

From 1993 to 2001 (figures available till 2001), the courts in India have on an average disposed of 15% of their trial cases (the average rate of convictions being 6% and acquittals being 9%), and carry over an average backlog of 81% pending cases each year.[1] As the officer's quote indicates, there is a long delay in cases coming up for hearing in the courts, apart from many adjournments and a long appeals procedure. It can take anything from 3 to 20 years for the courts to give a final ruling on any particular case.

All these factors contributed towards an increasing sense of frustration and despair on the part of the police and the public with respect to the processes of the criminal justice system. However, this sense of the "legal order as too slow, too ponderous, too indolent, too unaware, or too constrained to deal with 'the problem'" is not unique to Mumbai. In other countries too, the police generally tend to view the administration of justice as "weak, inadequate, or inefficient" (Skolnick and Fyfe, 1993: 24–25).

Given the inefficiencies of the system and the loss of time, energy, resources, and manpower involved in vainly trying to prosecute criminals, there appeared to be a general gravitation towards adopting easier, short-cut, and more effective methods of dealing with "hardened" criminals or what Skolnick and Fyfe (1993: 25) call "taking the law into their own hands". Holdaway (1983: 112–113) quotes a similar view of one officer in his work, "when you have a legal system that allows people to get off and makes you break the law to get convictions, then you have to be slightly bent". Thus, a majority of officers justified their actions by attributing moral responsibility to a faulty legal system.

Organisational Directives

Some officers suggested that a tacit organisational policy encouraged *encounters*. The inference that senior officers' approval of *encounters* motivated officers in actively engaging in them can be drawn from the periods of intense activity or inactivity in this field that followed regime change in the organisation, allowing for the possibility that certain senior officers approved of *encounters* more than others.

Since 2003, following a major overhaul in the senior ranks in the service and reorganisation of the Crime Branch, the number of *encounters* has reduced, giving rise to the conclusion that subsequent police chiefs and senior officers were perhaps not in favour of encouraging them. However, officers, when questioned, expressed the view that the reason for a reduction in *encounters* even in the first half of 2002 was because they had managed to dampen the activities of organised gangs, and not because of some unwritten departmental policy. Interestingly, following the bomb

---

[1] Source: Crime in India series, 1993–2001, New Delhi: National Crime Records Bureau.

Table 7.1 Disposal of IPC cases by the Indian Courts

Year	Total no. of cases for trial (including pending cases)	Compounded or withdrawn	Convicted	% Convicted	Acquitted	% Acquitted	Total cases disposed	% Disposed	Pending cases	% Pending
1993	4,504,396	137,875	345,812	7.7	407,040	9.0	752,852	16.7	3,613,669	80.2
1994	4,759,521	148,231	316,245	6.6	420,552	8.8	736,797	15.5	3,874,493	81.4
1995	5,042,744	158,357	321,609	6.4	442,335	8.8	763,944	15.1	4,120,443	81.7
1996	5,297,662	201,156	318,965	6.0	524,623	9.9	843,588	15.9	4,252,918	80.3
1997	5,461,004	185,432	336,421	6.2	543,507	10.0	879,928	16.1	4,395,644	80.5
1998	5,660,484	179,511	335,036	5.9	560,378	9.9	895,414	15.8	4,585,599	81.0
1999	5,890,744	185,130	369,005	6.3	561,724	9.5	930,729	15.8	4,775,216	81.1
2000	6,023,134	168,938	390,223	6.5	542,958	9.0	933,181	15.5	4,921,710	81.7
2001	6,221,034	171,966	380,505	6.1	551,388	8.9	931,892	15.0	5,117,864	82.3

Source: Crime in India (1993, 1994, 1995, 1996, 1997, 1998, 1999, 2000, 2001)

blasts in New Delhi in November 2005, there has been resurgence in the demand for *encounters* and "encounter specialists" in some official circles and sections of the media (Balakrishnan, 2005a). Further, incidents such as the Mumbai terrorist attacks in November 2008, where nine terrorists holding the city hostage for over 48 h were shot dead, can only increase support for police *encounters*.

Personal Responsibility

Senior officers seemed to think they were personally accountable for the crime situation and that their own reputation as leaders and senior managers of the force was at stake if the police were not seen as being proactive in controlling organised crime. As one senior officer described it,

> There is no escape. You are placed in a situation where you cannot say, 'thus far and no further'. If there is a problem and people are getting killed, and people are getting extortion threats, how can you say that I am doing my best, but beyond this I cannot do anything? You see you will not be spared. There is no running away from this situation. You, and only you are responsible for this... You may even be charged with dereliction of duty, cowardice, or maybe even prosecuted for deliberately neglecting your duty. (T31: Senior Management)

There was some amount of exaggeration in the rhetoric employed by the officer, but it served to underline the sense of responsibility he and others felt towards controlling the crime situation and the importance they placed on own role in this process.

Hindu Philosophy

One of the more controversial reasons officers articulated for the use of *encounters* was the reference to their "dharma" (duty). Four officers said that their job was to do their duty (and clearly their duty was crime control) and not worry about the consequences of their action. One officer quoted these verses from the Bhagvat Geeta,[2] to illustrate his point:

> I firmly believe in the Geeta quote. "Yada yada hi dharmasya..." There is a reason that my birth has taken place, there is a reason why I must have come into the police service. So if great injustice is going on, I am not going to sit and think about means and ends... I am not going to have a dilemma like this. I have to achieve at that moment of time and see justice is done. (T25: Upper Middle Management)

---

[2] The Bhagvat Geeta contained within the Mahabharata is one of the oldest Hindu texts. A philosophical work, it "is the instruction given to the great bowman Arjuna by his kinsman and charioteer Krishna. Just as the great battle is about to begin, Arjuna feels unable to fight his cousins and teachers on the opposing side. Krishna teaches him that it is his caste duty to fight, and that in any case the self is eternal, and therefore no lasting damage will be done to the enemy" (Smith, 2003: 40).

Another officer felt that Hindu mythology idealised their Gods and heroes as "vanquisher of the evil". Most Puranic[3] stories have the theme of "good versus evil", with the inevitable result of the forces of "good" triumphing over the "evil" actor by killing him or her. The interviewee believed this to be the reason why officers were lauded by the organisation and the public as heroes, who, by killing evil doers were ridding society of a menace and were, ultimately, righteous in spirit. Another officer said:

> Some people do not deserve to stay on this earth, then by hook or by crook they should be eliminated in the interest of society. Sri Krishna told Arjuna during the Great War that he had to go out and fight and kill, even if the enemy were his own kinsmen. (T7: Lower Middle Management, active participant)

Killing in the name of "dharma" for the king (as protector of the people) or the ascetic warriors dedicated to the protection of the people has been an acceptable and revered feature of Hinduism (Vidal, Tarabout, & Meyer, 2003; Biardeau, 2003; Bouillier, 2003).

The other strand of this argument stresses the concept of "karma" (or deeds) and it was the opinion expressed by some officers that bad deeds committed by the "criminal" were responsible for the bad ending that he deservedly got in an *encounter*. At this stage, it could tentatively be said that the belief in the cycle of birth, death, and rebirth, that is the cornerstone of Hinduism, may contribute to the blithe disregard for human life that some officers expressed and that prevails in a large section of the society. This may be the reason police show disregard for the life of "criminals". Vidal et al. (2003) allude to certain Hindu traditions, where violence is justified in terms of a global order and the resulting peace enjoyed by people. This, combined with the absence of the "rights of man" in the Brahmanical tradition (Biardeau, 2003) results in a situation where "violence is not so much thought of in universal, 'moral' terms in relation to its victims, but rather in the context of a problematic directed towards limiting its inauspicious consequences *for the perpetrators*" (Vidal et al., 2003: 19).

As compared to countries predominantly influenced by the Christian ethic, where a person only has one life which is precious and has to be preserved and protected at all costs, life in India, by contrast, appears to be cheap. A few deaths shock and sadden, but do not rock either the system or the social conscience. It can be surmised that contempt for Indian lives and the repeated use of high levels of state violence sanctioned by departmental custom were entrenched in police procedures and mentality in the colonial era (Arnold, 1986: 233) and this spilled over in police attitudes of contempt towards the "others" (criminals) even in latter day policing.

The sense of calm and inevitability with which India responds to human fatalities resulting from disasters (earthquakes, floods, heat waves, and landslides), accidents, terrorist attacks, communal violence, and riots contrasts sharply with the demands

---

[3] The Puranas are sacred repositories of story, legend, and other religious information. It is believed that some of the Puranic mythical stories reflect historical events, and are the source of much of popular Hinduism as these texts codify practises, often incorporating local folk practises (Smith, 2003: 43).

for inquiries, commissions, changes demanded by groups, and interested parties as well as the media attention that accompany similar events in, for example, the UK.[4] There is need for further research (of a more religio-philosophical nature) to comment on whether some lives are considered to be more worth preserving than others ("criminals") that are deemed less deserving; and whether this has made officers more blasé towards the loss of lives of "hardened" criminals.

Personal Glory

A few officers admitted that *encounters* were not necessarily altruistic, but were "done" either in the pursuit of medals, promotion, status enhancement, or personal ego gratification, as the officer who articulated his self-image as being a bigger bully than any criminal illustrated. One officer unhesitatingly admitted police *encounters* were conducted

> Because we are idiots. We are doing it for personal glory. We are neither doing it for the nation, nor for the state, we are doing it for personal glory-period! ...Other officers have two or three encounters to their credit. I have none, because it has never happened that somebody has drawn a pistol on me, and I am not going to get the man in the night and kill him... I am criticised in every meeting [by senior officers]... [But] I am a rogue, I'll not do it, and you can go on criticising. (T6: Upper Middle Management)

Although this quote suggests that the officer disapproved of the general organisational attitude of encouraging *encounters*, and could withstand organisational pressure to conform, the same officer went on to admit, later in the interview, that when he had to supervise *encounter* cases involving subordinate officers, despite evidence of "wrongdoing", he did not officially either condemn the incident or take action against the errant officers concerned. When asked why he did not do so, he replied frankly:

> I have no guts, it is cowardice. We are responsible for the decline in the system. We have lost the courage to stand up and say we will not do these things. We take a certain pride in being able to say we can manage under all situations and conditions... I will not quit the system because I do not believe that leaving the world and going to the forest or to the mountain will improve the system. If things have to change then I have to stay in the system to be able to effect any change...Ninety per cent of my time I am working like a bloody pimp doing all sorts of dirty jobs that I don't want to. But at least ten per cent of the time I can stand up to anybody and take some bold decisions. Even if I can prevent one old woman from being unfairly thrown out of her home in a year, it is better than selling thousands of Cherry Blossoms [shoe polish], isn't it? (T6)

The officer believed that being within the system and doing some good (helping the weak) was worth having to bow down to all sorts of pressures in the organisation,

---

[4] A striking example was the Hatfield rail tragedy, which is considered to be one of the worst in recent British rail history and continues to arouse passions and is commemorated years after its occurrence. There have been several disastrous railway accidents in India within the same period (with a much higher fatality rate) that seem to have been all but forgotten by the collective social conscience.

and was preferable to working in the corporate sector, which he perceived as not contributing to social welfare. This officer sought to excuse his lack of opposition to *encounters* by convincing himself that if he chose to question *encounters* and the conduct of the active participants and "specialists", he would be isolated and would perhaps have to leave the organisation in the end. He, therefore, was actually complicit in their continuance.

Very few other officers were willing to admit that *encounters* were the result of corruption, either moral or material. However, there were hints of this in many of the interviews and one Senior Management officer (T24) actually listed out officers by name who had been involved in either "talking to Chhota Shakeel about killing some people on his behalf"; a constable who "was involved with the Arun Gawli gang", another constable, who "used to go and kill people while serving on the police force and was killed in an encounter", yet another officer "who used to be shooting people left, right and centre... the allegation was he had been doing it on behalf of some interested groups", and elaborated upon the kind of departmental actions he initiated against these policemen which ranged from being transferred out of Mumbai, unpopular postings as punishment, one rank demotion, and even dismissal from service in rare cases. However, he was also very clear that he did not believe criminal proceedings were necessary against these officers. I asked him why when he clearly believed one officer was acting as a "hired gun", that officer had merely been posted out and banished from ever working in Mumbai, whereas an ordinary civilian would have been held upon a murder charge under similar circumstances. The reply was that it was the policeman's job to use his weapon to protect self and others and that it was not meant for "civilians". The officer conveniently ignored the fact that he had just listed out the offences of officers who had killed for reasons other than self-defence, and equally contradictorily went on to add:

> There is a kind of exceptional viewing a policeman's conduct comes in for, i.e. rape in custody, you are liable for more punishment than the normal other. So the policeman is kept under a scrutiny, or a microscope, or a glasshouse. You are under constant scrutiny of the law and you are treated in a different way, giving you exemplary punishment because you have additional responsibility. (T24: Senior Management)

It almost seemed as if because policemen were under greater scrutiny than ordinary citizens, the officer felt justified to condone and minimise their offences wherever this could be "managed". Cultural factors like "solidarity", "not spilling the beans", and "sticking up for one another" seemed to operate to facilitate this kind of thinking (Reiner, 2000a: 92, citing similar findings by Punch (1985), Skolnick and Fyfe (1993), Kleinig (1996), and Newburn (1999)). There was little evidence to show that the organisation or senior officers considered transgressions by officers under their supervision as liable for criminal prosecutions. Another reason for this reluctance to prosecute "rogue" officers in a public forum like the courts would be the fear of opening up Pandora's box of "wrongdoing" at several levels, as well as admitting that there could be errors in the way *encounters* were conceptualised and conducted.

There was evidence in the interviews and reports in the media of accusations of three of the four types of corruption that Punch (1985) outlines: *predatory corruption*, where the police stimulate crime, extort money, and actively organise graft; that is the "meat eaters" (Knapp Commission, 1972) who exploit legitimate and illegitimate enterprises for pursuing illicit ends; *combative corruption*, falsifying or creating evidence, involve accommodations with some criminals and certain informants and uses "illicit means for organisationally and socially approved goals" (Punch, 1985: 13); and finally, *corruption as perversion of justice*, which involves lying under oath, intimidating witnesses, planting evidence on suspects, and involves "perversion of justice largely in order to avoid the consequences of serious deviant behaviour" (p. 14).

Historical evidence shows that when the actions of special squads are left unsupervised and unaccountable, inevitably there is corruption and moral and ethical degeneration of work practises. Punch (1985) describes such corruption scandals that rocked the New York Police department (involving Serpico and the Knapp Commission, Leuci and the Special Investigating Unit); the London Metropolitan Police (involving the Times Investigation into the Criminal Investigation Department, the Drugs Squad, and the Obscene Publications Squad); and the Amsterdam Police (involving the Plain Clothes Squad, the Drugs Squad, etc.). Similarly, it appeared that the actions of "encounter specialists" in the Crime Branch were open to doubts and questions, which incidentally, no one was raising openly. Developments in Mumbai post 2003 showed that corruption had spread to the highest level in the police force and the rot had set in deep (Chaturvedi, 2004).

Good Intentions

The all-enveloping argument that police officers only acted in good faith and with good intentions covered every other justification in the accounts. Officers' preoccupation with good intentions bears an important influence on the overall police discourse on *encounters* and served as a catchall phrase to excuse all mistakes and excesses on the part of the police.

Overall, there were no significant differences between officers' justifications regardless of their roles or extent of participation in *encounters*. Broadly similar themes ran through all accounts across gender and rank – a significant finding because it implies that these accounts had become so internalised within the ethos of the organisation as to be accepted and retold by officers irrespective of rank, gender, or status. Shearing and Ericson (1991, reprinted 2005: 231) cite Bayley and Bittner's (1984) work which concluded that "The same stories crop up too often, suggesting that they have become part of the mythology of policing passed on uncritically from officer to officer". On the other hand, one officer had a more practical explanation for why he thought the same *encounter* account was being re-used by the police:

> Sometimes you feel that ok, the last time this story sailed smoothly and then you are also under pressure of work. So when you want to file a case, make various reports which have to go to the government and all that, you tend to take the easier way out, a tried and tested method. Or sometimes a man thinks that this kind of story is liked by the press, so ok this puts me in a better light, makes me a hero... So a genuine thing gets distorted and as you rightly say people get into a right mess while trying to play around with the facts. (T35: Senior Management)

Hunt and Manning (1991, cited in Foster, 2003: 206) found that not only do officers whose conduct is questionable, lie, but their colleagues are also expected to collude with the lies. When accounts are used retrospectively as justifications and excuses, it may facilitate them being used prospectively to construct new lies and it would take a lot of self-reflection on the part of officers to "tell the truth, rather than to passively accept and use lies when they are taken-for-granted and expected" (Hunt & Manning, 1991, 2003: 151). Even in my sample, only a few officers were willing to reflect on the truth and deviate from the "standard" *encounter* stories.

Although justifications used by active participants and facilitators were similar, there were subtle differences in the way they talked about *encounters*. Active participants openly spoke of *encounters* or (what they perceived to be) more politically astute term "operations", to denote cases where more planned, controlled, and meticulously conducted processes occurred rather than hot-headed, random violence by the police. The planning and meticulousness did not refer to cold-blooded plans for killing but were used to indicate that the police had identified and observed the target, convinced themselves of his "criminality", had laid a trap to ostensibly arrest him, but had to unfortunately kill him in self-defence. There were no doubts; rather there was pride when they talked of *encounters*. Facilitators and supervisors, interestingly, appeared more cynical about the use of the term "operations", its implications and the underlying messages of professionalism that the use of the term was supposed to give out. This was indicated in the self-conscious way in which they used the term, as if not entirely convinced it was more politically correct.

The Denial Framework

The main body of police justifications for *encounters* and the overt, dominant public narrative was one of the denials of police excesses or wrongdoings. Despite growing evidence and awareness about the questionable and doubtful circumstances surrounding *encounters*, police officers rarely overtly accepted that *encounters* were a euphemism, in many cases, for police executions. Officers used classic denial techniques (Sykes & Matza, 1957) to account for and to justify their actions (Scott & Lyman, 1968). Denial theory "claims to understand not the structural causes of the behaviour (*the* reasons) but the accounts typically given by deviants themselves (*their* reasons)" (Cohen, 2001: 58). Interviews with police officers and "claimsmakers" explored *their* reasons and showed that in Mumbai denial paved the way for police deviance to exist unchallenged.

Cohen's (2001) analysis of the Theory of Denial is particularly apposite to explain how not just individuals, but organisations, governments, media, and the public, can simultaneously know and not know about atrocities committed by state actors and to identify the mechanisms that operate in normalising such events in the social consciousness to the extent that they are not even recognised as being objectionable in a democratic society. Cohen seeks to understand how actors, agencies, and states live with the knowledge of atrocities around them and how do they explain it to themselves and to others. He uses the term "denial" to cover a whole range of phenomena – from lying, repressing, blocking or shutting out, wilfully misunderstanding, ignoring the implications of the knowledge of suffering or atrocities, or finding convenient rationalisations to explain themselves, and justify their conduct.

Cohen's experience in Israel led him to observe that the immediate official mainstream response to accusations of abuses was *outright denial, renaming, justification,* but there was no outrage even from the liberals. He further observed that soon there was a tone of acceptance towards these abuses. As a result of the report published by the Israeli Human Rights organisation, "a taboo subject was now discussed openly. Yet very soon, the silence returned. Worse than torture not being *in* the news, it was no longer news. Something, whose existence could not be admitted, was now seen as predictable" (Cohen, 2001: xi). These words could equally be applicable to the reaction and attitude towards *encounters* in Mumbai. The theory of denial tries to make sense of this apparent "normalisation" of atrocities. "The most familiar usage of the term 'denial' refers to the maintenance of social worlds in which an undesirable situation (event, condition, phenomenon) is unrecognised, ignored or made to seem normal" (p. 51).

Cohen begins his analysis by acknowledging that he uses the code word "denial" to cover many different states and situations. Denial, he argues, occurs at different levels and on various dimensions. As in Cohen's (2001: 3–20) work, denials (of "wrongdoings") in the data on *encounters* were analysed along the dimensions described by him.

Based on whether the denier is conscious or unconscious of the position he/she is adopting, there can be three possibilities about the truth-value of any statement of denial of wrongdoings in *encounters*: either it is a true statement; or it is blatant falsehood or lying; or it is a strange combination of knowing and not knowing (Cohen, 2001: 3–6). Accordingly, those officers who genuinely believed that *encounters* were chance occurrences and happened in self-defence were telling the truth when they denied that *encounters* are engineered. In contrast, those officers who were well aware that *encounters* were not quite the chance occurrences they were made out to be, but were the result of a deliberate strategy, were lying when they denied that *encounters* were engineered. However, the "strange combination of knowing and not knowing" is the most interesting state. In this case, denial is understood as an unconscious defence mechanism of coping with guilt, anxiety, and other uncomfortable emotions – that is when the psyche blocks off unpleasant and uncomfortable information. Whether this is done consciously or unconsciously is debatable as it could even be "willed omission" or inattention. In such situations, "we are vaguely aware of choosing not to look at the facts, but are not quite conscious of just what we are evading" (Cohen, 2001: 5).

Cohen suggests:

> Government bureaucracies, political parties, professional associations, religions, armies and the police all have their own forms of cover-up and lying. Such collective denial results from professional ethics, traditions of loyalty and secrecy, mutual reciprocity or codes of silence. Myths are maintained that prevent outsiders knowing about discreditable information; there are unspoken arrangements for concerted or strategic ignorance. It may be convenient not to know exactly what your superiors or subordinates are doing. (Cohen 2001: 6)

This could be accurately describing the situation in Mumbai. Unlike the outright refusal to accept wrongdoings by the few officers termed "deniers" earlier, a majority of the officers, seemed to be resorting to this subtler version of denial, where either they deliberately did not want to know the details of the *encounter* but were vaguely aware that there were several lacunae in the official account given out in the press release or in the First Information Report; or justified that the illegality was more than compensated by the "rightness" of the action, leading to the conclusion that there actually was no ethical wrongdoing.

Cohen (2001: 7–9) explains that there are three possibilities regarding *what* is being denied: literal, interpretive, and implicatory denial. Thus, in Mumbai, when officers (in possession of the facts of the case) denied that there is any sort of wrongdoing in *encounters*, they were engaging in literal denial. On the other hand, some officers did not deny that *encounters* could be more than just the chance of exchange of fire, but asserted that the "criminals" were a potential threat, or were generally known to possess sophisticated weapons and hence were fair game to be eliminated first. Thus, by saying that the *encounter* was not the straightforward killing it appeared, they engaged in interpretive denial. By changing words, using euphemisms and technical jargon, and citing mitigating circumstances, officers tended to give the occurrence a more acceptable version (i.e. acceptable to the courts of law and the public). Finally, officers who denied neither the facts nor the conventional interpretation of what an *encounter* actually was, but denied or mini-mised the psychological, moral, or political implications of the act, were engaging in implicatory denial. Examples of implicatory denial are, "the 'criminal' deserved it", or that "the criminal justice system has failed" or that "the people and the politi-cians approve and demand police *encounters*", or "what can I do about it?"

In addition, denial occurred on three levels – personal, cultural, or official (Cohen, 2001: 9–11). In Mumbai, denial was personal when an officer denied any personal knowledge of "wrongdoings" in *encounters*. Official or institutional denial occurred when the police organisation or the government as a whole denied there was any "wrongdoing" in police *encounters*. In this case, denial was built into the ideological façade of the organisation and the state itself. Evidence of collective denial indicative of a broader, widespread failure by the public and media to openly acknowledge uncomfortable or discriminatory behaviour collaborated with official denial through the coverage of these events argued the existence of cultural denial at the social level.

Cohen (2001: 12–13) suggests the time scale for the denial process can be either historical or contemporary. *Encounters* are a recent phenomenon, where denial can also be the result of information overload or compassion fatigue due to constant exposure to similar stories of atrocities within a short period of time. One officer said, "Initially encounters were few and there was media interest in them, but since then they have gone up, then the same-same news is repeated, probably they are not finding it newsworthy now". (T28: Inspector, active participant). Another officer said, "Encounters are just one of the many problems around me, I cannot react to any more news items about yet another 'hardcore criminal' killed". (T21: Sub Inspector). Some officers, on receiving news of yet another *encounter* tended to block it from their consciousness without really reflecting on the complexities of the situation.

Denials are part of the rhetoric not just of perpetrators, but of victims and bystanders too (Cohen, 2001). The focus here is on denial accounts of perpetrators (active participants, facilitators, and supervisors) and bystanders including both internal, immediate bystanders (police officers not involved in *encounters*) and external bystanders, that is external to the organisation but internal to the society ("claimsmakers") are included.

Cohen (2001: 51) distinguishes between micro denial that takes place at an individual level and macro denial that takes place at societal level. The phenomenon of *encounters* was never hidden, or unacknowledged in the sense of being absent from official records or media coverage, but it was hidden to the extent that no one other than the officers involved either directly or indirectly (as supervisors or facilitators) were really aware of the actual facts – to that extent it was normalised, contained, and covered-up. The analysis focuses on micro denials – at the level of individual officers and individual "claimsmakers". According to Cohen, micro denials are the individual's way of being able to give, what they think will be acceptable accounts to victims, friends, family, journalists, other criminal justice professionals, public inquiries, human rights organisations, international queries, and allow them to live with their conscience.

Cohen's model sees denials being part of wider motivational "accounts" – these accounts being, "not some mysterious internal states but typical vocabularies with clear functions in particular social situations".[5] Agreeing with Cohen (2001: 58) that "there is no point in looking for deeper, 'real' motives behind these verbal accounts", the interview material is examined as "*initial* guides to behaviour", where the account given by an actor is "not just another defence mechanism to deal with guilt, shame, or other psychic conflict after an offence has been committed; it must, in some sense, be present *before* the act. That is, to make the process sound far more rational and calculating than it usually is" (p. 58). It is difficult to distinguish between rationalisations (that take place ex post facto) and justificatory accounts that existed when the action (*encounter*) was being contemplated or occurred, and there may be differences of opinion whether what is judged to be justificatory accounts are not, in fact, rationalisations.

For example, the justification that Hindu mythology and tradition eulogises "the good vanquishing the evil", could be presented as a motivating, justifying factor to readily employ deadly force before the occurrence of *encounters*, or as a mitigating, rationalising factor, after the event in order to excuse it. It was also evident that accounts were used as devices *before* the act to lay the groundwork for making future *encounters* more acceptable and justifiable to the public, as well as *after* the act to protect the individuals from self-blame and blame from others. It is difficult to ascertain which justificatory devices were constructed *before* and which *after* the act.

---

[5]Cohen citing Wright-Mills (1940).

Justifying *Encounters*

Accounts as justifications and accounts as excuses are subtly distinguishable. Justifications are when "one accepts responsibility for the act in question, but denies the pejorative quality associated with it", whereas excuses are "accounts in which one admits that the act in question are bad, wrong or inappropriate, but denies full responsibility" (Cohen, 2001: 59).[6] Further, excuses are "passive, apologetic and defensive", whereas justifications are "active, unapologetic and offensive; they deny pejorative meanings, ignore accusations or appeal to different values and loyalties" (p. 59). However, this distinction does not always work and what may be considered to be an excuse may actually be a justification. For example, one officer said,

> I am happy I am not part of that team doing the shooting. I am also glad I am not taking the decisions at higher levels. I am simply ensuring that the paperwork is done as best as possible to protect the department's name. I am not doing a personal favour to anybody... I am doing what I can to see that the department does not get a bad name. (T34: Inspector, Facilitator, recorded verbatim in notes)

The sentiments expressed in this quote may actually be an active "appeal to higher loyalties" – an active and vigorous justification. On the other hand, the same account may actually be an excuse (the real reason for facilitating may be inability to challenge the system and organisation), but could be presented by the officer or interpreted by his audience, as justification, in order to establish and reinforce the cornerstone of all justifications – that is the action was done in good faith and for "noble" reasons.

Arguments put forward by officers to justify why *encounters* happened and were acceptable, were repeated often, and sounded so well-rehearsed that they had become part of the whole myth of effective policing. Accounts aimed not only to make *encounters* acceptable, but also to make them credible and reasonable, especially those that invoked the notion of "self-defence". One officer explained scant police injuries and virtual absence of casualties in *encounters* by invoking superior firearms training and professionalism on behalf of the police,

> Always the question is asked when gangsters fire, why no police officer is injured? There are always two or three instances in a year when police officers are injured or they get shot in police firing. ...So for a gangster... when the police announce their presence, morally he is always down, he cannot concentrate on his target, and that has an effect...the fellow [criminal] is always under tension, he cannot concentrate, he always shivers and there is less chance of him hitting his target. But the policeman, when he is trained and when he is tuned and mentally prepared, he can always hit a target. (T26: Upper Middle Management)

Table 3.6 showed the official figures recorded by the National Crime Records Bureau of police personnel killed on duty, if we contrast these numbers with the statistics quoted by the same interviewee earlier claiming nearly 300 criminals died in *encounters* between 1999 and 2001, we see stark disproportion. Interestingly,

---

[6] Cohen citing Scott and Lyman (1968).

almost all officers interviewed felt that the firearms training was generally inadequate and the weapons and ammunition, antiquated. It may be the case that "encounter specialists" received additional training, and protective gear, and also that they were in a position of advantage as the "pursuer" as compared to the "pursued". But there seemed to be a little or no support for the claim that police officers were better trained, prepared, and equipped to react when under fire as events in the Mumbai terror attacks of November 2008 showed. On the other hand, many officers said that "criminals" possessed sophisticated weaponry and methods of communication, which placed the police under an inherent disadvantage with dealing with organised criminals.

Cohen uses and expands upon Sykes and Matza's (1957) analysis of justifications for deviant behaviour based on the techniques of neutralisation and suggests that political accounts of atrocities follow the same logic as those of ordinary deviance. In Mumbai too, there was public knowledge that *encounters* between police and "criminals" occurred, but there was generalised refusal in narratives to accept that any of these were deliberately engineered killings. Even those who admitted to *encounters* being engineered sought to diminish their illegitimacy by using various justifying factors. Rhetorical devices employed by the officers could be categorised as:

Denial of Knowledge

The classic "I did not know" defence was used by some officers, the deniers in the sample, who maintained that only those actually involved in an *encounter* were aware of the facts of the case and were in a position to comment on whether a particular *encounter* was "genuine" or not. Since they themselves had never been in an *encounter* situation, they felt that they did not have the requisite knowledge to say whether or not *encounters* were deliberate police killings. As non-participant bystanders, they could legitimately use this argument to deny knowledge of *encounters*. It is possible that there might have been a few officers genuinely unaware of the realities behind *encounters*, or were not in a position to know the exact details of any particular incident, but given how the organisation operates it would be reasonable to assume that even an ordinary constable was aware of the fact that there was more to *encounters* than put forward for public consumption, not least because of the large death toll. However, by not having the power or evidence to do anything tangible on the basis of rumours or grapevine information, these officers preferred to deny any knowledge of *encounters*, thus either suspending their judgement or avoiding facing any awkward issues of having to square their conscience with uncomfortable knowledge of "wrongdoings".

Some senior officers (supervisors and/or facilitators) kept themselves shielded from the details of an *encounter*. Their arguments were akin to President Reagan's classic defence of "plausible deniability" as employed in the Iran Contra case, which involved "giving general policy guidelines and letting the details without his specific knowledge be carried out by others" (Hagan, 1997: 76). Similarly, some senior officers were interested in the effective impact of police actions, and deliberately turned a blind eye to the exact nature of these operations just so they could soothe their own conscience. Shielding themselves also meant that they were not lying when they said that they did not actually know whether any illegalities occurred during *encounters*. This is classic self-deception at work – the officer obviously knows that something unsavoury is going on, but precisely because he knows it, he withdraws from asking for any details that would entail facing up to an unpalatable truth about the nature of *encounters*.

Denial of Responsibility

The classic denial of responsibility defence, "It was an accident", or "I don't know why I did it", or "I don't know what came over me" were obviously denials officers could not use. They lack credibility. "Accidents" that led to the loss of life at the hands of the police were just not acceptable. For example, even when there have been cases of mistaken identity or accidental shooting, the police invariably tried to prove otherwise – as the Rathi case in Delhi demonstrated. In this case, Assistant Commissioner of Police (ACP) S.S. Rathi, faced murder charges along with nine other officers in the Connaught Place (New Delhi) *encounter* case for allegedly gunning down two businessmen in a case of mistaken identity in 1997. All ten officers were found guilty under sections 302 (murder), 307 (attempt to murder), and 193 (punishment for fabricating false evidence), read with 120-B (criminal conspiracy) of the Indian Penal Code (IPC) by the Delhi High Court in October 2007.[7]

Officers were at pains to demonstrate that their actions were the result of deliberate planning and careful targeting, but denied responsibility for *encounters* in other indirect ways. This technique was the one employed for the most part in accounting for *encounters* where officers accepted that the action was taken with full cognisance, but the motivation for the action was provided by others, that is they were either provoked by the "criminal" (victim precipitation) or had employed deadly force in self defence, or were fulfilling society's expectations of crime control. The ultimate responsibility for the use of deadly force lay with others and not active participants or facilitators. As an extreme example, one officer sought to deny responsibility by saying,

> If a man has to die, God has already written it. A man is by birth a normal human being; circumstances and God has confirmed him as a criminal and he is not going to change and he has to die and he will die. I am not going to bother about the consequences of that act because I have done what is necessary. (T25: Upper Middle Management)

Thus, the officer made *encounters* sound almost as if they were *fait accompli*, given that God and the deeds of the "criminal" had condemned him to certain death at the hands of the "righteous" police.

---

[7] See, for example *The Hindu* (2007), 'Shooting Case: 10 Policemen held guilty', October 10, 2007.

Very few officers explicitly mentioned that *encounters* followed from organisational directives. We can only indirectly surmise on the basis of statistical evidence that a tacit policy encouraging *encounters* was supported by some police chiefs (when *encounters* were high), and discouraged by other Commissioners in the years there was a lull. One Crime Branch "encounter specialist" explained,

> Now the [present] DCP [Deputy Commissioner of Police] is posted since two or three years and the Joint Commissioner has been here for some time. In eight or ten months these people will go away and new people will be appointed. There will be a new set-up, they will look at us ['encounter specialists'] differently, they will put a label on us that we are these officers' men, this Commissioner's man…So for a few months we will have some hassle. Then somebody big will be killed, they will need us, they will call us and say – now do this job? (T27: Inspector, "encounter specialist")

The officer was aggrieved about being unfairly labelled as being more loyal to the previous incumbents of the office by the new set of officers replacing them. He spoke of the suspicion and lack of trust that "encounter specialists" had to overcome before demonstrating that their loyalty was to the job and not to particular officers.

The quote also revealed internal tension within the department where other officers tried to influence newly appointed senior officers against "encounter specialists", envying their special privileges. The officer appeared to be saying that *encounters* were "done" when senior officers demanded a suitable police response to some sensational crime. Whether officers actually carried out *encounters* on the directives of senior officers, that is whether these were "crimes of obedience" was analysed using Kelman and Hamilton's (1989) model. They suggest that crimes of obedience result from the three processes of authorisation, dehumanisation, and routinisation, factors that are very evident in hierarchical organisations like the police and the military. A closer look at the implications in some of the articulations of the officers' accounts revealed that all these factors were present in the Mumbai police and contributed to some extent, to the situation in Mumbai.

Authorisation

Encounters were responsive to changes in police leadership and police policy. Since 2003, accompanied by changes in police leadership, the number of incidents has fallen and activities of "encounter specialists" curtailed (Varia, 2008). However, only a few officers specifically mentioned that they were involved in *encounters* as a result of organisational directives, "If the CP (Commissioner) says do it, then we will do it. As I said, it is a policy decision. It is not for me, it is the decision of the organisation" (T27: Inspector, "encounter specialist").

Officers appeared confident of senior officers' support because the whole system tacitly encouraged *encounters*. One officer said, "In Mumbai our senior officers support us in a good way. In every case of encounter, they give us correct guidance and our colleagues also give help and it is considered good work" (T19: Sub-Inspector, active participant). The certainty that the organisation and senior officers sanctioned such actions removed the moral element of decision making on part of the individual officers: they were merely obeying the orders of higher authorities, which allowed them to deny responsibility for the act. Even when officers denied responsibility, they remained aware of the moral and ethical dubiousness of the action. One officer claimed, "It hasn't happened so far. I don't think mistakes can happen, and even if they do senior officers will support us. So I am quite confident that we cannot get into any trouble because our intentions are not bad, we have no personal motives" (T29: Sub Inspector, active participant).

Dehumanisation

Dehumanisation is the process whereby enemies or "victims" are placed outside one's moral universe, thus making them fair game as victims of atrocities. When officers expressed opinions such as – "they deserved it" – or "if they are criminals what else can they expect" – they were effectively absolving themselves of the need to accord alleged "criminals" normal human rights and obligations. Most officers felt that a human rights regime meant criminal's rights were being protected at the cost of victim's rights and their actions redressed this imbalance. Another viewpoint suggested was that supporting "criminals" would only result in encouraging further criminal activity,

> Now Human Rights and other social organisations, they should really think about this – this particular criminal, of what value or worth is he? How many people has he harassed so far and whether he is capable of attacking the police in this manner? If you are planning to promote the cause of such criminals... by maligning or demoralising the police, then it is natural that such criminal tendencies will be on the rise and the number of criminals will increase. (T17: Inspector)

This officer was making a value judgement that "criminals" were not worth being supported by Human Rights organisations at the expense of demoralising the police.

Routinisation

Once initial moral restraints have been overcome, it becomes easier to commit atrocities routinely. This was true for the "encounter specialists". The number of "criminals" killed by them is openly acknowledged in magazine and newspaper articles.[8] It was almost as if these officers did not think of their "victims" as individuals with a personality and a life, but as one more notch on their belt. One "encounter specialist" is quoted as having said, "I don't enjoy killing, but after we shoot some mobster, his victims look at me like God. That's the best part of the job" (Perry, 2003).

Cohen suggests three other processes aid the denial of responsibility: appeals to *conformity, necessity and self-defence*, and *splitting*. The appeal to conformity was

---

[8] See, for example Perry (2003), Balakrishnan (2005a, 2005b), and *The Times of India* (2006a, 2006b).

not explicitly used by officers in general, but from my own experience and from informal conversations with police officers of various ranks, it is clear that "everyone else was doing it" is a powerful motivator for actions as extreme as the use of deadly force. One senior officer said,

> Sometimes, we have to win a very important case, where if we don't, the consequences can be disastrous. I find everybody else is doing it [using morally dubious methods]. In the sense all the other players in that game are doing it so the question is if you are bogged down by that then you are losing before your very own eyes...I go by the philosophy of the Geeta – even killing was advised if it was part of your duty... So that is a need based response of the police. I suppose it happens in America and a few other countries also which face a similar kind of problem. (T31: Senior Management)

The officer used the argument that because (in his perception) killing in the line of duty is prescribed in some religious texts; police in other countries are doing so in similar situations; and fellow officers are gaining fame and reputation ("getting ahead") by using deadly force, it becomes a matter of conformity to follow where others lead even in the illegal use of deadly force. Some officers hinted that they were aggrieved because they felt persecuted for engaging in *encounters* when others were getting away with similar actions. Since there were numerous "encounter specialists", picking on one particular individual for disciplinary action "when everyone else is doing it" becomes very difficult for senior officers who want to control abuse of force.

One officer said that she had been very unhappy about an *encounter* in her jurisdiction (led by the Crime Branch) and had made it clear to senior officers that she did not approve of these actions. Since then, "They have ensured that there are no encounters in this area" the officer declared proudly. The question why the officer had not raised serious, official objections in that particular case in the first place remained unasked primarily because it might be perceived as if the officer's actions were being judged. The answer might originate either in a misplaced sense of loyalty to the organisation, or because the officer just wanted to conform to the organisational culture and not to rock the boat. She went on to say after the interview was officially over that she did often agonise over whether speaking openly about these issues was being disloyal to the organisation.

Another officer said,

> If I ever raised any objections to any of the actions taken, they would have countered me with questions like – 'were you present there, then how can you say this?' You must know that senior officers do not appreciate it if a junior officer questions their policy or decisions. So I would be told to just shut up and stay out if I was not willing to be party to it... You do it because otherwise you would not have got support for your dissension or because there is some sort of loyalty towards your subordinates or the organisation. (T33: Upper Middle Management, verbatim notes from unrecorded interview)

The most common justification for *encounters* was the use of deadly force in self-defence. Apart from being the only legal justification for this action, it also takes away the responsibility for the act from the officer. By saying it often enough some officers believed that the mere fact that "criminals" were in possession of a weapon, justified the pre-emptive use of deadly force. The fact that almost half the active participants accepted wrongdoing showed their confidence and belief in the "correctness" or appropriateness of their actions.

> If someone is caught with a weapon in his hand, then he is not keeping that weapon in order to go to the temple, is he? He is keeping it to murder someone. If a weapon is found, then, it is not the case that he is an innocent person and you are planting a weapon and killing him. That is a personal issue. There is no question of making a mistake if they are carrying a weapon. Then there cannot be any ulterior motive. If we do anything in good faith then there will not be a mistake. (T27: Inspector, encounter specialist)

The officer was establishing the alleged criminal's guilt on the basis of posses-sion of a weapon, regardless of whether the "criminal" had used it on that particular occasion. *Encountering* such a person was perhaps considered justifi-able by the officer. The interviewee also appeared to imply that if a police officer planted a weapon/s on the dead person then that was a personal decision or choice of the officer concerned, and might have been done to cover-up errors that arose out of mistaken identity or excess use of force. The officer was merely engaging in what Young (1975) calls "negotiation of reality" where the officer was jumping the gap between theoretical and empirical guilt by making assumptions about the alleged criminal. However, what remained unarticulated was whether action taken in "good faith" could be extended to actually planting evidence in order to prove the officer's conviction that the *encountered* person was guilty of intent if not possession. Moreover, the justification cited by the officer is a travesty of the self-defence justification. Mere possession of a firearm, not use of it, was considered to be offence enough to merit being killed according to the officer.

Officers expressed another aspect of denial when they invoked necessity and the fact that someone had to do this dirty work. This "cleaning the scum off the streets" sentiment expressed by some officers embodied Hughes' (1961) conception of police work being "dirty work". One "encounter specialist" reportedly declared in a press interview: "A bullet for a bullet...It's the only language they (criminals) understand...Criminals are filth...and I'm the cleaner" (Perry, 2003).[9] Other officers interpreted that *encounters* were necessary because the police were perforce, solely responsible for crime control. The failure of the criminal justice system was the biggest factor contributing to the appeal of this argument.

Splitting is the third way in which an individual tries to deny responsibility by "means-end" dissociation, where individuals think of themselves as a cog in the machine, a cog that does routine tasks that may facilitate atrocities. However, not wanting to think of the resulting atrocities, they merely see it as doing one's job. Thus, when one Inspector (T34) said that he was merely aiding in the facilitation of *encounters* for the sake of the organisation, he was not merely appealing to higher loyalties, but was also denying responsibility. By saying that he did not pull

---

[9] Inspector Pradeep Sharma talking to Alex Perry, *Time Magazine*, 2003.

the trigger, but just ensured that the paperwork was in order or manipulated to be in order, the officer implied that his role in the process was not as morally loaded as that of the officer actually doing the killing. This is denial of responsibility in atrocities by splitting up the self's contribution to the process as being a mere facilitator, a passive vessel obeying orders, and is one way of dissociating oneself from the process.

Denial of Injury

Gross political atrocities cannot easily allow for typical denial of injury justifications ("no one really got hurt", or "that was ordinary business practise") used by ordinary delinquents (Cohen, 2001: 95). However, the way perpetrators deny injury is by asserting that the victims belonged to a devalued group in society (usually an ethnic out-group). In Mumbai, organised criminals were the out-group who deserved the treatment they received from the police. Officers were obviously aware that their actions caused death but sought to neutralise this or turn it into a moral blind spot by emphasising the beneficial aspects of *encounters* for society. Culling a few criminals brought safety and security to the larger society, and therefore from a utilitarian perspective such action was less injurious considering it promoted general welfare.

Another officer sought to use the argument, "in the circle of life and death, this person's bad deeds brought upon this bad ending to his life and that he ought to be relieved of this sinful existence and be given a chance to start again in a new birth" (T8: Sub Inspector). The Hindu doctrine of the cycle of birth, death, and rebirth was effectively twisted around by this officer to give credence to his actions and deny moral injury to the victim from a broader perspective.

Denial of Victim

Cohen describes the melodramatic discourse of political atrocities, where historically blaming the other is the dominant theme:

> 'history' proves that the people whom you call victims are not really victims; we, whom you condemn, have been the 'real' victims; they are, in the 'ultimate' sense, the true aggressors; therefore they deserve to be punished; justice is on our side. (Cohen 2001: 96)

This could be the story as told by the Mumbai police, when they talk about the damage done by "criminals" to the social fabric and how the rights of the people need to be safeguarded against the activities of these criminals. This argument not only denies victim status to the alleged criminal, but also denies them their basic human rights by asserting that protecting the rights of citizen victims is more important than protecting the rights of criminals. Thus, when one officer said that

"Some people do not deserve to stay on this earth" (T7: Lower Middle Management), he was denying "criminals" their right to existence.

This is a double pronged denial mechanism, where on the one hand officers denied the victims by saying that they deserved to suffer because of what they had done. On the other hand officers glossed over the fact that "criminals" or actual human beings were killed in *encounters*. Instead they talked in terms of "crime control" as a desirable goal, about how effective their actions were, and how dramatically they had succeeded in reducing criminal activities. In this way, officers were unconsciously or consciously removing the human element from the discourse, by not recognising the fact that human lives were lost as a result of "effective" actions taken by them.

Condemnation of Condemners

This technique of neutralisation questions the critics' right to criticise. Perpetrators seek to neutralise the legitimacy and authority of critics by casting aspersions on the intentions and integrity of those who dare to question their actions. As Cohen (2001: 98) points out, "the wrongness of *others* is the issue" not the legitimacy of police actions. Officers strongly condemned the antecedents of the Human Rights activists and NGOs who campaigned against police *encounters* and questioned the integrity of journalists and legal practitioners who had dared to question the use of deadly force. Lawyers, doctors, social workers, journalists, researchers, NGOs, and anti-police activists are categorised as "challengers" and "do-gooders", whom the police traditionally regard with hostility and suspicion (Reiner, 2000a: 94–95). Some officers were contemptuous of the critics, media, and NGOs. One said:

> Idiots, they are simply idiots and they are dishonest people. All media and all NGO's are dishonest. With due regards, there must be some honest, well-meaning people, the rest are poor jokers. Media is business. They are only interested in publishing what sells. They are not interested in anything beyond that – they do no social service or take up social causes, they are no crusaders – they just publish what is salacious and what sells…What are the NGO's doing – nothing… They are interested in furthering their personal goals, and making a quick buck. (T6: Upper Middle Management)

Another officer questioned the commitment and knowledge of people working for NGOs that were critical of police work, implying that they were only superficially involved in protesting about issues they had little understanding of. While some officers were willing to concede that there might have been some "wrongdoings" on behalf of the police, they were almost united in their contempt for activists and NGOs working in this field. A few officers even condemned what they saw as the hypocrisy of criminal justice practitioners, who were supposed champions of Human Rights but were more than willing to forget them when they themselves became victims of crimes.

> We have somehow double standards in society. If someone is affected, then he shouts. If my house is burgled and a suspect is arrested I will go and tell the police, "hit him, break his bones and recover my property". But if it happens in somebody else's house and I see a policeman hitting, I will say 'police are brutal'. (T18: Inspector)

Officers implied in their interviews that not only did biased individuals with an anti-police agenda use the rhetoric of human rights to further their personal or political gains and to discredit or humiliate the police, but that discourse-makers themselves did not possess integrity or respect for rights. Officers clearly reinforced Cohen's (2001: 98) contention that "External critics are attacked for being partial or are said to have no right to interfere". Officers added that only the criminally inclined and their beneficiaries could sympathise with the so-called "victims" and question police actions. One officer had this to say about public reaction to *encounters*, "Generally society will not support such a man [criminal], but a person's relatives or those who have got some benefit out of the criminal...they will call it a bad thing that the police killed him" (T10: Sub Inspector). Internal critics on the other hand were discouraged from speaking up against policies and forced into maintaining silence, as was the experience of one Upper Middle Management officer. The same officer went on to add:

> The greatest flaw with the police is that we think "wisdom goes with rank". Here it is believed that the more senior you are, the wiser you are and anybody junior to you knows nothing. Since in the police, hierarchy demands that command comes from the top, if you contradict seniors in public, then it creates a bad impression. And this is resented. (T33: Upper Middle Management, verbatim notes from unrecorded interview)

Appeal to Higher Loyalties

Police culture prizes solidarity. Moreover, since danger and isolation are regular features of police work (see, e.g. Reiner (2000a) and Bowling and Foster (2002)) appeal to higher loyalties strongly influences officer actions. Mutual support and protection of and by fellow officers and the organisation is of overriding the importance in police culture. During the interviews even when officers disapproved of *encounters*, they were very concerned about whistle blowing, or turning traitor. One officer was very dubious of even discussing these issues in the interview, though there was no doubt in her mind that police wrongdoing clearly existed. Another officer explained that the only reason he continued to support such actions was because of his loyalty to the department as he was grateful to the organisation for providing him with a job and status in society. One officer, who admitted to having a supervisory role in an *encounter* case that he disapproved of said:

> For me the dilemma would have been an ethical one – not a legal one. Law changes and has no meaning so I have no obligation to that... But if I had to take a stand, I would support my men...Also if I had betrayed them, I would have been a traitor to the organisation and no one, no subordinate would ever have any faith in me. The subordinates are only following orders, not doing anything for personal gain and they look upon their seniors to support

them. It would not have been correct if I had left their hand [meaning 'abandoned them'] when they were in trouble. But that does not mean that I approved of what they had done. (T25: Upper Middle Management)

The officer expressed his allegiance to the organisation and contempt for the law in no uncertain terms. He saw his own role as that of a protector or guide for his subordinate officers and felt that his obligation to fulfil his role was greater than any obligation to the law or the victim, or indeed to what was "right".

Moral Ambivalence

Cohen (2001: 99) suggests that the moral indifference of the perpetrators causes them to justify, not only to others, but also to themselves, the moral rightness of their actions. This research found no indifference, but ambivalence on the part of Mumbai police officers about their understanding of the moral and ethical issues involved in *encounters*. Klockar's (1980) classic "Dirty Harry" dilemma inherent in police work played itself out in this situation where an essential moral dilemma whether dirty means (*encounters*) justified good ends (controlling crime and social good) existed. Some officers felt that means and ends discussions were for others, whereas they were "men of action" and had to face the situation and be responsible for controlling crime. Hence they had no choice in the means-end debate. As one senior officer explained:

> I have seen many things going on, many wrong things being done. But sometimes… we have adopted means, which are not exactly legal, but perfectly moral. There is a difference. Everything, which is legal, is not necessarily moral and everything, which is illegal, is not necessarily immoral. Sometimes when achieving an end you adopt questionable means. I would not deny that yes, I had to sometimes resort to that – but never to serve my personal interest – strictly with a sense of duty. (T31: Senior Management)

Evidently, the officer did not have any qualms in adopting means that were not strictly legal in trying to achieve what he thought were morally superior ends. Punch (1985: 13) calls this type of police deviance *combative (strategic) corruption*, and is not confined to the Mumbai police alone.

Another senior officer reacted rather strongly to any suggestions that the police might be involved in "illegalities":

> But again I would like to reiterate that I don't believe in *encounters*, I don't encourage *encounters*. But when bullets are flying all over the city...if you don't fire a single bullet and start giving lectures from your moral high pedestal, then you will be a nincompoop, you will be an ineffective, sermonising police officer and we don't want you. You have no place, no relevance in the system – that's it! (T24: Senior Management)

The officer seemed to be implying that the situation in Mumbai was extraordinary in the days when organised crime was at its peak, that is it was as if bullets were flying across the city and people were in constant danger. The appropriate police response in the circumstances, according to him, seemed to be the use of deadly force with equal and opposite intensity as the criminals.

I am unsure if this officer was talking of the generic "you", or whether he was irked by the questions (and perceived value judgement) and had reacted to what he thought was a "moral high pedestal". The officer's irritated response may be indicative of my interview technique lacking polish, or his own overly defensive attitude towards the whole topic. On the other hand, the use of strong language made it clear that the officer did not have much respect for those who asked difficult questions and agonised over moral dilemmas, when "decisive action" was required to face the threat of increasing organised gang activities. It is also indicative of the fact that the officer approved of and would authorise "effective action" (regardless of the legality issue) under similar circumstances.

For others, dirty means were legitimate and justifiable if they provided a good end result. This stance was repeatedly stressed by the majority of officers interviewed, who emphasised the "good intentions" of officers. In this context, Cohen argues that perpetrators' actions do not arise out of a state of mindless conformity, but that:

> During the event, these perpetrators seem not to have reflected on its meaning; years later they may still profess not to understand why the event was so condemned. This might be an obvious lie... or a form of self-deception... The more frightening possibility is that they really saw nothing wrong at the time and behaved, like everyone else, without reflection. (Cohen 2001: 100)

The situation in Mumbai seemed to link with Cohen's second possibility, and displayed Cohen's interpretation of Arendt's concept of the "banality of evil". He suggests that:

> Far from minimizing the evil, she (Arendt) warns that unimaginable evil can result from a constellation of ordinary human qualities: not fully realizing the immorality of what you are doing, being as normal as all your peers doing the same things; having motives that are dull, unimaginative and commonplace (going along with others, professional ambition, job security), and retaining long afterwards the façade of pseudo-stupidity, not grasping what the fuss was about. (Cohen 2001: 100)

In Mumbai, as in other places in India where *encounters* were a regular occurrence, the enormity of the moral and ethical implications of police executions were neither articulated nor understood by officers. So inured were officers in the macho police culture, which routinely condemned Human Rights and Human Rights activists as "trouble makers" that they did not stop to think about what their actions actually meant and the extent to which they themselves had been infringing the law in the name of upholding it. The situation in Mumbai and the attitude of officers towards *encounters* was aptly described by Cohen as:

> Between those who actively refuse to see anything wrong and those who see everything as wrong, the vast majority in between can be nudged into acknowledging that something was wrong – yet *at the same time* sustain their denials. Cultures of denial encourage turning a collective blind eye, leaving horrors unexamined or normalised as being part of the rhythms of everyday life. (Cohen 2001: 101)

In Mumbai too, the police acted within a culture of denial and sought to normalise *encounters* as part of their jobs.

The Discourse of Official Denial

Inferences about the official position on *encounters* have been drawn from the interview data, as senior officers often talked in terms of the official policy. Some middle and lower ranking officers also fluctuated between talking about their own understanding of *encounters* and the organisational discourse on them. The police organisational discourse on *encounters* generally mirrored the three types of official denial mechanisms Cohen (2001: 101–116) identified, that is classic official denial, counter offensive, and partial acknowledgement.

The *literal* component of classic official denial, that is *encounters* did not happen, was not the case in Mumbai. However, other strands of classic official denial – both *interpretive* and *implicatory* – are similar to the ones found in Mumbai. It was not denied that *encounters* took place. Instead the assertion was it was not a form of extra-judicial killing but officers responding bravely in a situation that posed danger to their own lives. As Cohen (2001: 101) suggests, "Harm may be acknowledged, but its legal or common-sense meanings are denied". Thus, the organisation, by employing a combination of clever use of *euphemisms* (the use of the word *encounter* to suggest a chance or unplanned face-to-face coming with hardened, firearms-wielding "criminals"); *legalism* (ensuring that First Information Report describes the events in a certain sequence and all the subsequent paperwork is correct and accountable, thus implying that there can be no wrongdoings on the part of the police – what Cohen calls "magical denial"); *denial of responsibility* (since there is no official policy promoting *encounters*, subordinate officers cannot be said to have been authorised to conduct such actions, but instead derived their impetus from public expectation); and *isolation* (certain mistakes are acknowledged but are brushed aside as exceptions rather than the rule), sought to convey interpretive denial of police executions of alleged criminals.

Implicatory denials in officer accounts involved an acknowledgement that *encounters* happened, but they "happened" because they were in the interests of society at large; were necessary to control spiralling crime that threatened law and order as well as citizens' sense of security and confidence in the system; were nothing more than what the victim deserved; and/or were not routine. Another way of strengthening *implicatory* denial was the use of "advantageous comparison" (Cohen, 2001: 111). In terms of Mumbai, police actions (achieving the end result of making society safer) were asserted to be so much more morally superior to the actions of the "criminals" (spreading fear and insecurity), as well as the actions of the critics who had some personal agenda and political motivation in discrediting "brave" officers' actions. Officers also expressed their pride in the fact that as compared to other police forces in India, the Mumbai police's record in *encounter* cases was considered much better.

Classic official police denial is of mainly the *interpretive* and *implicatory* varieties, but there were elements of literal denial – denial not of the existence of *encounters*, but denial that there was any wrongdoing involved. As Cohen (2001: 103) suggests, literal denial is usually implied by attacking the reliability, objectivity, and credibility of the observers, victim/s, witnesses, journalists, activists all of whom are in various ways biased, selective, politically motivated, or else naïve, gullible, and easily manipulated. As one officer said:

> NGO's vigorously pursue these cases. Why? Because they want to show that they have done some work. This because they get foreign funding – they don't get much funding from India. Indian people will not give them any money so lovingly. (T4: Inspector, active participant)

The officer's perception seemed to be that issues of human rights of "criminals" appear to be of importance to NGOs funded by the West, to propagate their (western) conception of rights that considers everyone has an equal right to life and liberty. He appeared to suggest that Indian donors would support more worthwhile causes than those upholding the rights of hardened "criminals" or those who criticise proactive police actions against the latter.

This perception is in turn linked to the next kind of official denial, which is "counter offensive" and calls into question precisely the above qualities in the condemners. As the quote demonstrates the officer concerned was dismissive and contemptuous of the efforts of the NGO that tried to intervene in a particular case. Similarly, it was a generally held opinion that only those third parties who had a personal or political agenda in safeguarding the interests of a particular criminal or gang would question police actions in these cases, thus both dismissing the accusations as baseless and questioning the integrity of the critics themselves.

The third kind of official denial is "partial acknowledgement" by employing a variety of techniques like "spatial isolation" – there was grudging acceptance that certain *encounters* might have been problematic, but that these were occasional. It was generally accepted that "false" *encounters* happened in other parts of the country but officers pointed to the fact that no *encounter* in Mumbai had been subject to major public or legal scrutiny and criticism, with the exception of the Javed Fawda case, where police action was exonerated by the High Court (an assertion that was not entirely accurate). Another technique of denial adopted by some senior officers was "temporal containment", that is there might have been many *encounters* in the past decade or so, but as a result most of the gangs had been subdued and the number of *encounters* had gone down. Finally, even if some senior officers accepted that there might have been wrongdoing in these incidents, they asserted that they had taken stern action and disciplinary proceedings against the transgressors in an effort to "self-correct" the situation. This final technique of denial was framed as a partial acknowledgement of existing problems but mitigated by the assertion that it was also being corrected. One senior management officer emphatically assured me:

> Certain aberrations which are committed by our own policemen, when it comes to taking action or not, there is a moral dilemma. As a force we defend [actions of subordinate officers] ... but when it comes to individual things, we pull them up hard, very hard, you know. We take action, we take various corrective steps. (T24: Senior Management)

The officer then went to recount the number of cases in which he had taken official, departmental action against various errant officers, but did not favour criminal prosecution of the same.

Bystander Denial at Work

Situating *internal* bystander accounts – "claimsmakers" being internal to the society where the alleged atrocities are taking place – within the framework of denial shows how similar processes were at work here providing the support network for the police to use deadly force with impunity and without accountability. The term "bystander" according to Cohen (2001: 140) has pejorative connotations of passivity and indifference as opposed to similar terms such as onlookers, audience, spectators, or observers. However, the question that merits more detailed research in the future is whether bystanders in Mumbai were merely passive and/or indifferent, or whether they were (as some of the interview and anecdotal evidence showed) actively engaged in approving and encouraging police *encounters*. And if they were, what made ordinary, decent individuals (not just the elite "claimsmakers") approve of extralegal executions by the police?

Police *encounters* in Mumbai were not secret or unspoken operations like the "disappearances" in Argentina (Hinton, 2006) and there was little mobilisation of public opinion against them for many years. Sporadic incidents have and continue to give rise to demands for inquiries or greater police accountability,[10] in the media and other pressure groups. However, these disappear from the public domain rather rapidly. Whether the public did not know enough about *encounters*, or just lost interest in pursuing these cases, or whether there was a conspiracy to keep such items out of the public eye is debatable. However, the fact remained that there were no significant public protests, as compared to, for example, the intense media, public, and official scrutiny that followed the Jean Charles de Menezes shooting by officers of the London Metropolitan Police or the Sean Bell and Amadou Diallo cases in New York. Of course, the context of policing in London and New York is very different from that in Mumbai, as is the issue of routinely armed policing and the number of police shootings every year. Also, in a country beset by grinding poverty and other social problems, and in a city where the struggle to make a daily living occupied most people's energies, *encounters* might be of low priority. But one interpretation of the lack of protests in Mumbai could be that it was a form of moral passivity, which often takes the form of denial to sustain it. Whether this was a form of moral passivity of bystanders in Mumbai, that resulted either out of active support for actions of the perpetrators, or from fear and/or a sense of being helpless to fight it, is open to debate. Cohen's (2001) analysis of both the situational and cultural causes of what he calls internal bystander passivity is of relevance to understanding the public reaction to *encounters* in Mumbai.

Situational causes enumerated by Cohen (2001: 143) for why people in Mumbai might have remained mute spectators to the phenomenon of police *encounters* were found in the interview accounts of "claimsmakers". They put forward explanations for their own and the "general public's" inaction in allowing *encounters* to happen, which ranged from: *misperception* – not understanding or

---

[10] See 'Encounter victim's family seeks probe' in *The Times of India*, February 26, 2006.

misunderstanding what is happening; *diffusion of responsibility* – someone else can help; *fear* – of reprisals; *denial* – blocking out the significance of the event; *lack of empathy, boundaries* – victims (alleged gangsters who are in this case "victims" of the police) do not share the same moral universe; *psychic numbing* – lack of reaction due to overexposure to fact; *routinisation and desensitisation* – each further occurrence is predictable with no impetus to help; *no channel of help* – not knowing how to make a difference; and finally *ideological support* – sharing the world view of perpetrators.

Since the interviewees in my sample were people with some power and influence, they did not express their inability to stand up to the system, or challenge police actions as clearly as ordinary, common people might have done. People in Mumbai were certainly not living in a totalitarian regime, subject to direct state coercion or total information control. However, there might have been a certain resistance to getting involved in matters dealing with the police and the long-winded procedures of the courts. Another reason why people (and many of the interviewees) did not publicly denounce police *encounters* might have been because some sections of the public were not actually aware that *encounters* were a problem, or it might have been easier to pretend not to know than to acknowledge the existence of "wrongdoings" and feel the moral compulsion to do something about it. There were voices within the small sample that were critical of police *encounters* but they realised that without evidence to prove police malpractices, these could scarcely be controlled. Analysis of these interviews revealed how not only situational factors, but even a democratic political culture can be fertile ground for such denials to flourish. It could be argued that while there was support for *encounters* from some sections of society, there was perhaps indifference on the part of the majority that allowed for a discourse of denial to exist.

Summary

This chapter examines the language of denials and how the police, as individuals and organisationally, employed it to justify and present their actions as acceptable to themselves and to others. Denial theory was used to frame the analysis of the motivational and justificatory accounts of officers. Officer accounts of denial of *encounters* shifted along a spectrum, where on the one end they declared that all *encounters* were "bona fide", so there was no wrongdoing; and on the other end that *encounters* were justified on the grounds of being a "necessary evil" and employed similar techniques of neutralisation.

These accounts only partially answer the larger question – how do state actors commit acts of atrocities and how do they explain these to themselves and to others, and how do they get away with them? Wider situational, circumstantial, and cultural police-related factors which led to *encounters* becoming a socially accepted phenomenon will be identified and explored in Chap. 8. Drawing upon literature and theories related to police subculture, leadership, police brutality, and state violence, the wider issues of why and how a culture of police violence exists and flourishes in a democratic society are explored.

Chapter 8
Explaining *Encounters*: What Can We Do About Them?

Introduction

Police abuse of deadly force as a short-cut method to deal with burgeoning crime and terrorism remains a problem in several countries around the world. The research on police *encounters* in Mumbai uncovered the snapshot of a society that appeared complicit with the police in "cover-ups". However, police officers' perception of social consensus for *encounters* was not reflected unequivocally in interviews with "claimsmakers". There certainly wasn't unanimity or consensus between the two sets of interviewees about the desirability, legality, morality, or efficacy of *encounters*. Police officers believed that most of the public and politicians supported *encounters*, despite the fact that in some cases doubts and counterclaims by the media, activists and political opposition have questioned their legality. "Claimsmakers" too believed that general societal approval existed, though some interviewees personally did not approve of *encounters* as a policing policy. Lack of systematic large-scale public opinion surveys implies popular culture and opinion makers have a disproportionate influence on what passes as public opinion in Mumbai.

The research revealed that denial, incorporating classic techniques of neutralisation, was the mainstay of individual accounts of *encounters*, assuaging individual and collective conscience. Officers gave what they thought were plausible explanations ("their" reasons) for their audience (consisting of the media, politicians, the courts, and the public) to account for *encounters*. In this final chapter "the" reasons (underlying structural causes) (Cohen, 2001) as they were understood and explained by the interviewees for why circumstances in Mumbai appeared to be so conducive for *encounters* are discussed within the wider theoretical explanations for police violence. This chapter focuses on:

- Setting interviewees' (officers and "claimsmakers") explanations for *encounters* within the wider theoretical framework for police violence.
- Drawing upon past research in other locations and countries indicating similar factors affect police decisions to invoke force.

The aim of this would be to indicate that the underlying causes for use of deadly force put forward by the interviewees were neither whimsical nor particularly unique

J. Belur, *Permission to Shoot? Police Use of Deadly Force in Democracies*, DOI 10.1007/978-1-4419-0975-6_8, © Springer Science+Business Media, LLC 2010

to Mumbai. The chapter also briefly examines the relationship between control the police abuse of deadly force and issues of police leadership. Finally, drawing upon the experiences of other countries, policy recommendations for controlling police abuse of deadly force in Mumbai are made.

Explaining Police Use of Deadly Force

Denials of *encounters* cannot be dismissed as being fiction or simply rhetorical devices intended to exonerate deviant conduct. Explanations for *encounters* grouped as structural, cultural, organisational, and individual or psychological factors were discussed in Chap. 1. Various theoretical explanations for police violence contribute to furthering the understanding of the phenomenon by individually providing partial explanations for *encounters*. A synthesis of the various theoretical approaches, best provided by Chan's framework, would account for police *encounters* and also indicate how police reforms and policy changes can control police abuse of deadly force in a democratic society.

Police *encounters* have not been perceived as a major "problem" in India, barring a few cases because they have not been officially labelled as deviant acts. Unless there is widespread recognition of *encounters* as police deviance, they will continue to recur as unproblematic, indeed, valued behaviour. The phenomenon is a demonstration of the classic labelling theory that proposes, "Deviance is *not* a quality of the act the person commits, but rather a consequence of the application by others of rules and sanctions to an 'offender'…deviant behaviour is behaviour people so label" (Becker, 1963: 9). In Mumbai, since *encounters* were not considered deviant behaviour, officers engaging in them have not been labelled deviant.

However, *encounters* should be seen as problematic and a manifestation of police deviance not only by universal standards but according to the legal, ethical, and human rights standards that are notionally regarded as applicable for police actions in Mumbai. India aspires to achieve these international standards and in order to protect the police from litigation in the future, to maintain police legitimacy, and to protect citizens from arbitrary executions, *encounters* ought to be recognised as problematic. *Encounters* require explanation along two dimensions: what motivates officers to indulge in police killings (emphasising active agency factors); and what allows such killings to continue unchallenged in a democratic society (emphasising passive permissive factors). However, the boundaries between factors actively generating *encounters* (motivations) and those that passively allow them to continue (condonation) are blurred. For example, bystander (public) silence or lack of condemnation of abuse of force may be taken as silent support or active encouragement, via "non-talk as (approval) talk"; or as apathy, as in "not bothered to protest". Similarly the boundaries between "the" reasons for the existence of police *encounters*: structural, socio-cultural, organisational, and individual: are also blurred, sometimes with no clear-cut dividing lines between them. Thus, what may be perceived as a structural explanation (lack of accountability mechanisms) may also be a cultural or organisational explanation (lack of culture of accountability in the organisation) for *encounters* to occur.

Structural Reasons

Interviewees mentioned corruption, increasing class inequalities in Mumbai, and deepening divisions between communities in Mumbai as factors that increased social insecurity and fear of organised crime. Patel's (2003: 345) analysis of the political economy of Mumbai suggests that the decline of Mumbai's labour-intensive industries, the shifts to capital intensive industry, and the uneven growth of economic activity as a result of the processes of globalisation have furthered extreme social and spatial inequalities and have had "altogether negative implications for the poor and deprived in the city". The Bombay textile mill strike (1982–1984) where 75,000 workers lost their job and the subsequent decline of organised industrial employment increased further economic inequalities (van Wersch, 1992, 1995). Swaminathan's (2003) study of poverty and living standards in Mumbai concluded that the city displayed wide disparities in terms of income, housing, employment, education, sanitation, water supply, and nutrition. Others have also charted the complexities of globalisation, urbanisation, large-scale migration, changing economic opportunities, and the growing divide between Hindus and Muslims that have contributed to the skewed nature of social, political, and economic development in Mumbai (see, e.g. Blom Hansen, 2001; Desai, 2003; Grant & Nijman, 2003; Nijman, 2006; Patel, 2003; Varma, 2004). Corruption is endemic to all sectors in India, which is said to rank 84th in the list of 180 countries according to the Corruptions Perception Index[1] and the Indian police are considered the "most corrupt" sector in terms of public perception (Vittal, 2003).

Similar conditions of structural inequalities were found to account for police violence in countries like Argentina, Brazil, and Jamaica by Chevigny (1995). Chevigny (1995) found that although policing in the Latin American countries of Brazil and Argentina was different from that in Jamaica, and in the USA, there were several patterns of urban policing problems that were common. Problems arising out of immigration, colonialism, social dislocation and mobility, corruption, and a widespread fear of crime combined with disillusionment with the criminal justice system created an "explosive brew of state power and vigilantism" that allowed police to use extralegal methods to deal with crime (Chevigny, 1995: 142–143). For similar reasons, Harriott (2000) found that nearly 44% of the police force in Jamaica were in favour of retributive vigilantism in the form of summary execution of gun criminals. However, Chevigny attributes the difference between the levels of abuse of deadly

---

[1]*Press Trust of India* (2009), "India ranks 84th in global corruption perception list", http://www.ptinews.com/news/381377_India-ranks-84th-in-global-corruption-perception-list (accessed on 17 November 2009).

force in the USA and its profligate use in Brazil, Jamaica, and to a lesser extent Argentina, to social factors. All these countries experienced in common: strong class conflicts between the rich and the poor; impatience with the courts; a willingness to adopt extralegal methods to punish and deter combined with the government's disinclination to stop this kind of vigilantism; and a weak sense of citizen participation. However, the "sense of frightening economic crisis, the constant threat of poverty with no apparent exit that haunts the third world,…the near-panic fear of crime, abetted by the mass media and political leaders" was more prevalent in the latter countries as compared to the USA in the 1990s (Chevigny, 1995: 129). Hinton (2006: 33) and Chevigny (1995) suggest that police abuse of force is much greater in developing countries because "social instability, violent crime and inequality are problems of a much larger magnitude than in advanced countries". All these arguments apply equally to the situation in Mumbai (Shaban, 2004).

Socio-cultural Reasons

There were a variety of social and cultural explanations for police violence in Mumbai. Interviewees identified factors such as inadequate respect for the rule of law (preference for short-cut methods); the Hindu doctrine of karma and dharma and belief in cycle of death and rebirth (see, e.g. Biardeau 2003; Bouillier, 2003; Malamoud, 2003); a culture of indifference and apathy; widespread corruption (Vittal, 2003); and a culture of hero worship. These emerged as cultural factors contributing to the abuse of deadly force by the police, which in turn had an impact on social factors such as class and caste inequalities; inherited heritage of colonial policing; the impact of media-made moral panics; and rising public insecurity due to reported increase in organised crime activities that also encouraged police violence.

Hinton (2006) seeks explanations for the widespread existence of police violence in Latin American countries such as Brazil and Argentina in the socio-political relations that emerged in the post-colonial, military dictatorial regimes. Factors such as "uncivic attitudes towards public office, low levels of public accountability, and destructive forms of political competition" were endemic in both states and this implied that the lack of horizontal and vertical accountability as well as corruption resulted in police reforms being thwarted (p. 11).

Impact of colonial rule and consequences of the resulting policing style could be understood as structural factors affecting decisions to invoke force. However, the post-colonial police in India has inherited a certain mentality which has affected policing culture and attitudes (also see Dhillon, 2005; Verma, 2005), which is why it is discussed as a cultural factor affecting the use of force decisions. Mars (2002) suggests that police violence in Guyana prior to 1966 was aimed at population control under a colonial state authority. However, even after independence, the local state authority chose not to redefine the role and function of the Guyana police. It continued to function as an instrument of public intimidation and was deployed to repress political opponents. Mars (2002) suggests that the enduring influence of colonial rule in Guyana has contributed to strengthening and legitimising police violence as part of active state repression and prevented the development of policing as a public service by allowing police forces to emerge as instruments to further political tyranny.

Arnold (1992) discusses a similar development after 1947 in post Independence policing in India and suggests that once the Congress Party came into power at the Federal Centre "it sought to take over and strengthen the existing machinery of government, the better to consolidate its own position, reward its supporters and discomfort its adversaries" (p. 52). He suggests that after Indian Independence, the fledgling Congress government faced with a series of crises that threatened the unity and viability of the new nation state, such as – religious violence, communist insurrection, and industrial and agrarian unrests. Governments at the Centre and the states indefinitely postponed any possibility of a radical overhaul of the police organisation they had inherited from the British. Governments preferred to take over the colonial police organisation (and its colonial mentality) largely intact and promoted Indian officers, habituated to colonial policing roles and attitudes, to vacant senior posts formerly held by the British. Arnold concludes that there were no significant changes in police values and methods post Independence and that "the greatest value of the police to the new regime – as to its predecessor – was as an agency of coercion and intelligence" (p. 58). Thus, police violence in Mumbai could be said to have its roots in its colonial past (Blom Hansen, 2001: 151–152) characterised by: repression and coercion, belief in the value of periodic exhibitions of force, the interplay of police and military responsibilities, the equation of force with authority, the absence of public accountability, and the reliance upon supervisory and organisational systems of manipulation and control (Arnold, 1986: 235).

Added to socio-cultural factors, religious influences in the form of Hindu belief in the cycle of death and rebirth might have led to a more permissive policy on police use of deadly force being acceptable to a large section of the population. However, this proposition is difficult to prove or evidence. India has always expressed its commitment to protecting and upholding Human Rights as enshrined in the United Nations' Universal Declaration of Human Rights (1948). It could be argued that the ingrained inequality in the form of the caste system bred into Indian society for centuries combined with the doctrine of "karma" (one has to make reparations for one's deeds of the present and past lives) subconsciously clashes with equal access to the right to life for all. Perhaps it is a clash resulting from a struggle between the universal conception of rights (predominantly a Western conception) and cultural relativity of rights based on differences in socio-religious and cultural values. However, making any definitive statement on this would require further research.

Crime coverage occupies an important position in the media, and since a majority of people have no direct experience of crime (especially organised crime), the media provide important source of information and influence public opinion. Besides, Callanan (2005) suggests the crime situation is often distorted when portrayed by the media, which tends to promulgate simplistic ideological divides like good (the police) and evil (the alleged gangster), which gathers support for simplistic solutions like executing or incapacitating the criminal. During times of moral crisis, there is increased legitimacy for both institutions of social control and the media.

The latter, by "working in the best interests of the public by 'discovering' a potential threat, by alerting citizens to the issue, and by demanding government action" gains legitimacy, whereas "institutions of social control are legitimised as a necessary force to combat such menacing threats to public safety" (Callanan, 2005: 68).

Organisational Reasons

Organisational reasons for why *encounters* are supported can be of two types: external factors affecting the organisation's operational functioning and internal factors affecting the bureaucracy of the police.

External Factors Affecting the Organisation

Factors such as an overburdened criminal justice system; imbalance between the massive volume of crime and available police resources; lack of accountability structures; police subordination to the political executive; and public expectations emerged from the interviews as reasons for police using deadly force. The inability of the criminal justice system to cope with the demands of the crime situation is amply evidenced in the large number of cases pending final disposal in the courts throughout the country. Interviewees expressed widespread frustration resulting from the slow moving processes of the courts. Similar problems in other countries have sometimes led to police adopting other extra-legal methods to deal with crime (Chevigny, 1995) but the inadequacies of the criminal justice system combined with other factors created a unique police response of *encounters* in Mumbai. Also possibly, the desire on the part of officers to adopt short-cut solutions and deliver instant justice might have gained the approval of a large section of society.

A majority of the officers interviewed perceived the volume of crime to be very high as compared to the manpower and infrastructure provided to cope with it, especially since the extraordinary circumstances of a city gripped by organised crime demanded extraordinary measures to tackle it. It is questionable whether citizens actually shared this perception, due to the lack of public opinion surveys to establish the existence and depth of the "fear of crime". However, interviewees felt that the media conveyed the impression from the mid- to late 1990s that organised crime was out of control and that drastic measures were needed to control it.

Accountability structures in Mumbai though rudimentary, nonetheless existed. Whether they were functioning as they ought to was doubtful, given the lack of faith expressed in them by "claimsmakers" and the officers' dismissive attitude towards them. Lack of external or civilian oversight to the police complaints process has contributed to the fact that complaints have seldom resulted in conviction for officers (Table 8.1).

Judicial inquiries and courts can be formidable in demanding police accountability, but have been rarely so and as part of the accountability mechanism are often capricious

Table 8.1 Complaints against Mumbai police personnel and their disposal

Year	Number of complaints received	Departmental action	Judicial action	Found false	Persons sent up for trial	Persons whose trial was completed	Persons convicted	Persons acquitted
1995	146	59	87	0	87	1	0	1
1996	100	47	53	0	53	8	0	8
1997	73	27	46	0	46	17	2	15
1998	52	20	32	0	32	7	0	7
1999	59	22	37	0	37	7	0	7
2000	44	18	26	0	26	8	0	8
2001[2]								

Source: Crime in India (1995, 1996, 1997, 1998, 1999, 2000, 2001)

and politically expedient. Also since investigations into police misconduct are invariably conducted by police agencies themselves and because courts and commissions can only adjudicate on a case based on the facts and evidence placed before them, there is scope for a great deal of manipulation. The lack of an independent investigative agency makes it easier for officers to get away with abuse of force.

The police in Mumbai are not just formally accountable to the political executive, but even operational decisions defer to political compulsions. They carry out the wishes of the ruling executive but are not open to public scrutiny. It also means that politicians have a great deal of power in protecting officers by disallowing scrutiny by other central police agencies, by not commissioning a judicial inquiry into alleged misconduct, or by not sanctioning permission to prosecute officers under section 197 of the Code of Criminal Procedure (though this last power is rarely invoked). As a result, police officers remain confident that if they "act in good faith" and follow the tacit policies of the political party in power, they will be protected. The close nexus between the police and politicians and how it affects accountability was demonstrated when the Home Department in Maharashtra, acting on a recommendation of the Maharashtra State Human Rights Commission, had declared that inquiries into *encounters* would mandatorily be conducted by the State Criminal Investigation Department (CID). However, senior police officers appealed to the Minister in charge to reconsider this decision because of the "humiliation and embarrassment" that officers had to face in a number of cases, where the CID hastily arrested senior officers on registration of an offence but had to discharge them later (Marpakwar, 2007). The government is said to have accepted the suggestion of senior police officers and reportedly planned to issue fresh guidelines that in certain disputed cases special inquiries into *encounters* will be conducted by senior police officers rather than the CID.[3] However, political patronage for police use of force is fickle and could give way to public pressure should the occasion arise.

---

[2]From 2001, complaints against specific city police forces stopped being published. However, Crime in India (2001) shows that for the state of Maharashtra only one case of fake *encounter* was registered. No officers were reported to either been chargesheeted or convicted, as perhaps the case was still under investigation.

[3]*The Times of India* (2007), "Encounter deaths: now cops to probe", July 17, 2007.

Officers constructed their role and society's expectations from them to clearly imply that crime control was primarily police responsibility. This structural imbalance placed undue pressure on the police as sole agents to control crime, who were then forced to resort to extra legal or "innovative" methods. Merton's anomie theory (1938), when applied to the circumstances in Mumbai, could contribute to explaining *encounters* thus: crime control is a culturally approved goal for the police, but the means for achieving this goal are limited (in terms of inadequate infrastructure, manpower, criminal intelligence, and a tardy criminal justice system). As a result, the police seek innovative measures (*encounters*) to achieve a culturally approved goal (crime control). At a very superficial level, this theory perfectly explains why police officers are motivated to use illegal means to do what they clearly see as "doing their job". Merton isn't offering an account of the experience of deviance, but of its structural/cultural sources. He is concerned also with the issue of how cultures, subcultures, individuals assess the importance of achieving goals only via legitimate means. The relevance in this case seems to be that the Mumbai police interviews suggest not only a particular salience of crime control as a goal but less concern with the legitimacy of means, in their eyes and also in those of the "claimsmakers" and perhaps wider society. But the theory cannot explain why only a few officers feel the need to adopt deviant means, or that some officers might specialise in *encounters* for reasons other than fulfilling the goal of crime control.

Internal Bureaucratic Reasons

The reasons why the police organisation might implicitly condone *encounters* included: public expectations that the police solve the crime problem; inadequate resources to professionally tackle the serious nature of organised crime; a lack of emphasis on proper internal accountability structures; a policing style driven by ego/personality based cult; a preference for easy, short-cut methods to deal with complex problems. Given the reasons why Mumbai police officers might be working within an organisational culture which upheld the use of deadly force as desirable for dealing with gangsters, the classic "obedience to authority" thesis (Kelman& Hamilton, 1989; Milgram, 1974; Zimbardo, Haney, Banks, & Jaffe, 1973) could be advanced to explain *encounters*. This approach emphasises the link between authority and violence, strengthened further by the processes of routinisation and dehumanisation that "weaken the usual moral inhibitions against violence" (Kelman & Hamilton, 1989: 15). Similar processes worked in Mumbai to make the use of deadly force acceptable. By tacitly authorizing violence, senior police officers made it possible for subordinate officers to routinely (ab)use deadly force against "criminals" and "villains" who were deemed worthy of execution.

Personal policing experience and the interviews with officers indicated that a "personalistic" style of policing prevailed in Mumbai, implying personal preferences and styles of individual police leaders influenced organisational attitudes towards *encounters*. Officers mentioned that some police Commissioners encouraged *encounters,* leading to higher numbers of police killings, while others did not approve of them. This might explain why since 2003 Mumbai has witnessed fewer *encounters* every year.[4]

However, these theories provide only a partial explanation for police violence, primarily because they consider individuals indulging in "evil" acts doing so as puppets of their "circumstances" and do not stress the "agency" or volition of individuals (Foster, Haupt, & De Beer, 2005). A contrasting approach is adopted by Goldhagen (1995) who suggests with respect to the Holocaust that perpetrators may be willing, self-initiated, and active agents rather than victims of circumstances.[5] There does appear to be some credence to the concept of volition as one explanation for why some officers are more prone to use deadly force as against others who would prefer not to do so. The contrast of situational determinism vs. free choice is unnecessarily stark and surely there is an interdependence of structure and action (choice). Thus, not all police decisions to use force can simplistically be explained by the "obedience to authority" argument, but under similar circumstances, some officers choose to, while others refrain from, the use of deadly force.

Individual: Psychological Reasons

The discourse around *encounters* portrayed only a few officers as being responsible for a majority of *encounter* deaths. "Encounter specialists" in Mumbai did not appear to be publicity shy and were quite open about their excessive involvement in *encounters*, enjoying celebrity status in the media. This provided the motivation for a few officers to repeatedly use force. It also provided the opportunity for some senior officers and politicians to blame a few individuals in case things went wrong and there were inquiries into police actions. Thus, "heroes" would become "rotten apples" in the official and/or media discourse and held responsible for abuse of force when convenient or necessary.

However, the "banality of evil" thesis refutes the need for an individualistic theory of some special pathology to explain violence, instead it emphasises the ordinariness of those involved in "evil" practices (Conroy, 2000; Huggins, Haritos-Fatouros, & Zimbardo, 2002) and argues, "ordinary people are transformed by particular practices in their routine work environments into killers and murderers – they are not dispositionally predisposed towards violence" (Foster, Haupt, & De Beer, 2005: 56). In Mumbai, police officers and even "encounter specialists" were ordinarily recruited from among the general population and were not characterised by any particular preference for power or displayed any special inclination for violence before induction. This does not preclude the possibility that people with a certain authoritarian personality type were attracted to police work. Alternatively, it could be the case that the organisational and social context within which police officers in Mumbai operated

[4]See *The Times of India* (2004d).

[5]Goldhagen (1995) also looks at aspects of German history that might have contributed to participation in the Holocaust.

allowed ordinary individuals, who were so inclined, to indulge in or support illegal killings. This is merely speculative since an analysis of officers' background, life experiences, or personality was not the focus of this research.

Foster, Haupt, & De Beer (2005) prefer to adopt what they call a "relational" model to explain police and military violence in apartheid South Africa. In their approach, the emphasis on structural factors is counterbalanced by the concepts of "entitlement" and "interplay of multiple subjective identities". Thus, the "relational" approach suggests that a sense of entitlement (which "permits actors to do otherwise indefensible acts with a sense of righteousness" (p. 328)) combined with the complex interplay of various identities that officers have (nationalism, racism, anti-communism, Afrikaner identity, masculinity, and militarism (pp. 290–291)) act in ways that justifies the use of deadly force to the perpetrators in the South African context.

Huggins et al. (2002) seek explanations for the use of torture and abuse in types of "masculinity" in their study of Brazilian "violence workers" (state officials involved in killings and torture). Although "issues of masculinity do not readily leap off the pages of these accounts" as Foster, Haupt, & De Beer (2005: 286) remark about their work with officers in South Africa, there was a subtle sub-text and hints of all three masculinity types (Huggins et al.) were reflected in my sample. Active participants with "personalistic" masculinity talked in terms of caring for and providing relief for the "victims of organised gangsters", of "doing good" by cleaning "scum off the streets" and did not like to think of themselves as murderers but as the friend/protector (elder brother) of people. Officers (active participants and facilitators) who stressed achieving organisational targets and who compartmentalised work and self into separate categories, "institutional functionaries" who thought of *encounters* purely as a means to control crime (thus rationalising the achievement of good ends even at the cost of approving bad means) displayed a "bureaucratic" personality. Also officer accounts about their colleagues who were neither committed to society nor to the organisation but acted completely in ways that promoted their self-interest fell into the category of those who possessed a "blended" personality. Huggins et al. (pp. 232–269) put forward their conception of violence workers as ordinary men doing evil deeds and where the "interplay and interdependence" of historical and political factors, sociological and organisational influences, and social-psychological processes create the right circumstances for the resulting violence. The next section examines how the interdependence among socio-political, structural, and cultural factors created the right circumstances for *encounters* in Mumbai, using Janet Chan's (1996, 1997) theory of *field* and *habitus*.

The Synthesis

A more rounded explanation for police violence would necessarily be complex and multidimensional. It ought to involve explanations at the individual, organisational, situational, political, and social levels and the various theoretical approaches described above combine some or all of these factors to account for police violence.

One of the many useful approaches to "understanding what the problem is" and to answering "what can be done about it", is Janet Chan's exposition of the *field* and *habitus* approach based on Bourdieu's original concept. Developing the thoughts of previous policing scholars (e.g. Skolnick's 1966 work on police deviance) Chan (1996, 1997) suggests that the *field* of police work consists of historical relations between certain social groups and the police, anchored in the legal powers and discretion police are authorised to exercise and the distribution of power and material resources within the community. *Habitus*, on the other hand, is closer to what has earlier been described as cultural knowledge. It is a system of "dispositions", which integrate past experience and enable individuals to cope with a diversity of unforeseen situations; dispositions can be either coherent and systematic, or "ad hoc" when triggered by particular "encounters" in the field (Wacquant, 1992: 18–19, cited in Chan, 1996: 115). *Habitus* allows for creation and innovation within the *field* of police work, while at the same time being limited by the *field*. Thus, Bourdieu's theory recognises the interpretive and active role played by police officers in relating policing skills to the social and political context of policing (Chan, 1996: 115). It also allows for the existence of multiple cultures since officers in different organisational positions operate under different sets of *field* and *habitus*. Applying Chan's framework to explain police use of deadly force in Mumbai suggests: use of violent, short-cut methods are "dispositions" (*habitus*) affecting police behaviour that emerged in response to the particular socio-cultural and historical conditions created by burgeoning organised crime in Mumbai (*field*). Chan's approach highlights the impact social, cultural, and historical factors have on the police organisation and individual officers which lead to the abuse of deadly force becoming acceptable.

Chan uses old arguments explaining police deviance with new terminology whereby police violence is envisaged as the result of the interaction between society's demand that the police control crime (social, structural, and cultural factors), the interests of the police organisation to be seen as being effective (organisational and cultural factors), and inclinations of certain officers to employ deadly force more readily than others (individual and psychological factors) that result in *encounters*.

Change strategies according to Chan (1996) involve organisational restructuring, changes to recruitment and training, development of community-based programmes, as well as broader socio-legal changes. The debate is not whether rule-tightening or changing culture is more important (both clearly are) and while tightening the law might be easier to achieve than changing police culture, the results of both could be unpredictable (Chan, 1996: 131).

The concept of *field* extends beyond the formal rules and laws governing policing and includes socio-cultural conditions in which policing is conducted. Policing a society that upholds a punitive culture, encouraging retributive use of deadly force against "criminals", and does not emphasise police accountability for such actions, is conducive to cultivating a disposition to readily employ deadly force as a solution to the crime problem. Thus, the question of reforms, of what can be done about police violence, begs a multi-pronged approach. In Mumbai, in order to change the *habitus* (dispositions to use violence and illegal short-cut methods), conditions in the *field* (socio-cultural and legal factors) also ought to be changed.

This would involve large-scale social transformation, including police reforms, legal reforms, as well as an attitudinal change in the way society perceives and reacts to *encounters*. Chan gives an agenda for change.

Police Reforms

Prescriptive studies on police use of deadly force offer solutions to curb the phenomenon at the individual, organisational, and situational level depending upon the particular theoretical approach adopted. Thus studies advocating the "rotten apple" or "fascist pig" explanation for police violence advocate reforms at the level of the individual officer prescribing attitude and psychological tests to be included as part of the recruitment process to ensure only the most "suitable" candidates are chosen for the job. Better training and sensitising programmes are also part of the solution to ensure that individual officers are given an opportunity to renew their commitment to the rule of law and human rights (Grant & Grant, 1996). However, Worden (1996) found "little consistency between officers' attitudes and behaviours, and little consistency in each officer's behaviour from one incident to another" which ties in with Waddington's (1999b) view that police canteen culture need not and does not, in actual fact, affect behaviour. Thus, solutions that sift out "unsuitable" candidates at the recruitment stage (via psychological tests) and emphasise training and sensitising officers though useful are not the whole solution to curbing excessive use of force.

Research that locates the source of violent behaviour of officers in the police sub-culture and organisational ethos, either put forward solutions that emphasise training and placing administrative controls to ensure no abuse of force is tolerated, or suggest that real change can come about only when police culture can be changed to ensure that tolerating or encouraging deviant behaviour is prohibited (Chan, 1997; Fyfe, 1986; Reiner, 2000a). Some studies concluded that introduction of administrative controls via new guidelines and procedures succeeded to a large extent by bringing down the use of deadly force in New York, Kansas City, and Atlanta (Fyfe, 1979; Sherman, 1983). Sherman's (1983) research showed that the reduction in shooting was only in dubious cases, but shots fired in more serious, life-threatening circumstances (what might be termed as "non-elective" shootings in Fyfe's terminology) obviously remained the same. There is, nevertheless, general agreement among policing scholars that cultural change possibilities are very limited without structural change. There is also recognition in the literature that traditional organisational reforms may not bring about such a change as the culture originates in the nature of police work itself and not particular forces or organisations (Toch, 1976; van Maanen, 1974).

Klockars (1996: 16) mentions three obstacles that stand in the way of restricting excessive use of force by the organisation: the first is the "code" (Muir, 1977); the second is the "CYA" (cover your ass) syndrome endemic in police organisations, which means officers will behave in ways that will not expose them to criticism; and the third is the widely held belief that a "good" supervisor is one who will "back up" an officer in a tight situation or when he/she makes a mistake.

But Klockars feels that these obstacles are difficult to remove because of the fundamentally punitive orientation of the quasi-military administrative structure of police departments, where violation of rules leads to punishment every time. Also the occupational culture is such that a supervisor will earn the loyalty and support of his colleagues and subordinates if he covers for them and protects them when they flout the rules. Klockars' (1996) solution is simple, not every instance of use of excessive use of force need be punished, but the way forward in controlling its use is in identifying instances of use of force on every occasion.

Studies that focus on analysing the situational aspect of the violent police–citizen interaction advocate solutions whereby officers who have better control on the nature of the encounter are able to process information better and take adequate precautions to ensure that the outcome of a chance encounter is not violent (Fridell & Binder, 1992; Scharf & Binder, 1983). Fyfe (1986) suggests that in order to reduce unnecessary violence, the police role must be defined as one of a diagnostician and they must learn that role thoroughly as well as use the principles of tactical knowledge and concealment to reduce the likelihood of having to resort to deadly force, before they actually confront someone who may be armed and dangerous. Klinger (2005) applies Perrow's Natural Accident Theory to explain violent outcomes to police–citizen interactions. Recognising police–citizen interactions as social systems, Perrow's (1984) argument that systems are more likely to have problems that lead to negative outcomes as their elements become more tightly coupled and interactively complex, can explain how officers can avoid using violence by concentrating on tactics of police work. By keeping things simple, involving as few people as possible, and not getting too close, cops can avoid unnecessary shootings (Klinger, 2005). These micro-situational analyses seem directed at factors that make some officers unnecessarily prone to shoot (*habitus*) compared to others in fundamentally the same position (*field*) because of these informational and tactical deficiencies and are thus, complementary to the broader explanations for police violence.

A final category of studies that look at the use of force decisions by police officers in moral terms – as a moral dilemma between bad means and good ends – advocate more ethical policing to ensure that officers choose the most appropriate solutions to the "dirty Harry" problem. Klockars (1996) makes the point that the "dirty Harry" dilemma is a genuine ethical problem that cannot be ultimately resolved. As a result, officers violating legal rules must accept that they will be held to account, as with conscientious objectors, civil disobedience or say mercy killings by doctors. But if the authorities and public concur with the moral and situational assessment of the police, the verdict will not be punitive. Dellatre (2002: 197) feels that

> Once we go beyond the law for a noble purpose rather than a selfish one, we may feel that we have committed ourselves to illegal means, as further extremes become natural…This can be the beginning of substantial erosion. There is a fine line in these things, but once you step over it, you tend to justify subsequent acts by the former one.

Refusing to step over this line would not be morally tainting, in Delattre's opinion. But it can lead to tragic outcomes in specific cases, which is why it is a genuine dilemma. On the other hand, he feels that even officers who have employed illegal methods as a last ditch attempt – at great personal sacrifice, without regard to self-interest cannot be regarded as tainted, because the nature of police work sometimes demands such actions (Delattre, 2002). It is only flattering and arrogant self-appraisals that justify actions as being entirely noble that are the cause of noble cause corruption. Kleinig (1996) feels that while going down the "slippery slope of corruption" may be dangerous, it need not imply an inevitable descent to the bottom, as officers are capable of judging when to draw the line.

Tackling the problem of police abuse of deadly force has been attempted by developed countries like the USA, the UK, and Canada as well as developing democracies like Brazil, Argentina, and South Africa. The difference in the approach has been at the various levels at which the problem is perceived and addressed. For example in the USA, the UK, Canada, and Australia, which have more established democratic traditions, accountability mechanisms exist but the emphasis is on fine-tuning them or making them more refined to suit the purpose. In developing countries in the Latin America or South Africa, the problems are more fundamental of propagating a culture of democratic accountability to the rule of law and the people, of setting up proper accountability mechanisms in the first place, and also reforming management and supervision practices to ensure greater independence from political interference and ensure more professionalism. Such reforms would require changes in the *field*, that is the social context and problems facing the police.

The studies discussed are useful in their applicability to the Indian police if the "problem" of *encounters* has to be tackled not just symptomatically but by addressing the root causes of illegal use of deadly force. We have seen that the causes of abuse of deadly force are embedded in the individual and organisational level, flowing from the socio-political and cultural environment in which policing is conducted. Recognising that the discourse of denial at individual, organisational, and societal levels masks a deep-rooted problem in the role and public expectations from the police in a democratic society is the first step in controlling *encounters*. While some of the justifications in police discourses were anchored in fact (e.g. frustration arising out of an ineffective criminal justice system), the dominant discourse on *encounters* was fundamentally a form of denial that allowed extra-legal use of police force to be acceptable.

Changes have to be introduced within the police organisation and at the leadership level, as a first step towards addressing the problem of excessive use of deadly force. In order to do so, one must look a little deeper at the malaise that grips policing in general in the Indian context. The main problems with the Indian police have been identified by Verma (2005: 163) as: "the elitist nature of the police leadership, the politicisation of the department, unaccountability to the people, and outdated management practices have all combined to make corruption endemic and even acceptable within the organisation". Verma goes on to suggest that change can be brought about by "major transformation of organisational structure, management practices, supervision procedures, decentralisation of power, creation of local accountability system, even a change in role, and functions of the police in society" (pp. 163–164). Issues that have been identified and sought to be addressed in the eight National Police Commission Reports submitted between 1978 and 1981 and other committees such as the Padmanabhaiah Committee Report (2000) and the Soli Sorabjee Report on Police Reforms (2006). These reports have recommended specific reforms in diverse areas such as recruitment, training, promotions, tenure, transfers and postings of officers, increasing functional autonomy of officers, encouraging professionalism, enhancing credibility, addressing politicisation and criminalisation of the police, introducing a new system for evaluation performance, and new accountability structures. However, these recommendations have remained paper exercises, with state governments being unwilling to implement wide-ranging changes that would shift the balance of power away from politicians and in favour of police officers (Verma, 2005). A Public Interest Litigation (PIL) requesting implementations of police reforms filed by a few high-profile retired senior police officers in the Supreme Court has after 10 years resulted in a historic decision by the Court in September 2006 directing the Union of India to implement the recommendations of the National Police Commission in order to ensure that the police are accountable primarily to the law of the land and the people (Raghavan, 2006). Despite judicial activism police reforms in India remain unaddressed even in 2009. However, hope remains, as the Union government has to ensure compliance with the Court's directives, sooner rather than later.

Many of the recommendations given by these committees address some of the basic problems that lead to poor policing practices in India. Unless some of the fundamental issues in reforming the police organisation and expectations from the police are addressed, for example, introduction of an independent accountability structure, more refined recommendations that lead to fine-tuning accountability structures, or introducing specific controls on individual use of force incidents would be premature. A review of various police accountability structures in places as wide ranging as Philadelphia, Abuja, and Sao Paolo, all conclude that a strong system of police accountability with well-functioning structures at internal, governmental, and societal levels is essential to control the use of force and should be part of regular governance of police powers and not merely a result of a demand of the aggrieved (Stone, 2007). India can draw upon these lessons to inform its reform process.

It would appear that specifically controlling deadly use of force would be easier to achieve if some of the requisite police reforms already recommended are put in place. However, as the experience of introducing police reforms in Brazil and Argentina show, the failure to professionalise the police is closely linked to enduring political patterns of patronage, unholy alliances, and impunity, where political self-interest is paramount and successive governments are quick to introduce new policies without addressing deficiencies in the old ones (Hinton, 2005). Without political support and the will to introduce reforms and make them successful, change is unlikely to occur even in the Indian context as has been demonstrated by the past record of state governments since Independence.

The experience in South Africa shows, despite organisational and environmental imperatives to improve management and supervision of the South African Police Service, the requisite change from traditional styles to more participatory forms of management has not occurred due to its militaristic legacies, traditions of contestation, and non-corporate cultural conventions (Marks & Fleming, 2004).

The colonial legacy of police violence, strict adherence to a traditional hierarchical command, and control structure combined with subordination to political wishes has additionally weakened organisational and environmental imperatives to adopt changes that remain weak in the Indian context.

The Role of Police Leadership

It is clear that there is a definite relationship between the top police leadership and the emphasis placed on *encounters* as a method of dealing with organised crimes. There have been some Police Commissioners who openly declared their support for officers who were involved in "genuine" *encounters* and it seemed to be the case that there was a special dispensation to certain officers to carry out these activities unimpeded. In their interviews, some officers admitted as much. It might have been the case that the nature and extent of organised crime group activities were such during the late 1990s that they demanded drastic measures to be taken by the police to reassure the public. On the other hand, it may just have been the nature of leadership, which encouraged the use of *encounters* in preference to processing these "criminals" through the criminal justice system. However, since a change in the leadership in 2003 and subsequent corruption scandals that rocked the Mumbai police, there has been a curb on *encounters* whose numbers have reduced drastically (though they have not been completely eliminated). One explanation could be the fact that the new leadership has posted the so-called *encounter* "specialists" out of the Crime Branch to regular police stations.[6] Another explanation given by the police for the fall in *encounters* has been that they had already eliminated a whole cadre of criminals, so much so that very few active members remained. Also the fear of *encounters,* officers were convinced, meant that there was a slowing down in new recruitment to the organised gangs. There is, however, no evidence to support this.

Fear and insecurity of crime that appeared rampant in the late 1990s also seems to have abated judging from the newspaper and media reports on the subject, being now replaced by the fear of terrorism and terrorist attacks that have besieged Mumbai in the past few years,[7] culminating in the powerful serial blasts affecting six commuter trains and one railway platform on July 11, 2006 killing over 200 persons and injuring more than 714 persons[8] and the Mumbai terror attacks in November 2008 in which over 195 people, including senior police officers died.[9] Thus, the nature of crime and security concerns has changed in Mumbai over the past decade.

Whatever the explanation for the fluctuations in the numbers of *encounters* over the period under study (1993–2003), a direct link between the priorities of the

---

[6]See, for example *The Times of India* (2006b).

[7]See, for example *The Times of India* (2003a).

[8]See, for example: "Mumbai blasts death toll reaches 200", posted online by the Press Trust of India, July 12, 2006.

[9]See, for example Alderson (2008).

leadership of the police organisation and the use of *encounters* as a crime control measure cannot be ruled out. Though some commentators suggest that changes in legislation and rules are more effective in reducing officer discretion and increasing accountability (Foster, 2003, citing her forthcoming work, Brogden, Jefferson, & Walklate, 1988; Grimshaw & Jefferson, 1987; Marks, 1999), a change in leadership style can be instrumental in bringing about a change in police culture and practices more effectively, and without which additional legal restrictions or more stringent accountability mechanisms may not work as well. However, police organisations the world over have struggled to break with leadership styles based on "authoritarian, centralised control of mindless subordinates" (Cowper, 2004: 113), and it is difficult for police leaders with little effective leadership or management training to find alternatives to "top-down decision making and total submission to ensure their authority and status" (Cowper, 2004: 119) when confronted with crisis situations. Marks (2005) suggests in the context of transforming the South African police that "directive leadership" based on "participatory management" which involves "close and careful supervision coupled with clear and understandable directives during operations" and "agreed upon performance indicators, formulated with rank-and-file participation" (p. 251) would prove beneficial in transforming organisations via leadership changes. Similarly Long (2003) suggests a change of leadership style from "transactional" (emphasis on satisfying more bureaucratic and legal requirements) to "transformational", (emphasising inspirational motivation and participatory change on a reciprocal basis between subordinates and leaders).

A Final Word

The police use of deadly force in circumstances described as *encounters* in Mumbai have for many years now been widely and largely without question accepted as the correct and effective response to controlling increased organised crime. However, *encounters* which were once prized and acknowledged as individual and organisational achievements (during the period under study 1993–2003) are in the past few years gradually emerging as contested territory with questions being raised about whether officers abuse deadly force as a last resort to control crime or whether murkier motives (corruption and self-interest/aggrandisement) are at work here. Since these developments have occurred in the recent past, it is difficult to ascertain the precise reasons for the change, especially since there is no particular incident[10] that marked a change in attitudes. However, factors such as increasing public awareness of Human Rights issues as a result of greater activism on behalf of Human Rights Commissions and the Courts; changing political equations; conclusion of trials in older cases of *encounters* that ended in conviction of a few police officers;

---

[10]Incidents like the attack on the Twin Towers in September 2001 in the USA or the July 2005 bombings in London that heralded a sea change, in the direction opposite to that in Mumbai, towards police use of force issues in these countries.

more awareness on behalf of the media; and change in police leadership, might have been responsible for the change. The research suggests that in Mumbai police *encounters* were unquestioned and police officers continued to operate in an atmosphere that lacked rigorous accountability to either the rule of law or the public for a number of years. Interviews with police officers and "claimsmakers" revealed a discourse of denial that existed: accounts that enabled officers to explain to their audiences why *encounters* were justified and inevitable in the effort to fight crime.

This research in one Indian city draws on Sykes and Matza's original work on techniques of neutralisation and fits officer accounts within Cohen's framework of denial, making it one more example contributing to the literature that seeks to demonstrate that deniability is endemic to societies as diverse as Nazi Germany, apartheid South Africa, dictatorial regimes in Brazil and Argentina; societies that have something to deny, to justify, to cover up. Atrocities when committed by state actors and condoned by the political machinery have to be explained and made acceptable to the public, and this was done in Mumbai, like in other contexts, by denying that *encounters* were unjustified either on legal, and/or moral grounds. Unless the police recognise their discourse as denial, they will contribute to the violence if they do not "articulate a clear and consistent democratic role for the police" (Bonner, 2008).

When I started the research in 2001, *encounters* figured prominently in the news and print media, and the research was considered to be very topical in Mumbai. Even though the number of *encounters* has declined in Mumbai since then, police *encounters* were back in the public discourse with the criminal conviction of ten police officers in Delhi for criminal conspiracy and murder. There was furore in the Lok Sabha (Lower House of Parliament) when three high-ranking officers of the Indian Police Service (IPS) were arrested for their involvement in the fake *encounter* of Sohrabuddin Sheikh in the state of Gujarat.[11] The latest blow for *encounters* is the perceived adverse judgement of the High Court of Andhra Pradesh in February 2009, which made it mandatory for every *encounter* to be registered as a case against the police officers involved (i.e. a case of murder) even if the police investigation or magisterial inquiry did not substantiate any charges against police officers involved. The judgement further ruled that police investigation of *encounters* ending in Final Reports (implying charges were not substantiated) are not conclusive and magisterial inquiries in *encounter* cases are not a substitute for registration and investigation of such cases.[12] The judgement aroused a great deal of emotion among police circles across India and officers from Andhra Pradesh appealed against the High Court's judgement to the Supreme Court of India. The grant of an interim stay on the operation of the High Court's judgement by the Supreme Court has been hailed by officers as a positive development. The High Court judgement was presumably stayed on the grounds of causing anguish and distress of police officers involved in risky situations

---

[11]See, for example: "Gujarat fake encounter issue rocks Lok Sabha", Press Trust of India Report, in *India Today on the Net*, April 27, 2007. http://www.indiatoday.com/itoday/20070305/ newsallFullStory.php?id=6209 (accessedOctober 20, 2007).

[12]Writ Petition No. 15419 of 2006 and others *A.P. Civil Liberties Committee Vs. the State of A.P* http://www.judis.nic.in/andhra/qrydisp.asp?tfnm=6376 (accessed September 17, 2009).

and restricting operational freedom of police officers to deal with extreme situations including terrorist threats like the Mumbai terror attacks on 2008.

Encounters that appear to have been normalised and grounded in necessity in Mumbai, ought no longer to be so. The conditions that give rise to the necessity of *encounters* need to be addressed and unless the process of "normalisation" and "cover-ups" is exposed, which means, unless *encounters* are seen as problematic and addressed as such, they will continue to occur (maybe not continually but in periodic cycles) and pose a danger to the right to life, one of the most basic of human rights that a democratic country has the obligation to secure, protect and promote.

Chapter 9
Appendix: Methodology

The research began in 2001, the year in which police *encounters* peaked in Mumbai, and police use of deadly force was in the forefront of media reports. Although *encounters* were not a new phenomenon in Mumbai, there was no deep examination into the issues involved in either police or public circles. This research attempts to do just that, drawing on the accounts of some of the actors involved in *encounters*, those bystanders to them and those who influenced the social processes that contributed to making *encounters* both acceptable and desirable.

The motivation to study *encounters* is embedded in my experiences as a police officer in the North Indian state of Uttar Pradesh, notorious for "*encounters*" of "dreaded" criminals in the late 1970s and 1980s. At the National Police Academy and in the first few years of service, I found that the implicit values in the organisation stressed on machismo; hailing officers who had been involved in *encounters* as heroes or "real officers", worth emulating. In addition, faced with working conditions in the field, the inadequacies of the criminal justice system, the lack of scientific training and infrastructure made available to the police, and the sheer volume of crime, *encounters* came to become justifiable.

However, observations of what actually went on behind the scenes in *encounters* made me rethink my attitude towards them. Were other officers also troubled by similar moral dilemmas? *Encounters* required deeper understanding as it was evident that there were some very strong forces at work, influencing ordinary individuals into condoning and even encouraging *encounters* as an acceptable means of crime control.

As a serving officer, I felt the need to seek a "deep understanding" of the topic by speaking to other officers, in order to explore or to check my understandings and whether they were shared by other members or participants; "to check, stimulate, or inspire" my own self-reflections, and to "go beyond commonsense explanations"; in order to "grasp and articulate the multiple views of, perspectives on, and meanings of some activity, event, place, or cultural object" (Johnson, 2002: 106). In order to do so, a qualitative approach to the topic seemed most relevant for the research. The focus of this research was on officers' perceptions and accounts of *encounters*, ways in which they explained, excused, or justified their conduct, official and personal discourses through which they reconciled the arbitrary use of deadly force with their moral conscience and professional ethics.

Having a strong personal and emotional motive for undertaking the research proved to be a great incentive to do the research itself, but also created the potential for a flawed study. I needed to guard against "selective observation" and "premature closure" (Lawrence, 2000a: 4–5), "personal biases", and "theoretical predispositions" (Patton, 2002: 51) during the research. I had to think about the "interviewer effect", and resolve issues of power, gender, and status, what Schwalbe and Wolkomir (2002: 206) call "interview as threat" situation. I, the researcher, was a senior ranking woman police officer and my interviewees were police officers of various ranks (subordinate, colleagues, and senior ranks), and a group of people whom I call "claimsmakers", who varied in the social status and power they enjoyed. Thus, each interview was unique in the personal dynamics and power relations that set its parameters. Apart from being aware that "gender filters knowledge" (Fontana & Frey, 2000: 658), I was also aware that being an Indian Police Service officer might constitute a barrier in the interviews (see Johnson, 2002: 107). There was also a danger that respondents would tailor their responses to what they thought would suit my purpose. In practice, I negotiated around these issues by trying to set the tone of the interview as one of friendly discussion. Most officers were flattered on being asked their opinion on a variety of issues and did not hesitate to speak out. However, a few remained on guard, preferring not to have an open discussion. "Claimsmakers" too were interested in discussing such an interesting topic with a woman police officer.

Access

The research was intentionally overt to avoid undergoing the stress involved in researching a manifestly sensitive topic covertly (see, e.g. Holdaway, 1983). Access was sought openly through the formal channels. Being a serving officer proved advantageous as I was given instant and unconditional access by the incumbent Commissioner and I remain indebted to him for his generous support. The entire organisation was to be accessible for research. The receipt of official sanction of the leader meant there were no bureaucratic obstacles thereafter. However, once initial access had been successfully negotiated, it was necessary to constantly "renegotiate access to the... individual members of the organisation" (Buchanan, Boddy, & McCalman, 1988: 59). All officers approached assented to being interviewed, but their willingness to be open and honest during the interviews depended upon the interpersonal relationship developed during the process. In most cases, a common operational policing background helped build bridges quite swiftly. Ostensibly my rank automatically established my legitimacy and credibility and I was viewed as "one of them". The Mumbai police were virgin research territory and I was not asked any questions (in fact no one even read the research synopsis); no guarantees were expected; and any opening remarks about confidentiality and anonymity were waved aside. The trust reposed by the interviewees made me even more obliged to treat the material with care. Some officers interviewed were too well known to disguise their identity sufficiently, but names, places, and references to particular incidents have been carefully anonymised.

My researcher role was that of an "outside insider" (Brown, 1996; Reiner, 2000b) – a serving officer researching another force. Jones (1980), Holdaway (1983), and Young (1991) suggested the problems with being an inside researcher were exposing the processes behind the "secrecy" that shrouds police work and the apprehension of causing damage to people who had co-operated during the research if the findings were made public. As an "insider" my experience and knowledge of the culture gave me deeper insight into the topic, but I was worried about accusations of whistle blowing. The other major issue that I struggled with during the research was maintaining objectivity and guarding against agreeing with officers' worldview uncritically since I shared many of their cultural assumptions.

Interviews

I was mainly interested in understanding how actors perceived the situation and constructed accounts about the issues around *encounters*. The field research was divided into two sections: interviews with police officers conducted during the summer of 2002 and interviews with a group of people I call "claimsmakers" conducted over the summer of 2003. The interviews were semi-structured and open ended generally ranging between 45 min and 2 h.

Police Officers

In-depth interviews were carried out with 38 police officers (33 men and 5 women) from the Mumbai Police. These included four Senior Management (including the Commissioner and Joint Commissioners of Police); eight Upper Middle Management (Additional and Deputy Commissioners of Police); five Lower Middle Management (Assistant Commissioners of Police); ten Inspectors; and 11 Sub Inspectors.

Seven Upper Middle Management (UMM) and all Senior Management (SM) belonged to the Indian Police Service, two officers (one each from the Upper Middle Management (UMM) and Lower Middle Management (LMM) levels) had risen from the ranks of Sub Inspector, and the others were recruited as Constables or Sub Inspectors (SI) and had risen to their present ranks through promotion. The five women officers interviewed were mainly from the ranks of Sub Inspector, Inspector, and Deputy Commissioner of Police.

The sample of police interviewees was selected using *quota* (various ranks), *purposeful* (those who had some experience of *encounters*), and *snowball* (being referred on to meet other officers who were considered "experts" on some of the issues being researched) sampling (see, e.g. Lawrence, 2000a, 2000b; Patton, 2002; Warren, 2002). Of the nine zones in the city, four were selected randomly and interviews were carried out with officers of different ranks, along with officers from the Crime Branch; added to these were senior officers in the Commissioner's office, as well as senior officers who had in previous capacities, been closely associated with police *encounters*. The initial and subsequent response I received from all officers was overwhelmingly positive. Access had to be negotiated with individual officers by explaining the purpose and aims of the research. The interviews were conducted in their offices and police stations.

"Claimsmakers"

Eighteen in-depth interviews (14 men and 4 women) were conducted with a group of persons I call "claimsmakers". Best (1991) calls promoters, activists, professional experts, and spokespersons involved in forwarding specific claims about a phenomenon "claimsmakers". I have used the term because people interviewed ought to be critics, or "social conscience keepers" on the issue (of *encounters*) and could potentially influence policy ("policing policy shapers"). My sample included four journalists (representing the English broadsheets, Marathi broadsheets, and the tabloid press), three retired judges of the Mumbai High Court, and the Supreme Court of India, two lawyers (a public prosecutor and one representing the "encountered victim"), two political leaders (from the Ruling Party and the Opposition), two representatives of Industrial Associations, three Human Rights activists (representing Non-Governmental Organisations), one Criminologist, and one Academic who was a member of the State Human Rights Commission.

These interviews were conducted as a sample of the formal articulation of public opinion on police *encounters*. The sample is not representative of the general public, in fact they may be quite the opposite as they represent the opinions of "elite" groups also called the "chattering classes" or the "intelligentsia" in India. Most of the "claimsmakers" interviewed were significant players in the political and social life in Mumbai who created, influenced, as well as reflected general public opinion. These interviews certainly gave a flavour of and in some cases, reaffirmed opinions that I had heard expressed in ordinary everyday conversations with friends, neighbours, shopkeepers, domestic help, doctors, taxi drivers, etc. My interactions with citizens were also an informal way of triangulating and validating the interview data of this group.

Snowball sampling was used to contact most of the interviews with "claimsmakers" interviewed. Starting out with one contact (who was not an interviewee) I was directed on to others, and subsequently other contacts flowed smoothly. Most interviews were conducted in the residences or offices of the interviewees (the choice was theirs).

Taping and Transcribing

At the beginning of every interview, permission was sought to tape record the interview. Only two police officers refused, and for one interview the recorder malfunctioned. Some interviewees said during the interview that they would prefer that the material they were just about to disclose was not used; others asked me to switch off the tape for a few minutes while they said something which they thought was "unsafe"; while others would reveal quite a lot of confidential information after the tape recorder was switched off. Notes were made both during the interview and during the informal discussions, with the permission of the interviewee. This "unrecorded" data was as important as that derived from the tape recordings (Warren, 2002: 91–92).

Interviews were mainly conducted in English, however, some officers were more comfortable speaking in Marathi, and others interspersed Hindi in their comments. Interviews were translated literally and then transcribed, without trying to smoothen the edges, neaten, and correct the grammar (Alldred & Gillies, 2002). This has sometimes resulted in slightly strange phrases and metaphors that are alien to the English language, but make perfect sense given their vernacular origin and context.

Analysis

There were three main phases of the analysis: classifying the interview material into relevant codes or categories; identifying and exploring the links between inter-related categories; and, interpreting and analysing emerging links, generating explanations at a more abstract and generalised level.

The analysis was done mainly within the "constructivist–interpretivist paradigm" (Denzin & Lincoln, 1994: Introduction), which recognises that social reality is constructed by social actors and in order to understand the world of meanings, one must interpret it. Thus, the goal is to "understand the complex world of lived experience from the point of view of those who live it" (Schwandt, 1994: 118). Patton (2002: 98) citing Guba and Lincoln's (1988) primary assumptions of constructivism suggests that phenomena can be only understood in the context in which they are studied, and neither the problem nor solutions can be generalised across time and space. While this is true to a large extent, at the same time there can be generalisations across contexts and countries and learning from the experiences of others.

To further explore these shared cultural meanings around language, "*domain analysis*" was used. This analytic strategy, according to Coffey and Atkinson (1996: 90) "explore[s] the linguistic symbols or 'folk terms' used by social actors, both individually and collectively". The aim is to identify "patterns and systems of folk terms as a mechanism for understanding the cultural knowledge of a particular social group". Spradley (1979, 1980) describes a domain structure as having four characteristics – a core term or overall category title; two or more included folk terms that belong to the category; a semantic relationship that links the core term to the included terms; and a boundary or parameter, the terms of which should be defined by the native informant/social actor (Coffey & Atkinson, 1996: 91). Coffey and Atkinson also suggest that Spradley's concept of the linguistic symbol having a triad of elements – the actual symbol, the referent, and the relationship between the symbol and the referent – helps in trying to explain the relationship between different labels attached to *encounters*, and how they are understood by different actors. In this case, *encounter*, is the symbol, representing police killing of criminals in self-defence;

the referent is the recognition of the fact that these killings are actually deliberate; and the elationship between the symbol and referent are the conditions under which a particular *encounter* would be accepted or rejected as justifiable by the one making this judgement. Thus according to Spradley's (1979, 1980) domain structure, the core term *encounter* includes three folk terms such as "genuine" *encounters* and "fake" *encounters* that are in common usage by the police and members of the public alike, as well as my own term "bona fide" *encounters*. One of the aims of the research was to explore how these terms were semantically related in the perception of the police and of the public, and to determine the parameters by which the terms were defined by these social actors. Further Coffey and Atkinson explain that, the symbols may be thought of as *organising schemes* (Tesch, 1990: 139), and the analysis aims to identify the rules and relationships among the symbols. In this context, a *domain* refers to a set of symbols that share meaning in some way.

Lyman and Scott (1970: 112) suggest that the construction of accounts as part of everyday talk is done by actors to explain unanticipated, untoward, and unexpected behaviour – these explanations are situated accounts, dependent upon the status of the actors and the physical and social location, and are standardised within cultures and subgroups; hence, accounts can be useful in exploring the situated culture within which they are embedded.

An exploration of interview accounts would help get a better insight into not only how police culture engenders, but also how societal values and norms create conditions for the tolerance and acceptance of repeated occurrences of *encounters* in India. The ultimate aim of the analysis was to move from the level of distilling a "substantive theory" (using Glaser and Strauss' (1968) distinction) accounting for the police use of deadly force in Mumbai, to linking this with the more generic "formal theory" of the police use or abuse of force in a wider context.

The main theoretical orientation of the analysis was the *grounded theory* approach (Bottoms, 2000; Glaser & Strauss, 1968). This enabled me to draw theory from the evidence gathered in the field, which evolved through an inductive process, rather than either proving or disproving any pre-existing hypothesis that led the research process (Cresswell, 1998: 241).

Reisman (1979) advocates that research into deviant behaviour should not be undertaken from a taken-for-granted worldview as this would involve implicit judgements about the legitimacy of behaviour and would influence the types of questions asked. He feels that researchers should study deviant behaviour in a value-neutral manner because what appears deviant may actually be very rational or necessary to those being studied. By assuming a taken-for-granted world view (that all police are corrupt) and supporting prevailing social norms, scientific objectivity is lost and one is liable to miss the point that the deviance may be symptomatic of a deeper social, systemic malaise that needs attention. While there could be another argument that scientific objectivity might neither be desirable nor achievable in social sciences research, it is true that by labelling police *encounters* as deviant at the outset, one may miss the fundamental point that there is a mismatch between society's expectations from the police force and the legal provisions and the capacity of the police to deliver, given their limited resources and powers. Interviews were conducted and analysed value – neutrally, that is understanding the perspective of the respondent without being judgemental or biased. Even though it is not possible to view police abuse of deadly force as anything other than undesirable, it can be studied and understood, using a medical analogy, like a disease, in order to be cured.

Reliability and Validity

Reliability and validity are important issues in any research. Following Silverman (1993: 146–149) reliability was addressed in this qualitative study in three ways. First, during the entire course of the field work, notes were kept about the conditions under which the interview took place, the attitude and demeanour of the interviewees, their willingness or otherwise to discuss some of the more sensitive issues openly. Secondly, reliability in interviews was ensured by asking broadly the same set of questions to the respondents. Most of the interviews were taped and in those rare cases when they were not, meticulous notes were taken. Finally, transcripts were made and while these may not be perfect; the attempt was made to keep the translations and transcription as close to the exact words used by the respondents, as possible.

Reliability and validity were perennial problems as the study cannot be replicated. Also other researchers in the field may not have the same access or response from the field. Undoubtedly, the analysis was influenced to a large extent by personal experience and observation; however, the typical pitfalls, that is a tendency to select field data to fit preconceptions of the phenomenon and a tendency to select field data, which are conspicuous because they are exotic, at the expense of less dramatic (but possibly indicative) data (Fielding & Fielding, 1986), was avoided.

Validation of the research findings has been attempted through the methods of *triangulation* and *reflexivity* (Sapsford, 1996; Silverman, 1993). Triangulation was sought through collecting data from several sources – interviews with police officers and with "claimsmakers", media reports, official statistics, personal experience, observation, and introspection. The broader conclusions that have been arrived at as a result of the analysis are based on representative patterns emerging from the data, and not on stray remarks or anecdotal evidence. However, anecdotal evidence has been used to illustrate points that have a wider consensus among those interviewed.

Ethical Issues

There were numerous ethical dilemmas in the research including: consent, deception, privacy, identification, confidentiality, and spoiling the field (Punch, 1986).

Confidentiality and Anonymity

The fact that the subject under scrutiny was so local and specific to the city of Mumbai, it would have been nearly impossible to disguise the identity of the city and the force. Also it has been very difficult to cloak the identity of various officers, who might be easily recognisable by insiders (either correctly or mistakenly), or are such public figures that their identity might have been inadvertently revealed (Punch, 1998: 176). Also troubling was the amount of very sensitive material that had been divulged during the interviews, with little or no demands for guarantees of confidentiality or anonymity by police officers.

Power and Consent

Though the Police Commissioner as "gatekeeper" had left subordinate officers with little choice about participating in the research, they still retained the power to talk as little or as much as they wanted to. Most of the officers interviewed were not weak and powerless, on the contrary – while they were expected to be subservient to authority vis-à-vis their position in the hierarchy, they were still capable of retaining power in the interview situation.

Trust

Researching the police is generally problematic, as the experience of past researchers has indicated (Reiner, 2000b). This appeared to be true in the Indian context – "In general, Indian police officers are reluctant to be formally interviewed on matters pertaining to policing practices and strategies for academic research purposes. This is because policing is seen as a matter of state security that may be compromised by revelations" (Mukhopadhyaya, 1997: 5). The culture of secrecy, distrust of outsiders, suspicion, and cynicism (Bowling & Foster, 2002; Reiner, 2000a) are difficult barriers to overcome in any type of research. However, my experience with the Mumbai police was in total contrast to what I had been led to expect, and as mentioned, being an "outsider–insider" (Reiner, 2000b) proved to be very useful in bringing down the barriers to some extent, with the officers and others.

The guiding principle of my research was not to shock or reveal "dark and murky" deeds of the police, but to explore an issue that is of social and sociological significance: that is how police use of deadly force goes unchallenged and is even tacitly encouraged in an open and democratic state like India, that would like to be seen as a champion of Human Rights in the international arena.

Bibliography

Adams, K. (1995). Measuring the prevalence of police abuse of force. In W. Geller & H. Toch (Eds.), *And justice for all: Understanding and controlling police abuse of force*. Washington, DC: Police Executive Research Forum.

Adams, K. (1999). Research agenda on police use of force. In Adams, K., et al. (Eds.), *Use of force by police: overview of national and local data*. National Institute of Justice. Retrieved from http://www.ncjrs.gov/pdffiles1/nij/176330-1.pdf.

Adler, P. A., & Adler, P. (2002). The reluctant respondent. In J. Gubrium & J. Holstein (Eds.), *Handbook of interview research*. Thousand Oaks, CA: Sage.

Agnes, F. (1996). The Busti that did not yield. In J. McGuire, P. Reeves, & H. Brasted (Eds.), *Politics of violence: From Ayodhya to Behrampada*. Thousand Oaks, CA: Sage.

Aiyar, S. S. A. (1998, July 19). The state, by other means. *Sunday Times of India* (New Delhi Edition).

Aiyar, S. & Koppikar, S. (1997, December 22). Triggering controversy. *India Today*.

Albanese, J., Das, D., & Verma, A. (Eds.). (2003). *Organized crime: World perspectives*. New Jersey: Prentice Hall.

Alderson, A. (2008, November 29). Mumbai attacks: Taj Mahal siege ends as death toll rises to 195. *The Telegraph*. Retrieved July 12, 2009, from http://www.telegraph.co.uk/news/worldnews/asia/india/3535230/Mumbai-attacks-Taj-Mahal-siege-ends-as-total-death-toll-rises-to-195-Bombay-India.html.

Alldred, P., & Gillies, V. (2002). Eliciting research accounts: Re/producing modern subjects. In M. Mauthner et al. (Eds.), *Ethics in qualitative research*. Thousand Oaks, CA: Sage.

Allen, N. (2004, November 2). Met in crisis and protesting officers lay down arms. *The Independent*. Retrieved August 24, 2009, from http://www.independent.co.uk/news/uk/crime/met-in-crisis-as-protesting-officers-lay-down-arms-531778.html.

Allport, F. (1937). Toward a science of public opinion. *Public Opinion Quarterly, 1*(1), 7–23.

Alpert, G. (1989). Police use of deadly force: The Miami experience. In R. Dunham & G. Alpert (Eds.), *Critical issues in policing: Contemporary readings*. Prospect Heights, IL: Waveland.

Amir, M. (1971). *Patterns of forcible rape*. Chicago, IL: University of Chicago Press.

Anechiarico, F. (1991). Beyond bribery: The political influence of organized crime in New York City. In C. Fijnaut & J. Jacobs (Eds.), *Organized crime and its containment: A transatlantic initiative*. Boston: Kluwer.

Arnold, D. (1986). *Police power and colonial rule: Madras 1859–1947*. Delhi: Oxford University Press.

Arnold, D. (1992). Police power and the demise of British rule in India, 1930–1947. In D. Anderson & D. Killingray (Eds.), *Policing and decolonization: Politics, nationalism and the police 1917–1965*. Manchester: Manchester University Press.

Babbie, E. (1986). *Observing ourselves: Essays in social research*. Prospect Heights, IL: Waveland.

Baker, A. (2009, April 25). One year after acquittal in Sean bell shooting, lives remain in limbo. *The New York Times*. Retrieved June 10, 2009, from http://www.lexisnexis.com.

Balakrishnan, S. (2005, September 28). Encounter specialist on cops' wanted list. *The Times of India.*

Balakrishnan, S. (2005, October 31). Delhi blast: D-company under scan. *The Times of India.*

Balakrishnan, S. (2006, November 22). We are gangsters, not terrorists, says Shakeel. *The Times of India.*

Banks, R., Eberhardt, J., & Ross, L. (2006). Discrimination and implicit bias in a racially unequal society. *California Law Review, 94*(4), 1169–1190.

Bassis, M., Gelles, R., & Levine, A. (1982). *Social problems.* New York: Harcourt.

Baumer, E. (2008). An empirical assessment of the contemporary crime trends puzzle: A modest step towards a more comprehensive research agenda. In *Understanding crime trends: Workshop report, committee on understanding crime trends* (pp. 127–176). The National Academies. Retrieved July 24, 2009, from http://www.nap.edu/catalog.php?record_id=12472#toc.

Bayley, D. (1969). *The police and political development in India.* Princeton, NJ: Princeton University Press.

Bayley, D. (1986). The tactical choices of police patrol officers. *Journal of Criminal Justice, 14,* 329–348.

Bayley, D. (1996). Police brutality abroad. In W. Geller & H. Toch (Eds.), *Police violence: Understanding and controlling police abuse of force.* New Haven, CT: Yale University Press.

Bayley, B., & Bittner, E. (1984). Learning the skills of policing. *Law and Contemporary Problems, 47*(4), 35–39.

Becker, H. (1963). *Outsiders: Study in the sociology of deviance.* London: Free Press of Glencoe.

Becker, H. (Ed.). (1964). *The other side: Perspectives on deviance.* London: Free Press of Glencoe.

Beckett, K. (1997). *Making crime pay: Law and order in contemporary American politics.* Oxford: Oxford University Press.

Bedi, K. (1998). *Its always possible: Transforming one of the largest prisons in the world.* New Delhi: Sterling.

Bedi, K. (2003). *Jaisa maine dekha.* New Delhi: Phyujana Buksa.

Beehr, T., Ivanitskaya, L., Glaser, K., Erofeev, D., & Canali, K. (2004). Working in a violent environment: The accuracy of police officers' reports of shooting incidents. *Journal of Occupational and Organizational Psychology, 77,* 217–235.

Benney, M., & Hughes, E. (1984). Of sociology and the interview. In M. Bulmer (Ed.), *Sociological research methods: An introduction* (2nd ed.). Basingstoke: Macmillan.

Best, J. (1991). *Images of issues: Typifying contemporary social problems.* New York: Aldine de Gruyter.

Best, J. (1995). *Images of issues: Typifying contemporary social problems* (2nd ed.). New York: Aldine de Gruyter.

Best, J. (1999). *Random violence: How we talk about new crimes and new victims.* Berkeley: University of California Press.

Bhatt, C. (2001). *Hindu nationalism: Origins, ideologies and modern myths.* Oxford: Berg.

Biardeau, M. (2003). Ancient Brahminism, or impossible non-violence. In D. Vidal, G. Tarabout, & E. Meyer (Eds.), *Violence/non-violence: Some Hindu perspectives.* New Delhi: Manohar, Centre De Sciences Humaines.

Binder, A., Scharf, P., & Gavin, R. (1982). *Use of deadly force by police officers: Final report.* Washington, DC: National Institute of Justice.

Birch, M., & Miller, T. (2002). Encouraging participation: Ethics and responsibilities. In M. Mauthner et al. (Eds.), *Ethics in qualitative research.* Thousand Oaks, CA: Sage.

Bishop, G. (2005). *The illusion of public opinion: Fact and artifact in American public opinion polls.* Lanham: Rowman and Littlefield.

Bittner, E. (1970). *The functions of the police in modern society.* Chevy Chase, MD: National Institute of Mental Health.

Bittner, E. (1975). *The functions of the police in modern society.* New York: Jason Aronson.

Bittner, E. (1979). *The functions of the police in modern society.* USA: National Institute of Mental Health.

Bittner, E. (1990). Florence Nightingale in pursuit of Willie Sutton. In *Aspects of policework.* Reprinted in Newburn, T. (Ed.). (2005). *Policing: Key readings.* Devon: Willan.

Bittner, E. (1991). The functions of the police in modern society. In C. Klockars & S. Mastrofski (Eds.), *Thinking about police: Contemporary readings* (2nd ed.). New York: McGraw-Hill.

Block, A., & Chambliss, W. (1981). *Organizing crime*. New York: Elsevier.

Blom Hansen, T. (2001). *Wages of violence: Naming and identity in postcolonial Bombay*. Princeton: Princeton University Press.

Blumberg, M. (1989). Controlling police use of deadly force: Assessing two decades of progress. In R. Dunham & G. Alpert (Eds.), *Critical issues in policing: Contemporary readings*. Prospect Heights, IL: Waveland.

Bode, N. (2009, April 25). Sean bell way plan stirs anger. *Daily News* (New York). Retrieved July 10, 2009, from http://www.lexisnexis.com.

Boni, N. (1998). *Deployment of women in policing*. Paymeham, SA: National Police Research Unit.

Bonner, M. (2008). State discourses, police violence and democratisation in Argentina. *Bulletin of Latin American Research, 28*(2), 227–245.

Bonner, M. (2009). Media as social accountability: The case of police violence in Argentina. *International Journal of Press Politics, 14*(3), 296–312.

Bottomley, K., & Pease, K. (1986). *Crime and punishment: Interpreting the data*. Milton Keynes: Open University Press.

Bottoms, A. (2000). The relationship between theory and research in criminology. In R. King & E. Wincup (Eds.), *Doing research on crime and justice*. New York: Oxford University Press.

Bouillier, V. (2003). The violence of the non-violent, or ascetics in combat. In D. Vidal, G. Tarabout, & E. Meyer (Eds.), *Violence/non-violence: Some Hindu perspectives*. New Delhi: Manohar, Centre De Sciences Humaines.

Bourdieu, P. (1979). Public opinion does not exist. In A. Mattelart & S. Siegelaub (Eds.), *Communication and class struggle: An anthology in 2 volumes*. New York: International General, International Mass Media Research Centre.

Bourdieu, P. (1990). *In other words: Essay towards a reflexive sociology*. Cambridge: Polity.

Bovenkerk, F. (1991). Organized crime and the sex and gambling business in the Netherlands. In C. Fijnaut & J. Jacobs (Eds.), *Organized crime and its containment: A transatlantic initiative*. Deventer: Kluwer.

Bowden, T. (1978). *Beyond the limits of the law: A comparative study of the police in crisis politics*. Harmondsworth: Penguin.

Bowling, B., & Foster, J. (2002). Policing and the police. In M. Maguire, R. Morgan, & R. Reiner (Eds.), *Oxford handbook of criminology*. Oxford: Oxford University Press.

Box, S. (1983). *Power, crime and mystification*. London: Routledge.

Breuil, B., & Rozema, R. (2009). Fatal imaginations: Death squads in Davao City and Medellin compared. *Crime, Law and Social Change, 52*, 405–424.

Brewer, J. (1994). *Black and blue: Policing in South Africa*. Oxford: Oxford University Press.

Brinks, D. (2008). *The judicial response to police killings in Latin America: Inequality and the rule of law*. Cambridge: Cambridge University Press.

Broderick, J. (1973). *Police in a time of change*. Morristown, NJ: General Learning.

Brogden, M. (1987). The emergence of the police – the colonial dimension. *British Journal of Criminology, 27*(1), 4–16.

Brogden, M., Jefferson, T., & Walklate, S. (1988). *Introducing policework*. London: Unwin Hyman.

Brown, M. (1981). *Working the street*. New York: Russell Sage.

Brown, M. (1984). Use of deadly force by patrol officers – training implications. *Journal of Police Science and Administration, 12*(2), 133–140.

Brown, J. (1996). Police research: Some critical issues. In F. Leishman, B. Loveday, & S. Savage (Eds.), *Core issues in policing*. London: Longman.

Brown, J., & Heidensohn, F. (2000). *Gender and policing: Comparative perspectives*. Hampshire: Macmillan.

Browning, C. (1993). *Ordinary men: Reserve police battalion 101 and the final solution in Poland*. New York: Harper Collins.

Brunson, R. (2007). "Police don't like black people" African-American young men's accumulated police experiences. *Criminology and Public Policy, 6*(1), 71–101.

Bryman, A. (1988). *Quantity and quality in social research*. London: Unwin Hyman.

Buchanan, D., Boddy, D., & McCalman, J. (1988). Getting in, getting on, getting out, and getting back. In A. Bryman (Ed.), *Doing research in organizations*. London: Routledge.

Bulmer, M. (1988). Some reflections upon research in organizations. In A. Bryman (Ed.), *Doing research in organizations*. London: Routledge.

Bumgarner, J., Lewinsky, W., Hudson, W., & Sapp, C. (2006). An examination of police officer mental chronometry. *The Scene: Journal of the Association for Crime Scene Reconstruction, 12*(3), 11–26.

Bunsha, D. (2007, May 18), Fake encounter. *Frontline*, 24(9). Retrieved from http://www.flonnet.com/fl2409/stories/20070518002303400.htm.

Button, J. (2005, July 30). Collateral damage. *The Sydney Morning Herald*.

Cain, M. (1970). On the beat. In S. Cohen (Ed.), *Images of deviance*. Harmondsworth: Penguin.

Cain, M. (1973). *Society and the policeman's role*. London: Routledge and Kegan Paul.

Caldeira, T. (2000). *City of walls: Crime, segregation and citizenship in Sao Paolo*. Berkeley: University of California Press.

Callanan, V. (2005). *Feeding the fear of crime: Crime-related media and support for three strikes*. New York: LFB Scholarly Publishing LLC.

Campbell, B. (2000). Death squads: Definition, problems, and historical context. In B. Campbell & A. Brenner (Eds.), *Death squads in global perspective* (pp. 1–26). New York: St. Martin.

Carrabine, E., Iganski, P., Lee, M., Plummer, K., & South, N. (2004). *Criminology: A sociological introduction*. London: Routledge.

Cavender, G. (2004). Media and crime policy: A reconsideration of David Garland's the culture of control. *Punishment and Society, 6*, 335–348.

Chadha, M. (2005, October 20). Police say no to festival. *BBC News*. Retrieved from http://www.news.bbc.co.uk/1/hi/world/south_asia/4361676.stm.

Chambliss, W. (1989). *On the take: From petty crooks to presidents*. Bloomington: Indiana University Press.

Chambliss, W. (1994). Policing the ghetto underclass: The politics of law and law enforcement. *Social Problems, 41*(2), 177–194.

Chan, J. (1996). Changing police culture. *British Journal of Criminology, 36*, 109–134.

Chan, J. (1997). *Changing police culture*. Cambridge: Cambridge University Press.

Chan, J. (2000). Backstage punishment: Police violence, occupational culture and criminal justice. In T. Coady, S. James, S. Miller, & M. O'Keefe (Eds.), *Violence and police culture*. Carlton South, Victoria: Melbourne University Press.

Charles, M. (2001). The growth and activities of organised crime in Bombay. *International Social Science Journal, 53*, 359–367.

Chatterton, M. (1979). The supervision of patrol work under the fixed points system. In S. Holdaway (Ed.), *The British police*. London: Edward Arnold.

Chaturvedi, S. (2004, March 23). Telgi scam quantum put at Rs. 33,000 crores. *The Tribune, Chandigarh*. Retrieved from http://www.tribuneindia.com.

Cheh, M. (1996). Are lawsuits an answer to police brutality? In W. Geller & H. Toch (Eds.), *Police violence: Understanding and controlling police abuse of force*. New Haven, CT: Yale University Press.

Chevigny, P. (1990). Deadly force as social control: Jamaica, Argentina and Brazil. *Criminal Law Forum, 1*(3), 389–425.

Chevigny, P. (1995). *Edge of the knife: Police violence in Americas*. New York: New.

Chevigny, P. (1996). Changing control of police violence in Rio de Janeiro and Sao Paulo, Brazil. In O. Marenin (Ed.), *Policing change, changing police*. New York: Garland.

Choongh, S. (1997). *Policing as social discipline*. Oxford: Clarendon.

Coffey, A., & Atkinson, P. (1996). *Making sense of qualitative data*. London: Sage.

Cohen, S. (1972). *Folk devils and moral panics*. London: MacGibbon and Kee.

Cohen, S. (1996). Crime and politics: Spot the difference. *British Journal of Sociology, 47*(1), 1–21.

Cohen, S. (2001). *States of denial: Knowing about atrocities and suffering*. Cambridge: Polity.

Coleman, C., & Moynihan, J. (1996). *Understanding crime data: Haunted by the dark figure*. Maidenhead: Open University Press.

Conroy, J. (2000). *Unspeakable acts, ordinary people*. New York: Knopf.

Converse, P. (1987). Changing conceptions of public opinion in the political process. *Public Opinion Quarterly, 51*(4), 12–24.

Cop on the run finds an ally in Bollywood. (2006, January 23). *The Times of India*

Correll, J., Park, B., Judd, C., Wittenberg, B., Sadler, M., & Keesee, T. (2007). Across the thin blue line: Police officers and racial bias in the decision to shoot. *Journal of Personality and Social Psychology, 92*(6), 1006–1023.

Cowan, R., Campbell, D., & Dodd, V. (2005, August 17), The death of Juan Charles de Menezes. *The Guardian*. Retrieved July 10, 2009, from http://www.lexisnexis.com.

Cowper, T. (2004). The myth of the 'military model' of leadership in law enforcement. In Q. Thurman & J. Zhao (Eds.), *Contemporary policing: Controversies, challenges and solutions*. Los Angeles: Roxbury.

Cox, E. (n.d.). *Police and crime in India*. London: Stanley Paul & Co.

Crandon, G., & Dunne, S. (1997). Symbiosis or vassalage: The media and law enforcers. *Policing and Society, 8*(1), 77–91.

Crank, J. (1998). *Understanding police culture*. Cincinatti: Anderson.

Cresswell, J. (1998). *Qualitative inquiry and research design: Choosing among five traditions*. Thousand Oaks, CA: Sage.

Crime in India. (1993). New Delhi: National Crime Records Bureau.

Crime in India. (1994). New Delhi: National Crime Records Bureau.

Crime in India. (1995). New Delhi: National Crime Records Bureau.

Crime in India. (1996). New Delhi: National Crime Records Bureau.

Crime in India. (1997). New Delhi: National Crime Records Bureau.

Crime in India. (1998). New Delhi: National Crime Records Bureau.

Crime in India. (1999). New Delhi: National Crime Records Bureau.

Crime in India. (2000). New Delhi: National Crime Records Bureau.

Crime in India. (2001). New Delhi: National Crime Records Bureau.

Das, D. (1993). *Policing in six countries around the world*. Chicago: University of Illinois.

Das, A.K. (1998, June 16). Working for the wrong cause. *Times of India* (Bombay Edition).

Davis, G. R. (2004). *Shantaram*. UK: Little Brown.

Dawood brother to fight polls. (2004, September 21). *The Times of India*.

Delattre, E. (2002). *Character and cops: Ethics in policing* (4th ed.). Washington, DC: AEI.

Denzin, N., & Lincoln, Y. (Eds.). (1994). *Handbook of qualitative research*. Newbury Park, CA: Sage.

Desai, A. (2003). Urbanization and social stratification. In R. Sandhu (Ed.), *Urbanization in India: Sociological contributions*. New Delhi: Sage.

Deuskar, V. (1999). *Organized crime in India*. Unpublished research project under the Golden Jubilee Fellowship Scheme, SVP National Police Academy, Hyderabad.

Dhillon, K. (2005). *Police and politics in India – colonial concepts, democratic compulsions: Indian police 1947–2002*. New Delhi: Manohar.

Duncombe, J., & Jessop, J. (2002). 'Doing rapport' and the ethics of 'faking friendship'. In M. Mauthner et al. (Eds.), *Ethics in qualitative research*. Thousand Oaks, CA: Sage.

Ekblom, P., & Heal, K. (1982). *The police response to calls from the public* (Home Officer research and planning paper, Vol. 9). London: Home Office.

Ellis, C., & Berger, L. (2002). Their story/my story/our story – including the researcher's experience in interview research. In J. Gubrium & J. Holstein (Eds.), *Handbook of interview research*. Thousand Oaks, CA: Sage.

Engineer, A. A. (1995). *Lifting the veil*. Bombay: Sangam.

Ericson, R. (1981). *Making crime: A study of detective work*. Toronto: Butterworth.

Ericson, R. (1982). The police as reproducers of order. In *Reproducing order: A study of police patrol work*. Toronto: University of Toronto Press. Reproduced in Newburn, T. (Ed.). (2005). *Policing: Key readings*. Cullompton, Devon: Willan.

Ericson, R. (1989). Patrolling the facts: Secrecy and publicity in police work. *British Journal of Sociology, 40*(2), 205–226.

Farrington, D., & Dowds, E. (1985). Disentangling criminal behaviour and police reaction. In D. Farrington & J. Gunn (Eds.), *Reactions to crime: The public, the police, courts and prisons.* Chichester: Wiley.

Fielding, N. (1995). *Community policing.* Oxford: Oxford University Press.

Fielding, N., & Fielding, J. (1986). *Linking data* (Qualitative research methods, Vol. 4). London: Sage.

Fijnaut, C. (1991). Organized crime and anti-organized crime efforts in Western Europe: An overview. In C. Fijnaut & J. Jacobs (Eds.), *Organized crime and its containment: A transatlantic initiative.* Deventer: Kluwer.

Flick, U. (2002). *An introduction to qualitative research* (2nd ed.). London: Sage.

Fontana, A., & Frey, J. (2000). The interview: From structured questions to negotiated text. In N. Denzin & Y. Lincoln (Eds.), *Handbook of qualitative research* (2nd ed.). Thousand Oaks, CA: Sage.

Foster, J. (2003). Police culture. In T. Newburn (Ed.), *Handbook of policing.* Collumpton: Willan.

Foster, D., Haupt, P., & De Beer, M. (2005). *The theatre of violence: Narratives of protagonists in the South African conflict.* Oxford: James Curry.

Foster, J., Newburn, T., & Souhami, A. (2005). *Assessing the impact of the Stephen Lawrence inquiry* (Home Officer research study, Vol. 294). London: Home Office.

Freedland, J. (2006, July 7). How London carried on, G2. *The Guardian.*

Fridell, L., & Binder, A. (1992). Police officer decision making in potentially violent confrontations. *Journal of Criminal Justice, 20,* 385–399.

Friedrich, R. (1980). Police use of force: Individuals, situations and organizations. *Annals of American Academy of Political and Social Science, 452,* 82–97.

Friedrichs, D. (2000). State crime or governmental crime: Making sense of the conceptual confusion. In J. Ross (Ed.), *Controlling state crime* (2nd ed.). New Brunswick: Transaction.

Fyfe, J. (1978). *Shots fired: A typological examination of New York City police firearms discharges, 1971–75.* Unpublished PhD dissertation submitted to SUNY, Albany.

Fyfe, J. (1979). Administrative intervention on police shooting discretion: An empirical examination. *Journal of Criminal Justice, 7,* 309–323.

Fyfe, J. (1980). Geographic correlates of police shooting: A microanalysis. *Journal of Research in Crime and Delinquency, 17*(1), 101–113.

Fyfe, J. (1981a). Toward a typology of police shootings. In J. Fyfe (Ed.), *Contemporary issues in law enforcement.* Beverly Hills, CA: Sage.

Fyfe, J. (1981b). Race and extreme police–citizen violence. In R. McNeeley & C. Pope (Eds.), *Race, crime and criminal justice.* Beverley Hills, CA: Sage.

Fyfe, J. (1986). The split second syndrome and other determinants of police violence. In A. Campbell & J. Gibbs (Eds.), *Violent transactions.* Oxford: Basil Blackwell.

Fyfe, J. (1987). Police shooting: Environment and licence. In J. Scott & T. Hirschi (Eds.), *Controversial issues in crime and justice.* Newbury Park, CA: Sage.

Gamson, W., & Wolfsfeld, G. (1993). Movements and media as interacting systems. *Annals of the American Academy of Political and Social Science, 528,* 114–125.

Gardiner, S. (2007, January 10). Suspects as usual. *The Village Voice.* Retrieved July 21, 2009, from http://www.lexisnexis.com.

Gardiner, S. (2008, June 3). After the Sean bell case, Bloomberg still starves the NYPD watchdog. *The Village Voice (New York).* Retrieved July 19, 2009, from http://www.lexisnexis.com.

Garland, D. (1991). *Punishment and modern society.* Oxford: Clarendon.

Garland, D. (1996). The limits of the sovereign state: Strategies of crime control in contemporary society. *British Journal of Criminology, 36,* 445–471.

Garland, D. (2001). *The culture of control: Crime and social order in contemporary society.* Oxford: Oxford University Press.

Geller, W. (1982). Deadly force: What we know. *Journal of Police Science and Administration, 10,* 151–177.

Geller, W. (1989). *Civilians shot by Chicago police, 1974–1983, by reason for shooting and civilian race.* Chicago, IL: Police Executive Research Forum.

Geller, W., & Karales, K. (1981a). *Split second decisions: Shootings of and by Chicago police.* Chicago, IL: Chicago Law Enforcement Study Group.

Geller, W., & Scott, M. (1991). Deadly force: What we know. In C. Klockars & S. Mastrofski (Eds.), *Thinking about police: Contemporary readings* (2nd ed.). New York: McGraw-Hill.

Geller, W., & Scott, M. (1992). *Deadly force: What we know – a practitioner's desk-reference on police-involved shootings.* Washington, DC: Police Executive Research Forum.

Geller, W., & Toch, H. (1996). *Police violence: understanding and controlling police abuse of force.* New Haven, CT: Yale University Press.

Ghosh, S. (1991). *The Indian Mafia.* New Delhi: Ashish.

Ghosh, S. (1993). *Torture and rape in police custody: An analysis.* New Delhi: Ashish.

Gill, J., & Pasquale-Styles, P. (2009). Firearm deaths by law enforcement. *Journal of Forensic Science, 54*(1), 185–188.

Glaser, B., & Strauss, A. (1968). *The discovery of grounded theory: Strategies for qualitative research.* London: Weidenfeld and Nicolson.

Goffman, E. (1961). *Asylums: Essays on the social situation of mental patients and other inmates.* Garden City, NY: Anchor.

Goldhagen, D. (1995). *Hitler's willing executioners.* New York: Vintage.

Gossman, P. (2002). India's secret armies. In B. Campbell & A. Brenner (Eds.), *Death squads in global perspective: Murder with deniability.* New York: Palgrave Macmillan.

Grant, D., & Grant, J. (1996). Officer selection and the prevention of abuse of force. In W. Geller & H. Toch (Eds.), *Police violence: Understanding and controlling police abuse of force.* New Haven, CT: Yale University Press.

Grant, R., & Nijman, J. (2003). Post-colonial cities in the global era: A comparative study of Mumbai and Accra. In A. Dutt, A. Noble, G. Venugopal, & S. Subbiah (Eds.), *Challenges to Asian urbanization in the 21st century.* Dordrecht: Kluwer.

Green, P., & Ward, T. (2004). *State crime: Governments, violence and corruption.* London: Pluto.

Gregg, A. (2006). Shoot-to-kill: How far is too far in protecting citizens? *Penn State International Law Review, 25*(1), 295–316.

Grimshaw, R., & Jefferson, T. (1987). *Interpreting policework: Policy and practice in forms of beat policing.* London: Allen and Unwin.

Guba, E., & Lincoln, Y. (1988). Do inquiry paradigms imply inquiry methodologies? In D. Fetterman (Ed.), *Qualitative approaches to evaluation in education: The silent scientific revolution.* New York: Praeger.

Haberman, C. (2008, April 29). Cleared as criminals, but forever on trial. *The New York Times.* Retrieved June 10, 2008, from http://www.nytimes.com/2008/04/29/nyregion/29nyc.html.

Hagan, F. (1997). *Political crime: Ideology and criminality.* Boston: Allyand and Bacon.

Hall, S., Critcher, C., Jefferson, T., Clarke, J., & Roberts, B. (1981). The social production of news: Mugging in the media. In S. Cohen & J. Young (Eds.), *The manufacture of news: Social problems, deviance and the mass media.* California: Sage.

Hall, S., Critcher, C., Jefferson, T., Clarke, J., & Roberts, B. (1978). *Policing the crisis: Mugging, the state, and law and order.* London: Macmillan.

Hammersley, M. (1992). *What's wrong with ethnography: Methodological explorations.* London: Routledge.

Hannerz, U. (1969). *Soulside: Inquiries into ghetto culture and community.* New York: Columbia University Press.

Haritos-Fatouros, M. (2003). *The psychological origins of institutionalised terror.* London: Routledge.

Harring, S. (2000). The diallo verdict: Another 'tragic accident' in New York's war on street crime? *Social Justice, 27*(1), 9–18.

Harriott, A. (2000). *Police and crime control in Jamaica: Problems of reforming ex-colonial constablaries.* Barbados: University of the West Indies Press.

Harris, R. (1978). The police academy and the professional self-image. In P. Manning & J. Van Maanen (Eds.), *Policing: A view from the streets.* Santa Monica, CA: Goodyear.

Harris, N. (1995). Bombay in the global economy. In S. Patel & A. Thorner (Eds.), *Bombay: Metaphor for modern india.* Bombay: Oxford University Press.

Hernandez, D. (2003, February 5). Street where he lived and died now Amadou Diallo place. *The New York Times*. Retrieved July 10, 2009, from http://www.lexisnexis.com.

Herzog, S. (2000). Is there a distinct profile of police officers accused of violence? The Israeli case. *Journal of Criminal Justice, 28*(6), 457–471.

Hinton, M. (2005). A distant reality: Democratic policing in Argentina and Brazil. *Criminal Justice, 5*(1), 75–100.

Hinton, M. (2006). *The state on the streets: Police and politics in Argentina and Brazil.* Colorado: Lynne Rienner Publishers.

Hobbs, D. (1997). Criminal collaboration: Youth gangs, sub-cultures, professional criminals and organised crime. In M. Maguire, R. Morgan, & R. Reiner (Eds.), *The Oxford handbook of criminology* (2nd ed.). Oxford: Clarendon.

Hobbs, D. (2000). Researching serious crime. In R. King & E. Wincup (Eds.), *Doing research on crime and justice.* Oxford: Oxford University Press.

Hobbs, D. (2004). Organized crime in the UK. In C. Fijnaut & L. Paoli (Eds.), *Organized crime in Europe.* Dordrecht: Springer.

Holdaway, S. (1977). Changes in urban policing. *British Journal of Sociology, 28*(2), 119–137.

Holdaway, S. (1983). *Inside the British police.* Oxford: Blackwell.

Holdaway, S. (1996). *The racialization of British policing.* London: Macmillan.

Home Affairs Select Committee. (2005). Counter-terrorism and community relations in the aftermath of the London bombings, uncorrected transcript of oral evidence taken on 13th September 2005. Retrieved August 21, 2009, from http://www.publications.parliament.uk.

Horvath, F. (1987). The police use of deadly force: A description of selected characteristics of intra-state incidents. *Journal of Police Science and Administration, 15*(3), 226–238.

Huggins, M., Haritos-Fatouros, M., & Zimbardo, P. (2002). *Violence workers: Police torturers and murderers reconstruct Brazilian atrocities.* Berkeley: University of California Press.

Hughes, E. (1961). Good people and dirty work. *Social Problems, 10*(1), 3–10.

Hunt, J. (1985). Police accounts of normal force. *Urban Life: A Journal of Ethnographic Research, 13*(4), 315–341.

Hunt, J., & Manning, P. (1991). The social context of police lying. *Symbolic Interaction, 14*(1), 1–20. Reproduced in Pogrebin M. (Ed.). (2003). Qualitative approaches to criminal justice: Perspectives from the field. Thousand Oaks, CA: Sage.

Ianni, F., & Reuss-Ianni, E. (1972). *A family business: Kinship and social control in organized crime.* London: Routledge and Kegan Paul.

Independent Commission on the Los Angeles Police Department. (1991). *Report of the Independent Commission on the Los Angeles Police Department.* Los Angeles.

Independent Police Complaints Commission. (2006a). *Stockwell one: investigation into the shooting of Juan Charles de Menezes at Stockwell underground station on July 22, 2005.* Retrieved July 30, 2009, from http://www.news.bbc.co.uk/1/shared/bsp/hi/pdfs/08_11_07_stockwell1.pdf.

Independent Police Complaints Commission. (2006b). *The death of Harry Stanley – ICPP Decision.* Retrieved July 27, 2009, from http://www.ipcc.gov.uk/stanley_ipcc_decision_feb_06.pdf.

Independent Police Complaints Commission. (2007). *Stockwell Two: An investigation into the complaints about the Metropolitan Police Service's handling of public statements following the shooting of Juan Charles de Menezes on 22 July 2005.* Retrieved July 10, 2009, from http://www.ipcc.gov.uk/ipcc_stockwell_2.pdf.

Independent Police Complaints Commission. *Shootings by police.* Retrieved July 30, 2009, from http://www.ipcc.gov.uk/index/resources/evidence_reports/investigation_reports/the_stockwell_investigation/shootings_by_police.htm.

Innes, M. & Jones, V. (2006). *Neighbourhood security and urban change: Risk, resilience and recovery.* Joseph Rowntree Foundation. Retrieved from http://www.jrf.org.uk.

IPCS. (2005). *Non traditional security issues: Evolution of criminal gangs in Mumbai.* New Delhi: Institute of Peace and Conflict Studies.

Jacobs, J., & Panarella, C. (1998). Organized crime. In M. Tonry (Ed.), *The handbook of crime and punishment.* Oxford: Oxford University Press.

James, D. (1979). Police–Black relations: The professional solution. In S. Holdaway (Ed.), *The British police*. London: Edward Arnold.

Jefferson, T. (1987). Beyond paramilitarism. *British Journal of Criminology, 27*(1), 47–53.

Jefferson, T. (1990). *The case against paramilitary policing*. Milton Keynes: Open University Press.

Johnson, J. (2002). In-depth interviewing. In J. Gubrium & J. Holstein (Eds.), *Handbook of interview research*. Thousand Oaks, CA: Sage.

Johnson, M. (2003). *Street justice: A history of police violence in New York city*. Boston: Beacon.

Jones, M. (1980). *Organisational aspects of police behaviour*. Guildford: Gower.

Jones-Brown, D. (2007). Forever the symbolic assailant: The More things change the more they remain the same. *Criminology and Public Policy, 6*(1), 103–121.

Kane, R. (2007). Collect and release data on coercive police actions. *Criminology and Public Policy, 6*(4), 773–780.

Kappeler, V., Sluder, R., & Alpert, G. (1998). *Forces of deviance: Understanding the dark side of policing* (2nd ed.). Prospect Heights, IL: Waveland.

Katakam, A. (2005). In India at last. *Frontline, 22*(24): The Hindu.

Kelly, R. (1986). Criminal underworlds: Looking down on society from below. In R. Kelly (Ed.), *Organized crime: A global perspective*. New Jersey: Rowman and Littlefield.

Kelman, H., & Hamilton, V. (1989). *Crimes of obedience*. New Haven: Yale University Press.

Kennison, P., & Loumansky, A. (2007). Shoot to kill: Understanding police use of force in combating suicide terrorism. *Crime, Law and Social Change, 47*, 157–168.

Ketkar, P. (2004). Abu Salem: From tailor to don. New Delhi: Institute of Peace and Conflict Studies. Retrieved from July 23, 2009, from http://www.ipcs.org/article/terrorism/abu-salem-from-tailor-to-don-1318.html.

Khalidi, O. (2003). *Khaki and the ethnic violence in India*. New Delhi: Three Essays Collective.

Khan, A. A. (2004). *Surrender*. New Delhi: Thomson.

Khomne, R. (2002, March 23). Dombivili encounter deaths get curiouser. *The Times of India*.

Kleinig, J. (1996). *The ethics of policing*. Cambridge: Cambridge University Press.

Klinger, D. (2005). Social theory and the street cop: The case of deadly force. *Ideas in American Policing, 7*: Police Foundation.

Klockars, C. (1979). Dirty hands and deviant subjects. In C. Klockars & F. O'Connor (Eds.), *Deviance and decency: The ethics of research with human subjects*. London: Sage.

Klockars, C. (1980). The dirty Harry problem. *The Annals of the American Academy of Political and Social Science, 452*, 33–47.

Klockars, C. (1991). The dirty Harry problem. In C. Klockars & S. Mastrofski (Eds.), *Thinking about police: Contemporary readings* (2nd ed.). New York: McGraw-Hill.

Klockars, C. (1996). A theory of excessive force and its control. In W. Geller & H. Toch (Eds.), *Police violence: Understanding and controlling police abuse of force*. New Haven, CT: Yale University Press.

Klockars, C., & Mastrofski, S. (1991). The moral hazards. In C. Klockars & S. Mastrofski (Eds.), *Thinking about police: Contemporary readings* (2nd ed.). New York: McGraw-Hill.

Knapp, W. (1972). *The Knapp report on police corruption*. New York: Braziller.

Kolker, T. (2008, February 24). A bad night at Club Kalua: In the Sean bell shooting, 50 bullets and many truths. *The New York Times Magazine*. Retrieved July 9, 2009, from http://www.nymag.com/news/features/44458.

Kraska, P., & Kappeler, V. (1997). Militarizing American police: The rise and normalization of paramilitary units. *Social Problems, 44*, 1–18.

Kripalani, M. (2005). The business of Bollywood. In A. Ayres & P. Oldenburg (Eds.), *India briefing: Take-off at last?* New York: Asia Society.

Krishnamurty, S. (1996). *Human rights and the Indian police* (2nd ed.). Bangalore: R.R.

Lakshmi, R. (2003). Gun slinging police battle Bombay's mob. *Washington Post*.

Lawrence, N. (2000a). *Social research methods: Qualitative and quantitative approaches* (4th ed.). Boston: Allyn and Bacon.

Lee, J. (1981). Some structural aspects of police deviance in relations with minority groups. In C. Shearing (Ed.), *Organizational police deviance*. Toronto: Butterworth.

Leishman, F., & Mason, P. (2003). *Policing and the media: Facts, Fictions and Factions.* Cullompton: Willan.

Lele, J. (1995). *Hindutva: The emergence of the right.* Madras: Earthworm.

Levi, M. (2002). The organization of serious crimes. In M. Maguire, R. Morgan, & R. Reiner (Eds.), *The Oxford handbook of criminology* (3rd ed.). Oxford: Clarendon.

Levi, M., & Maguire, M. (2002). Violent crime. In M. Maguire, R. Morgan, & R. Reiner (Eds.), *The Oxford handbook of criminology* (3rd ed.). Oxford: Oxford University Press.

Levi, M., & Maguire, M. (2004). Reducing and preventing organised crime: an evidence based critique. *Crime, Law and Social Change, 41*(5), 397–469.

Lewinsky, W. (2002, May–June). Stress reactions related to lethal force encounters. *The Police Marksman,* 23–28.

Lewinsky, W. & Hudson W. (2003a). Time to start shooting? Time to stop shooting. *The Police Marksman.* September–October, 26–29.

Lewinsky, W. & Hudson, W. (2003b, November–December), The impact of visual complexity, decision making and anticipation. *The Police Marksman,* 24–27.

Lippman, W. (1925). *The phantom public.* New York: Harcourt, Brace.

Liska, A. (1992). *Social threat and social control.* Albany: State University of New York.

Liska, A., & Yu, J. (1992). Specifying and testing the threat hypothesis: Police use of deadly force. In A. Liska (Ed.), *Social threat and social control* (pp. 53–68). Albany: State University of New York.

Long, M. (2003). Leadership and performance management. In T. Newburn (Ed.), *Handbook of policing.* Cullompton: Willan.

Louis, E. (2009, February 1). He was shot down, we stood up. *The Daily News (New York).* Retrieved July 11, 2009, from http://www.lexisnexis.com.

Lueck, T. (2008, May 8). 216 Held in protests of police acquittals. *The New York Times.* Retrieved July 9, 2009, from http://www.nytimes.com/2008/05/08/nyregion/08bell.html.

Lyman, S., & Scott, M. (1970). *A sociology of the absurd.* New York: Appleton-Century-Crofts.

Maas, P. (1974). *Serpico.* London: Fontana.

Macdonald, J., Alpert, G., & Tennenbaum, A. (1999). Justifiable homicide by police and criminal homicide: A research note. *Journal of Crime and Justice, 22,* 153–166.

Maguire, M. (2002). Crime statistics: The 'data explosion' and its implications. In M. Maguire, R. Morgan, & R. Reiner (Eds.), *The Oxford handbook of criminology.* Oxford: Oxford University Press.

Mahmood, C. (2000). Trials by fire: Dynamics of terror in Punjab and Kashmir. In J. Sluka (Ed.), *Death squad: The anthropology of state terror* (pp. 70–90). Philadelphia: University of Pennsylvania Press.

Malamoud, C. (2003). Remarks on dissuasion in ancient India. In D. Vidal, G. Tarabout, & E. Meyer (Eds.), *Violence/non-violence: Some Hindu perspectives.* New Delhi: Manohar, Centre De Sciences Humaines.

Manning, P. (1977). *Police work.* Cambridge, MA: MIT.

Manning, P. (1980). *Police work: The social organization of policing* (2nd ed.). Prospect Heights, IL: Waveland.

Manning, P. (1997). *Police work* (2nd ed.). Prospect Heights, IL: Waveland.

Manning, P. (2003). *Policing contingencies.* Chicago: University of Chicago Press.

Manning, P., & Redlinger, L. (1977). Invitational edges of corruption: Some consequences of narcotic law enforcement. In P. Rock (Ed.), *Drugs and politics.* Rutgers, NJ: Society/Transaction Books.

Manning, P., & van Maanen, J. (Eds.). (1978). *Policing: A view from the street.* Santa Monica, CA: Goodyear.

Mark, R. (1978). *In the office of constable.* London: Collins.

Marks, M. (1999). Changing dilemmas and the dilemmas of change: Transforming the public order policing unit in Durban. *Policing and Society, 9*(2), 157–179.

Marks, M. (2005). *Transforming the Robocops: Changing police in South Africa.* Scottsville: University of KwaZulu-Natal Press.

Marks, M., & Fleming, J. (2004). As unremarkable as the air they breathe? Reforming police management in South Africa. *Current Sociology, 52*(5), 784–808.

Marpakwar, P. (2007, July 19). CID unlikely to investigate death. *The Times of India*. Retrieved from http://www.timesofindia.indiatimes.com.

Mars, J. (2002). *Deadly force, colonialism, and the rule of law: Police violence in Guyana*. Westport, CT: Greenwood.

Masselos, J. (1996). The Bombay riots of January 1993. In J. McGuire, P. Reeves, & H. Brasted (Eds.), *Politics of violence: From Ayodhya to Behrampada*. New Delhi: Sage.

Matthews, R. (2003). Rethinking penal policy: Towards a systems approach. In R. Matthews & J. Young (Eds.), *The new politics of crime and punishment*. Cullompton: Willan.

Matulia, K. (1985). *A balance of forces* (2nd ed.). Gaithersburg, MD: International Association of Chiefs of Police.

McConville, M., & Shepherd, D. (1992). *Watching police, watching communities*. London: Routledge.

McCulloch, J. (2001). *Blue army: Paramilitary policing in Australia*. Melbourne: Melbourne University Press.

McKenzie, I. (2000). Policing force: Rules, hierarchies and consequences. In F. Leishman, B. Loveday, & S. Savage (Eds.), *Core issues in policing* (2nd ed.). Harlow, Essex: Longman, Pearson Education.

Mehra, A. (1985). *Police in changing India*. New Delhi: Usha.

Mehta, S. (2005). *Maximum city: Bombay lost and found*. New Delhi: Penguin.

Melossi, D. (2004). The cultural embeddedness of social control: Reflections on a comparison of Italian and North American cultures concerning punishment. In T. Newburn & S. Sparks (Eds.), *Criminal justice and political cultures: National and international dimensions of crime control*. Cullompton: Willan.

Menzies, K. (2000). State crime by the police and its control. In J. Ross (Ed.), *Controlling state crime* (2nd ed.). New Brunswick: Transaction.

Merton, R. (1938). Social structure and anomie. *American Sociological Review, 3*, 672–682.

Meyer, M. (1980). Police shootings at minorities: The case of Los Angeles. *Annals, 452*, 98–110.

Milgram, S. (1974). *Obedience to authority*. New York: Harper and Row.

Miller, T., & Bell, L. (2002). Consenting to what? Issues of access, gate-keeping and 'informed' consent. In M. Mauthner et al. (Eds.), *Ethics in qualitative research*. Thousand Oaks, CA: Sage.

Miller, S., & Blackler, J. (2005). *Ethical issues in policing*. Aldershot: Ashgate.

Miller, L., & Braswell, M. (1992). Police perceptions of ethical decision making: The ideal vs the real. *American Journal of Police, XI*, 27–45.

Mills, T. (1973). The detective. In T. Wolfe (Ed.), *The new journalism*. New York: Harper and Row.

Milton, C., Halleck, J., Lardner, J., & Albrecht, G. (1977). *Police use of deadly force*. Washington, DC: Police Foundation.

Morgan, R., & Newburn, T. (1997). *The future of policing*. Oxford: Clarendon.

Muir, K. (1977). *Police: Streetcorner politicians*. Chicago: Chicago University Press.

Mukhopadhyaya, S. (1997). *Conceptualising post-colonial policing: An analysis and application of policing public order in India,* Unpublished PhD thesis submitted to the University of Leicester.

Nair, P. (2002). *Combating organised crime*. New Delhi: Konark.

Nath, T. (1981). *Forty years of Indian police*. New Delhi: Concept.

National Police Commission Report. (1983). *Eighth and concluding report of the national police commission*. New Delhi: Controller of Publication, India.

Newburn, T. (1999). *Understanding and preventing police corruption: Lessons from the literature*. London: Home Office Policing and Reducing Crime Unit.

Nigam, S. (1963). *Scotland yard and the Indian police*. Allahabad: Kitab Mahal.

Nijman, J. (2006). Mumbai's mysterious middle class. *International Journal of Urban and Regional Research, 30*(4), 758–775.

O'Driscoll, C. (2008). Fear and trust: The shooting of Juan Charles de Menezes and the war on terror. *Millennium – Journal of International Studies, 36*, 339–360.

Panorama. (2006). When cops kill? BBC productions. Retrieved August 23, 2009, from http://www.news.bbc.co.uk/1/hi/programmes/panorama/6048250.stm.

Patel, S. (1995). Bombay's urban predicament. In S. Patel & A. Thorner (Eds.), *Bombay: Metaphor for modern India*. Bombay: Oxford University Press.

Patel, S. (2003). Bombay/Mumbai: Globalization, inequalities, and politics. In J. Gugler (Ed.), *World cities beyond the west: Globalization, development and inequality*. Cambridge: Cambridge University Press.

Patton, M. (2002). *Qualitative research and evaluation methods* (3rd ed.). Thousand Oaks, CA: Sage.

Pearson, G. (1983). *Hooligan: A history of respectable fears*. London: Macmillan.

Pedicelli, G. (1998). *When police kill: Police use of force in Montreal and Toronto*. Montreal: Vehicule.

Pendse, S. (2003). Satya's Mumbai; Mumbai's satya. In S. Patel & J. Masselos (Eds.), *Bombay and Mumbai: The city in transition*. Oxford: Oxford University Press.

Perrow, C. (1984). *Normal accidents: Living with high-risk technologies*. New York: Basic.

Perry A. (2003, January 6). Urban cowboys. *Time Magazine*.

Pettigrew, J. (2000). Parents and their children in situations of terror: Disappearances and special police activity in Punjab. In J. Sluka (Ed.), *Death squad: The anthropology of state terror* (pp. 204–225). Philadelphia: University of Pennsylvania Press.

Phillips, A. (2008, June 9). NYPD changes sought in wake of Sean Bell shooting. *The New York Sun*. Retrieved July 19, 2009, from http://www.lexisnexis.com.

Pineda, N. (2009, May 30). Calls for probe of police shootings. *Eyewitness News*. Retrieved July 9, 2009, from http://www.abclocal.go.com/wabc/story?section=news/local&id=6839933.

Potter, G. (1994). *Criminal organizations: Vice, racketeering, and politics in an American city*. Illinois: Waveland.

Prasannan, R. (1996). Great NGO fraud: Most of the funds they get never reach the poor. *The Week, 14*, 28–38.

Pratt, J. (2001). Emotive and ostentatious punishment. *Punishment and Society, 24*(4), 407–439.

Pugliese, J. (2006). Asymmetries of terror: Visual regimes of racial profiling and the shooting of Juan Charles de Menezes in the context of the war in Iraq, *Borderlands Ejournal, 5*(1). Retrieved August 10, 2009, from http://www.borderlands.net.au/vol5no1_2006/pugliese.htm.

Punch, M. (1979). *Policing the inner city*. London: Macmillan.

Punch, M. (1985). *Conduct unbecoming: The social construction of police deviance and control*. London: Tavistock.

Punch, M. (1986). *The politics and ethics of fieldwork*. Thousand Oaks, CA: Sage.

Punch, M. (1996). *Dirty business: Exploring corporate misconduct*. London: Sage.

Punch, M. (1998). Politics and ethics in qualitative research. In N. Denzin & Y. Lincoln (Eds.), *The landscape of qualitative research: Theories and issues*. Thousand Oaks, CA: Sage.

Punch, M. (2000). Police corruption and its prevention. *European Journal on Criminal Policy and Research, 8*(3), 301–324.

Punch, M., & Naylor, T. (1973). The police: A social service. *New Society, 24*, 358–361.

Punwani, J. (2003). My area, your area: How riots changed the city. In S. Patel & J. Masselos (Eds.), *Bombay and Mumbai: The city in transition*. Oxford: Oxford University Press.

Punwani, J. (2005, October 21). Police rotten from within. *The Times of India*.

Purandare, V. (1999). *The SENA story*. Mumbai: Business.

Raghavan, R. (2004, September 25). Understanding crime. *Frontline, 21*, 20.

Raghavan, R. (2006, October 7). Landmark order. *Frontline, 23*, 20.

Raghavan, R. (2007, May 5). Hall of shame. *Frontline, 24*(9).

Rai, V. N. (1998). *Combating communal conflicts*. New Delhi: Renaissance.

Rajagopalan, K. (2000). *Different strokes: Events, episodes and experiences of a police officer*. New Delhi: K.A. Rajagopalan.

Rao, V. (2006). Risk and the city: Bombay, Mumbai and other theoretical departures. *India Review, 5*(2), 220–232. Retrieved July 28, 2009, from http://www.pdfserve.informaworld.com/299766_751306972_756738178.pdf.

Rattanani, L. (1997, November 3). No brakes for bullet train? *Outlook*.

Rawlinson, P. (1998). Mafia, media and myth: Representations of Russian organised crime. *The Howard Journal, 37*(4), 346–358.

Rebeiro, J. (1998). *Bullet for bullet.* New Delhi: Viking, Penguin.

Reiman, J. (1979). Research subjects, political subjects, and human subjects. In C. Klockars & F. O'Connor (Eds.), *Deviance and decency: The ethics of research with human subjects* (Sage annual reviews of studies in deviance, Vol. 3). Beverly Hills: Sage.

Reiner, R. (2000a). *The politics of the police* (3rd ed.). Oxford: Oxford University Press.

Reiner, R. (2000b). Police research. In R. King & E. Wincup (Eds.), *Doing research on crime and justice.* New York: Oxford University Press.

Reiner, R. (2002). Media made criminality: The representation of crime in the mass media. In M. Maguire, R. Morgan, & R. Reiner (Eds.), *The Oxford handbook of criminology* (3rd ed.). Oxford: Oxford University Press.

Reiner, R. (2003). Policing and the media. In T. Newburn (Ed.), *Handbook of policing.* Cullompton: Willan.

Reiner, R., Livingstone, S., & Allen, J. (2000). No more happy endings? The media and popular concern about crime since the Second World War. In T. Hope & R. Sparks (Eds.), *Crime, risk and insecurity.* London: Routledge.

Reisman, M. (1979). *Folded lies.* New York: Free.

Reiss, A., Jr. (1968). Police brutality – answers to key questions. *Transactions, 5*(8), 10–19.

Reiss, A., Jr. (1977). Foreword. In A. Simpson (Ed.), *The literature of police corruption.* New York: John Jay.

Reiss, A., Jr. (1995). Reflections on policing systems and police cooperation in Europe. In J. Brodeur (Ed.), *Comparisons in policing: An international perspective.* Aldershot: Avebury.

Reuss-Ianni, E., & Ianni, F. (1983). Street cops and management cops: The two cultures of policing. In M. Punch (Ed.), *Control in the police organization.* Cambridge, MA: MIT.

Rivera, G. (1999, March 17). New information about Amadou Diallo, the West African man shot 41 times by police, in Rivera Live. *CNBC News Transcripts.* Retrieved July 19, 2009, from http://www.lexisnexis.com.

Robin, G. (1963). Justifiable homicide by police officers. *Journal of criminal Law, Criminology and Police Science, 54,* 225–231.

Rock, P. (2002). On becoming a victim. In C. Hoyle & R. Young (Eds.), *New visions of crime victims.* Oxford: Hart.

Roshier, B. (1981). The selection of crime news by the press. In S. Cohen & J. Young (Eds.), *The manufacture of news: Social problems, deviance and the mass media.* California: Sage.

Ross, J. (2000a). Controlling state crime: Towards an integrated structural model. In J. Ross (Ed.), *Controlling state crime* (2nd ed.). New Brunswick: Transaction.

Ross, J. (2000b). *Making news of police violence: A comparative study of Toronto and New York city.* Westport: Praeger.

Rostker, B., Hanser, L., Hix, W., Jensen, C., Morral, A., Ridgeway, G., et al. (2008). *Evaluation of the New York City police department firearm training and firearm-discharge review process.* Centre on Quality Policing: Rand Corporation. Retrieved July 23, 2008, from http://www.rc.rand.org/pubs/monographs/2008/RAND_MG717.pdf.

Roy, B. (1994, October 7). Spirit of volunteerism: The new parasites. *Indian Express* (New Delhi Edition).

Rustamji, K. (1992). The wrong test of policing. In J. Guha Roy (Ed.), *Policing a district.* New Delhi: Indian Institute of Public Opinion.

Samuel, R. (1981). *East end underworld: The life and times of Arthur Harding.* London: Routledge and Kegan Paul.

Sapsford, R. (1996). Reading qualitative research. In R. Sapsford (Ed.), *Researching crime and criminal justice.* Milton Keynes: The Open University Press.

Saraf, V. (1999). *Formation of Criminal Gangs in Major Cities.* Unpublished PhD thesis submitted to the Bureau of Police Research and Development, New Delhi, cited in Sarkar, S. & Tiwari, A. (2002). Combating organized crime: A case study of Mumbai city. *Faultlines,* 12, South Asia Terrorism Portal.

Sarkar, S. & Tiwari, A. (2002). Combating organized crime: A case study of Mumbai city. *Faultlines*, 12, South Asia Terrorism Portal. Retrieved from http://www.satp.org/satporgtp/publication/faultlines/volume12/Article5.htm.

Sassen, S. (2000). The global city: Strategic site/new frontier. In E. Isin (Ed.), *Democracy, citizenship and the global city*. London: Routledge.

Savage, S., Charman, S., & Cope, S. (2000). The policy-making context: Who shapes policing policy? In F. Leishman, B. Loveday, & S. Savage (Eds.), *Core issues in policing* (2nd ed.). Harlow, Essex: Longman, Pearson Education.

Savarkar, V. (1969). *Hindutva: Who is a Hindu?* Bombay: Veer Savarkar Prakashan.

Scharf, P., & Binder, A. (1983). *The badge and the bullet: Police use of deadly force*. New York: Praeger.

Schwalbe, M., & Wolkomir, M. (2002). Interviewing men. In J. Gubrium & J. Holstein (Eds.), *Handbook of interview research*. Thousand Oaks, CA: Sage.

Schwandt, T. (1994). Constructivist, interpretivist approaches to human inquiry. In N. Denzin & Y. Lincoln (Eds.), *Handbook of qualitative research*. Newbury Park, CA: Sage.

Scott, M., & Lyman, S. (1968). Accounts. *American sociological review, 33*, 46–62.

Scraton, P. (1987). *Law, order and the authoritarian state*. Milton Keynes: Open University Press.

Settle, R. (1990). *Police power: Use and abuse*. Northcote: Muxworthy.

Shaban, A. (2004). *City, crime and space: A case of Mumbai megalopolis*. Mumbai: Centre for Development Studies, Tata Institute of Social Sciences.

Shapland, J., & Hobbs, D. (1989). Policing on the ground. In R. Morgan & D. Smith (Eds.), *Coming to terms with policing*. London: Routledge.

Shearing, C. (1981). Subterranean processes in the maintenance of power. *Canadian Review of Sociology and Anthropology, 18*(3), 283–298.

Shearing, C. & Ericson, R. (1991). Culture as figurative action. Reprinted in Newburn, T. (Ed.). (2005). *Policing: Key readings*. Devon: Willan.

Sherman, L. (1980). Causes of police behaviour: The current state of quantitative research. *Journal of Research in Crime and Delinquency, 17*(1), 69–100.

Sherman, L. (1983). Reducing police gun use: Critical events, administrative policy and organizational change. In M. Punch (Ed.), *Control in the police organization*. Cambridge: MIT.

Sherman, L., & Cohen, G. (1986). *Citizens killed by big city police, 1970–1984*. Washington, DC: Crime Control Institute.

Sherman, L., & Langworthy, R. (1979). Measuring homicide by police officers. *Journal of Criminal Law and Criminology, 70*, 546–560.

Shourie, H. (1995, June 18). Too many cooks spoil the broth. *Sunday Times of India* (New Delhi Edition).

Shrivastava, S. (1998, November 4). Bombay gets tough on gangsters. *BBC News*. Retrieved from http://www.news.bbc.co.uk/1/hi/world/south_asia/207828.stm.

Sillitoe, P. (1955). *Cloak without dagger*. London: Cassell and Company.

Silverman, D. (1993). *Interpreting qualitative data: Methods for analysing talk, text and interaction*. London: Sage.

Simmons, J., Legg, C., & Hosking, R. (2003). *National crime recording standard (NCRS): An analysis of the impact on recorded crime companion volume to crime in England and Wales 2002–2003, Home Office occassional paper*. London: Home Office.

Singh, J. (1999). *Inside the Indian police*. New Delhi: Gyan.

Singh, P. (2000). Organised crime. *Faultlines*, 5, South Asia Terrorism Portal. Retrieved from http://www.satp.org/satporgtp/publication/faultlines/volume5/fault5-10singh.htm.

Skogan, W. (1990). *Disorder and decline: Crime and the spiral of decay in American neighbourhoods*. New York: Free.

Skolnick, J. (1966). *Justice without trial: Law enforcement in democratic society*. New York: Wiley.

Skolnick, J. (1975). *Justice without trial: Law enforcement in democratic society* (2nd ed.). New York: Wiley.

Skolnick, J. (1994). A sketch of the policeman's working personality. In *Justice without trial: Law enforcement in democratic society* (3rd ed., pp. 41–68). New York: Wiley.

Skolnick, J. (2007). Racial profiling: Then and now. *Criminology and Public policy, 6*(1), 65–70.

Skolnick, J. (2008). Enduring issues of police culture and demographics. *Policing and Society, 18*(1), 35–45.

Skolnick, J., & Fyfe, J. (1993). *Above the law: Police and the excessive use of force*. New York: Free.

Sluka, J. (2000). State terror and anthropology. In J. Sluka (Ed.), *Death squad: The anthropology of state terror*. Philadelphia: University of Pennsylvania Press.

Smith, D. (2003). *Hinduism and modernity*. Oxford: Blackwell.

Smith, B. (2004). Structural and organizational predictors of homicide by police. *Policing: An International Journal of Police Strategies and Management, 27*(4), 539–557.

Sooryamoorthy, R., & Gangrade, K. (2001). *NGOs in India: A cross-sectional study*. Westport, CT: Greenwood.

Sorenson, J., Marquart, J., & Brock, D. (1993). Factors related to killings of felons by police officers: A test of the community violence and conflict hypotheses. *Justice Quarterly, 10*, 417–440.

Spradley, J. (1979). *The ethnographic interview*. New York: Holt, Rinehart and Winston.

Spradley, J. (1980). *Participant observation*. New York: Holt, Rinehart and Winston.

Srikrishna, B. (1998). *Report of the Srikrishna commission, volumes 1 & 2*. Mumbai: Government of Maharashtra.

Stone, C. (2007). Tracing police accountability in theory and practice: From Philadelphia to Abuja and Sao Paulo. *Theoretical Criminology, 11*(2), 245–259.

Sturcke, J. (2007, November 1). Met police guilty over de Menezes shooting. *The Guardian*.

Subrahmanium, V. (2002, December 4). Rape of justice. *The Times of India*.

Subramanium, C. (2000). *Indian police: A DGP remembers*. New Delhi: B.R.

Sudnow, D. (1965). Normal crimes: Sociological features of the penal code in a public defender office. *Social Problems, 12*(3), 255–276.

Surette, R. (1998a). Some unpopular thoughts about popular culture. In F. Bailey & D. Hale (Eds.), *Popular culture, crime & justice*. Washington: West/Wadsworth.

Surette, R. (1998b). *Media, crime and criminal justice: Images and reality*. Belmont, CA: Wandsworth.

Surrey Police. (2005). *The Fatal Shooting of Henry Bruce Stanley*, Report to the independent police complaints commission. Retrieved July 24, 2009, from http://www.ipcc.gov.uk/stanley_report_to_ipcc_03.02.06_for_publication.pdf.

Sutherland, E. (1949). *White collar crime*. New York: Dryden.

Swaminathan, M. (2003). Aspects of poverty and living standards. In S. Paterl & J. Masselos (Eds.), *Bombay and Mumbai: The city in transition*. Oxford: Oxford University Press.

Sykes, G., & Matza, D. (1957). Techniques of neutralization. *American Sociological Review, 22*, 664–670.

Takagi, P. (1974). A Garrison state in "democratic" society. *Crime and Social Justice, 1*, 27–33.

Taylor, I., Walton, P., & Young, J. (1973). *The new criminology: For a social theory of deviance*. London: Routledge and Kegan Paul.

Terrill, W. (2001). *Police coercion: Application of the force continuum*. New York: LFB Scholarly Publishing LLC.

Terrill, W., & Mastrofski, S. (2002). Situational and officer based determinants of police coercion. *Justice Quarterly, 19*(2), 215–248.

Tesch, R. (1990). *Qualitative research: Analysis types and software tools*. London: Falmer.

The Aguiar Commission Report: Police encounters in Bombay. Retrieved July 24, 2009, from http://www.altindia.net/augiarcommission/aguiar.html.

The Guardian. (2005, October 20). Policemen escape charges over table leg killing. Retrieved September 24, 2009, from http://www.guardian.co.uk/uk/2005/oct/20/ukcrime1.

The Hindu. (2005, April 26). Protests over minor's rape continue in Mumbai.

The Indian Express. (1999, February 28). HC rejects 'biased' Aguiar report. Retrieved February 19, 2009, from http://www.indianexpress.com/ie/daily/19990226/ige26048p.html.

The Indian Express. (2001, December 29). Mumbai police pats itself as encounter deaths double, Mumbai.

The New York Times. (2006, November 28). A fatal police shooting in queens. Retrieved July 9, 2009, from http://www.nytimes.com/2006/11/27/nyregion/20061129_SHOOTING_GRAPHIC.html?_r=1.

The Pioneer. (2002, November 8). Do only terrorists have human rights?

The Post Standard. (2008, May 2). Deadly force: Sean Bell case should prompt reforms in training, accountability. Retrieved August 28, 2009, from http://www.lexisnexis.com.

The Sun. (2005, July 29). Juan Charles de Menezes may have had forged stamp in his passport. Retrieved July 10, 2009, from http://www.lexisnexis.com.

The Times of India. (1999, February 25). HC gives police clean chit in Javed Fawda shootout case.

The Times of India. (2002, February 27). 7 gangsters gunned down in encounter.

The Times of India. (2003, July 29). Chronology of Mumbai blasts since December 2002.

The Times of India. (2003, January 17). Inspector arrested for 1992 encounter.

The Times of India. (2003, January 15). Police official held in fake encounter case.

The Times of India. (2004, January 15). I want more cops to be nabbed by ACB: Pasricha.

The Times of India. (2004, October 19). Arun Gawli shoots down encounter fears.

The Times of India. (2004, September 21). City gangs enter political fray.

The Times of India. (2004, December 9). Encounter killings down to a trickle.

The Times of India. (2006, February 26). Encounter victim's family seeks probe.

The Times of India. (2006, June 29). Encounter cops among 120 shuffled.

The Times of India. (2007, July 17). Encounter deaths: Now cops to probe.

Thevar, V. (2006, July 16). Don of a new era. *The Telegraph,* Calcutta, Sunday. Retrieved from http://www.telegraphindia.com.

Thompson, T. (2005, August 21). The Stockwell shooting: Baptism by fire. *The Observer.* Retrieved July 10, 2009, from http://www.lexisnexis.com.

Thompson, T. & Phillips, T. (2005, August 14). Policing on trial: Death in stockwell. *The Observer.* Retrieved July 10, 2009, from http://www.lexisnexis.com.

Toch, H. (1976). *Peacekeeping: Police, prisons, and violence.* Lexington: Lexington.

Toch, H. (1996). The violence-prone police officer. In W. Geller & H. Toch (Eds.), *Police violence: Understanding and controlling police abuse of force.* New Haven, CT: Yale University Press.

Treverton, G., Matthies, C., Cunningham, K., Goulka, J., Ridgeway, G., & Wong A. (2009). *Film piracy, organized crime and terrorism,* Rand Corporation monograph series. Retrieved October 23, 2009, from http://www.rand.org/pubs/monographs/2009/RAND_MG742.pdf.

Uldricks, N., & van Mastrigt, H. (1991). *Policing police violence.* Dordrecht: Kluwer.

Vaikunth, V. (2000). *An eye to indian policing: Challenges and response.* Chennai: East West.

van Maanen, J. (1973). Observations on the making of policemen. *Human Organizations, 32,* 407–418.

van Maanen, J. (1974). Working the street: A developmental view of police behaviour. In H. Jacob (Ed.), *The potential for reform of criminal justice.* Beverley Hills, CA: Sage.

van Maanen, J. (1978). On watching the watchers. In P. Manning & J. van Maanen (Eds.), *Policing: A view from the street.* Santa Monica, CA: Goodyear.

Van Maanen, J. (1985). The asshole. In A. Blumberg & E. Niederhoff (Eds.), *The ambivalent force: Perspectives on the police* (3rd ed.). New York: Holt, Rinehart and Winston.

Van Wersch, H. (1992). *Bombay textile strike, 1982–83.* Bombay: Oxford University Press.

Van Wersch, H. (1995). Flying a kite and losing the string. In S. Patel & A. Thorner (Eds.), *Bombay: Metaphor for modern India.* Bombay: Oxford University Press.

Varia, T. (2008, March 26). Mumbai's encounter specialists out of favour. *IBN Live.* Retrieved June 23, 2009, from http://www.ibnlive.in.com/news/mumbais-encounter-specialists-out-of-favour/61960-3.html.

Varma, R. (2004). Provincializing the global city: From Bombay to Mumbai. *Social Text, 22*(4), 65–89.

Vaughan-Williams, N. (2007). The shooting of Juan Charles de Menezes: New border politics? *Alternatives, 32,* 177–195.

Verma, A. (2005). *The Indian police: A critical evaluation.* New Delhi: Regency.

Verma, A., & Tiwari, R. (2003). Organized crime: Perspective from India. In J. Albanese, D. Das, & A. Verma (Eds.), *Organized crime: World perspectives.* New Jersey: Prentice Hall.

Vidal, D., Tarabout, G., & Meyer, E. (Eds.). (2003). *Violence/non-violence: Some Hindu perspectives.* New Delhi: Manohar, Centre De Sciences Humaines.

Villejoubert, G., O'Keeffe, C., & Alison, L. (2006). Hindsight bias and shooting incidents. In S. Giles & M. Santarcangelo (Eds.), *Psychological aspects of legal processes* (pp. 17–24). London: IA-IP.

Virani, P. (1999). *Once there was Bombay.* New Delhi: Penguin.

Vitale, A. (2005). From negotiated management to command and control: How the New York police department polices protests. *Policing and Society, 15*(3), 283–304.

Vittal, N. (2003). *Corruption in India*. New Delhi: Academic Foundation.

Wacquant, L. (1992). Towards a social praxeology: The structure and logic of Bourdieu's sociology. In P. Bourdieu & L. Wacquant (Eds.), *An invitation to reflexive sociology*. Cambridge: Polity.

Waddington, P. A. J. (1987). Towards paramilitarism? Dilemmas in policing civil disorders. *British Journal of Criminology, 27*(1), 37–46.

Waddington, P. A. J. (1991). *The strong arm of the law*. Oxford: Clarendon.

Waddington, P. A. J. (1999a). *Policing citizens*. London: UCL.

Waddington, P. A. J. (1999b). Police (canteen) sub-culture: An appreciation. *British Journal of Criminology, 39*(2), 287–308.

Waegel, W. (1984). How police justify use of deadly force. *Social Problems, 32*(2), 144–155.

Walker, A., Kershaw, C., & Nicholas, S. (2006). *Crime in England and Wales 2005–6, Home Office statistical bulletin*. London: HMSO.

Walsh, J. (1977). Career styles and police behaviour. In D. Bayley (Ed.), *Police and society*. Beverly Hills, CA: Sage.

Warren, K. (2000). Death squads and wider complicities: Dilemmas for the anthropology of violence. In J. Sluka (Ed.), *Death squad: The anthropology of state terror* (pp. 226–247). Philadelphia: University of Pennsylvania Press.

Warren, C. (2002). Qualitative interviewing. In J. Gubrium & J. Holstein (Eds.), *Handbook of interview research*. Thousand Oaks, CA: Sage.

Warren, I., & James, S. (2000). The police use of force: Contexts and constraints. In T. Coady, S. James, S. Miller, & M. O'Keefe (Eds.), *Violence and police culture*. Carlton South, Victoria: Melbourne University Press.

Weber, M. (1904). The 'objectivity' of knowledge in social science and social policy. Reprinted in Whimster, S. (Ed.). (2004). *The essential Weber: A reader*. London, New York: Routledge.

Weinstein, L. (2008). Mumbai's development Mafias: Globalization, organized crime and land development. *International Journal of Urban and Regional Research, 32*(1), 22–39.

Westley, W. (1970). *Violence and the police*. Cambridge, MA: MIT.

Westmarland, L. (2002). *Gender and policing*. Cullompton: Willan.

Whimster, S. (Ed.). (2004). *The essential Weber: A reader*. London: Routledge.

White, M. (2001). Controlling police decisions to use deadly force: Reexamining the importance of administrative policy. *Crime and Delinquency, 47*(1), 131–151.

Wolfgang, M. (1959). *Patterns in criminal homicide*. Philadelphia, PA: University of Pennsylvania Press.

Worden, R. (1996). The causes of police brutality: Theory and evidence on police use of force. In W. Geller & H. Toch (Eds.), *Police violence*. New Haven, CT: Yale University Press.

Wright-Mills, C. (1940). Situated actions and vocabularies of motive. *American Sociological Review, 15*, 904–913.

Young, J. (1975). The police as amplifiers of deviancy. Reprinted in Henshel, R. & Silverman, R. (Eds.). *Perception in criminology*, Ontario: Columbia University Press.

Young, M. (1991). *An inside job*. Oxford: Clarendon.

Young, J. (1999). *The exclusive society*. London: Sage.

Young, J. (2003). Winning the fight against crime? New Labour, populism and lost opportunities. In R. Matthews & J. Young (Eds.), *The new politics of crime and punishment*. Cullompton, Devon: Willan.

Zaidi, S.H. (1999, January 21). Cops back to trigger-happy ways. *Indian Express* (Bombay edition).

Zimbardo, P., Haney, C., Banks, W., & Jaffe D. (1973, April 8). The mind is a formidable jailor. *New York Times Magazine*.

Zimring, F. (2007). *The great American crime decline*. Oxford: Oxford University Press.

Acts

Code of Criminal Procedure
Indian Evidence Act
Indian Penal Code Maharashtra Control of Organised Crime Act

Index

LaVergne, TN USA
14 January 2011
212465LV00003B/87/P